D0793508

ARAFAT

THE MAN AND THE MYTH

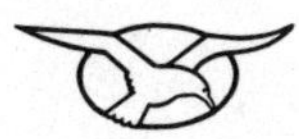

ARAFAT

THE MAN AND THE MYTH

THOMAS KIERNAN

W · W · NORTON & COMPANY · INC ·
New York

 Published simultaneously in Canada by George J. McLeod Limited, Toronto.
Printed in the United States of America

First Edition

The text of this book is set in Times Roman and Bauer Bodoni
Manufactured by The Haddon Craftsmen, Inc.
Designed by Jacques Chazaud

LIBRARY OF CONGRESS IN PUBLICATON DATA

Kiernan, Thomas
Arafat, the man and the myth.

Includes index.
1.Arafat, Yasir, 1929– 2.Jewish-Arab relations—1917– —History.
DS119.7K488 1976 322.4'2'0924 [B] 76–10298
ISBN 0–393–07503–6

1 2 3 4 5 6 7 8 9 0

Contents

PART II: AFTER ISRAEL

Foreword

This biography was conceived during the course of an interview I had in 1974 with Yasir Arafat in Beirut, Lebanon, while preparing an earlier book.* The time was a few months before Arafat's controversial appearance at the United Nations. He expressed an interest in cooperating on an English-language biography, principally, I suppose, because the kind of book he envisioned would in his mind advance the cause of Palestinian liberationism in the West, not to mention his own standing. Thereafter, through intermediaries in the Arab world, although I took pains to be very explicit about my idea of cooperation, his interest was reaffirmed.

By cooperation I was not, of course, thinking in terms of Arafat's authorization or approval of the eventual biographical narrative. That he had made a mystery of his past was well known; the mystery had become central to his popular mystique within the Arab world, and I resolved to uncover all I could about his life before proceeding to work directly with him on the book.

Toward that end I interviewed scores of people who had known him at various earlier stages in his life. I also examined as many documents as I could track down (they turned out to be precious few) which might shed further factual light on Arafat's life. Having collected and collated reams of facts, fancies, opinions, recollections, and anecdotes about him, mostly from those I interviewed, I then set out in May of 1975 to locate Arafat, sit down with him for the extended period I had been promised, and have him fill in whatever missing pieces there were in the portrait I had drawn.

Alas, things did not work out quite as I had hoped. Beirut, which was the location of Arafat's most frequently used headquarters, was

*Thomas Kiernan, *The Arabs: Their History, Attitudes, and Challenge to the Industrialized World* (Boston: Little, Brown, 1975).

a city locked in a murderous civil war between its Muslim and Christian populations. Arafat, I was told by my intermediaries, fearing for his life because of the involvement of Palestinian guerrillas in the fighting, had taken refuge in Damascus, the capital of Syria.

Would he see me there? I inquired. He is very preoccupied at the moment, came the answer, but if you want to take a chance, go to Damascus.

A trip to Damascus proved of little profit. Not because Arafat wouldn't see me, but because I learned that his concept of cooperation had all along been radically different from mine. So unwilling was he to go into the factual details of his life, so hopeful was he instead of getting me to re-create the mythological life he had invented for himself, that had I concurred in his notion of cooperation this book would have emerged not as biography but as press agentry.

I have thus relied in writing this biography mostly on the information I was able to elicit from relatives, acquaintances, and former acquaintances of Arafat whom I interviewed. I should note that many of these sources speak only Arabic and that my interviews with them were conducted through interpreters. Where I have quoted them in the book, I have not reproduced their answers and anecdotes verbatim as translated by the interpreters, for the simple reason that the interpreters themselves often spoke a convoluted English. Instead I have rephrased the anecdotes into a kind of ordinary conversational English for the sake of readability. Other sources spoke to me in English that was either halting or otherwise imprecise, and I have rephrased their remarks for the same reason.

It is my belief that to gain an understanding of the previously unknown life of Yasir Arafat, the reader should have at least a minimal sense of the exterior times and events that helped shape it. I have therefore tried to weave a historical thread through the narrative. It is my hope that the reader who has expert knowledge of the spare history I relate will not find it distractingly oversimplified, and that the reader who has heretofore been uninformed about Middle Eastern history will not find it simply distracting.

New York City T. K.

ARAFAT

THE MAN AND THE MYTH

Prologue

It was the morning of August 23, 1929. As the sun climbed toward noon over Jerusalem, a group of long-bearded Jews, frocked in black, carrying shawls and prayer books, turned a corner and made their way toward al-Haram al-Sharif. This was the Arabic name for the wall that surrounded the compound containing the al-Aqsa and Dome of the Rock mosques.

The mosques were the two most important Muslim holy sites in Jerusalem, itself the third holiest city of Islam. Built centuries earlier, they were in the process of being restored in the wake of a vast fund-raising campaign throughout the Islamic world.

The goal of the restorations was not purely religious. Although there had always been a Jewish community in Jerusalem and its environs, the previous thirty years had seen an increasingly systematic influx of Jews into Palestine, most of them from central and eastern Europe. Initially, the migration had been more or less spontaneous. But then it had assumed a rationale in the form of Zionism —a mix of religious and political ideology designed to give Europe's Jews a national homeland in Palestine, a haven in the land of their spiritual ancestors, far away from the oppression and persecution they had experienced for countless generations. Finally, in 1917, it had acquired a license in the form of the Balfour Declaration, which most Jews interpreted as Great Britain's commitment to the establishment of such a homeland. Many further took it as Britain's intention of helping to establish not just a national homeland but an independent, sovereign Jewish nation.

On this hot Jerusalem morning twelve years later, Zionism was the bête noire of the leaders of the local Muslim and Christian Arab population, a population which, despite the previous three decades' influx of Jews, outnumbered the Jews by nine to one. Foremost among the Arab leaders was a mercurial thirty-two-year-old politician and religious authority named Haj Amin al-Husayni.

Haj Amin was the scion of one of Jerusalem's largest and most important families, the Husaynis. Since the seventeenth century, almost without interruption, a member of this family had occupied the position of Grand Mufti of Jerusalem. "Mufti" was basically a prestigious religious title held by an Islamic scholar whose function was to lead the Muslim community, to oversee and administer its sacred places, and to be the highest local interpreter of the Sharia —the holy law of Islam, which, in many areas throughout the Arab world, until recently constituted the civil law as well.

Haj Amin's grandfather had been Mufti of Jerusalem, as had his father and his elder brother, Kamil al-Husayni. When his brother died, in 1921, Haj Amin, although barely out of his teens, presented himself as his brother's natural successor. So it was, then, that after some extensive but unsuccessful behind-the-scenes maneuvering on the part of Jerusalem's other leading family to get its representative named, Haj Amin was approved as Mufti by the British High Commissioner for Palestine. Ironically, the High Commissioner was Herbert Samuel, an English Jew and supporter of Zionism.

Haj Amin's appointment came after he had taken part in an Arab uprising against the British administration, in April of 1920, over the question of Britain's support of Zionism and its encouragement of Jewish immigration. The resentment of the Arabs of Palestine was not really rooted in the issue of Zionism, however. It had a long history, one that went back through centuries of colonial and imperial rule. The rise of Zionist aspiration and its support by Britain were simply the flaming match dropped onto a deep pile of kindling.

World War I had brought an end to centuries of Arab existence under the generally oppressive umbrella of the Turkish or Ottoman Empire. The Turks had taken the side of the Axis powers in the war against Britain, France, Russia, and (later) the United States. Britain and France had developed their own spheres of influence in the Arab world during the nineteenth century—Britain in Egypt, Iraq, and the Arabian peninsula; France in Syria and Arab-Berber North Africa. Britain especially had reason to defend its considerable interests in the Middle East from Axis penetration by the Germany-allied Turks.

In pursuit of this defense, England in 1916 persuaded Husayn ibn Ali, Grand Sharif of Mecca and leader of the most royal and powerful family of Arab Islam—the Hashemites—to revolt against the Ottomans. The strategy behind this was to divert the Ottoman armies from the north and thus make the defense of British interests there easier. In exchange for the Hashemite family's cooperation, Britain promised to install Husayn and his sons as the crowned heads of an independent and sovereign pan-Arab nation at the successful conclusion of the war. The nation, thought the Hashemites, was to encompass all Arabic-speaking lands east of Egypt, and was to include what are today Israel, Lebanon, Syria, Jordan, Iraq, and the Arabian peninsula.

The war ended successfully for the British, but the promise was never honored. At first it was fudged, then abandoned altogether. Instead Britain and France, aided by the United States, unilaterally apportioned the Arab world between themselves, creating new states and protectorates while attempting to extinguish the fires of Arab nationalism and self-determination they themselves had lit.

The fires refused to go out. Where they burned the fiercest was in what was to have been the geographical heart of the aborted pan-Arab nation, Syria. Under Turkish rule Syria, an Ottoman province, had had no distinct borders, but was generally perceived as covering all that land east of the Mediterranean between Turkey in the north and Egyptian Sinai in the southwest, with the equally indistinct frontiers of the Ottoman provinces of Arabia and Mesopotamia (Iraq) circumscribing it on its eastern extremity.

It was this large Syrian province that England and France parceled between them. Out of it, by means of artificial borders, they created four distinct territories: Palestine, Transjordan, Syria, and Lebanon.

The idea of an independent pan-Arab nation, free of the domination of both the Ottomans and Europe, had sprung up in Egypt and Syria during the latter part of the nineteenth century, mainly as a result of the communication of European political ideas that flowed from British and French colonization. From the time of the Crusades in the twelfth and thirteenth centuries until the penetration of England and France in the nineteenth, the Arab region had been a backwater on the global scene. Its culture and institutions had stagnated under the successive foreign medieval dynasties that ruled it. With its exposure to nineteenth-century European ideas, however—particularly the political and economic ideas of nationalism—the vast area began to stir. As it did so, Ottoman power was in the process of weakening through the twin engines of internal corruption and external warfare. By the beginning of the twentieth century the Arab world, though not yet throbbing with nationalist, self-determinist fervor, was aware that changes were coming.

By the time World War I broke out, that awareness had sharpened into hope. Hope was transformed by the British into expectation when, in 1916, they committed themselves to the establishment of Arab independence as a reward for the Hashemite revolt against the Turks. Indeed, Arab political thinkers and activists spent the following two years determinedly preparing themselves for statehood.

Among these was the youthful Haj Amin al-Husayni, who, representing one of the leading families of southern Syria, envisioned for himself a significant political role in the coming independent state, the capital of which would most likely be Damascus, or possibly even Jerusalem. But then came the Balfour Declaration, followed by the slicing off of southern Syria from Syria proper. Britain further divided southern Syria into two separate territories and named them Palestine (after the biblical land of the Philistines) and Transjordan. The rest of Syria remained to be haggled over by Britain, France, and the Hashemites.

Husayn and his sons made concession after concession to the Europeans in an attempt to come away with at least a piece of the pie. In so doing, they unwittingly acquiesced in the British and French designs on the Arab world. So far as Arab nationalists such as Haj Amin were concerned, they had been doubly betrayed—first by the British, then by their own leaders. When the first waves of immigrant Jews from Europe began to lap up on the shores of Palestine under the banner of the largely British-sponsored Zionist movement, the stage was fully set for conflict.

The first organized Arab reaction to Jewish immigration came in April, 1920. Haj Amin was at the forefront of the demonstrations, delivering himself of fiery speeches and inciting the Arab populace of Jerusalem to insurrection against the British administration and the Jewish settlers. For this a warrant was issued by the British for his arrest, as well as for the arrest of his closest collaborator, Aref al-Aref. The two fled to Damascus, where they found safe but temporary refuge among Syrian nationalists trying to prevent the Hashemites from relinquishing the remains of the pan-Arab dream.

Haj Amin's stay in Damascus was short-lived. Soon after his arrival the Hashemites were evicted from Syria by the French. Haj Amin, along with hundreds of other Syrian nationalists, was forced to go underground in Transjordan. He remained there until early in 1921, when Herbert Samuel was sent out from London to be British High Commissioner of Palestine. As part of his philosophy of reconciliation, Samuel granted amnesties to Haj Amin and al-Aref. Haj Amin returned to Jerusalem; shortly afterward, as a further gesture of conciliation, Samuel officially approved of his selection as Mufti of Jerusalem.

Although Samuel's intention was to neutralize a potential enemy by conscripting him into the British cause, the net effect of his tactic was just the opposite. Thereafter, using his prestige as Mufti and later as head of the Supreme Muslim Council, along with the large annual sums of money these positions brought him, Haj Amin toiled tirelessly to undo everything the British tried to establish in Palestine, particularly Zionist settlement.

From the beginning of his rule over the Supreme Muslim Council, Haj Amin tried to endow the anti-Zionist struggle with religious content. His efforts culminated in the events of August 23, 1929, at the wall that surrounded the compound of the two holy mosques.

Haj Amin had instituted the plan to restore the mosques in order to re-establish the primacy of Islam over all of Palestine and to counter the increasingly vocal religious claims of the Zionists to a portion of Jerusalem. Toward this end he had raised vast sums of money within the Muslim world, interlacing his religious appeals with political invective against real and imagined Jewish designs on the city.

It happened that a portion of the wall surrounding the mosque compound was also a remnant of the ancient and sacred Temple Wall of Jewish religious lore. Yet it was not only the mosques themselves but the entire compound that was Islam's most revered site in Jerusalem. To have Jews conducting their prayers at the holy al-Haram al-Sharif, which was included in the restoration project, would be tantamount to Islamic funds being used to subsidize a religion of infidels. Thus went the spirit of Haj Amin's fund-raising appeals over the course of several years.

So powerful was the cumulative effect of these appeals that on that late August morning in 1929, as the file of devout Jews shuffled through the narrow streets of Jerusalem toward what they considered to be *their* sacred prayer wall, the news of their route and intentions crackled along the local Muslim grapevine like a call to arms. By the time the dozen or so Jews arrived at the wall, they were surrounded by hundreds of Muslim Arabs. And no sooner did the first Jewish supplicant open his prayer book than he was pounced upon by a score of the nearest Arabs.

What followed was the most painful combat Jerusalem had seen since the days of the Crusades. The violence spread throughout the city, gangs of Arabs armed with clubs and daggers fanning out into the Jewish quarter to kill and maim as many Zionists as could be found. The British authorities appealed to Haj Amin to step in and put an end to the carnage. The Mufti shrugged, as if helpless to stop what he had been the prime instrument of.

The following day the bloodletting spread beyond Jerusalem. A few days later an Arab mob murdered fifty-nine Jewish settlers in Hebron, south of Jerusalem, while the historic Jewish town of Safed, in northern Galilee, was also hard hit. Dozens of other Zionist settlements throughout Palestine were victimized, and by the time the British civil authorities were able to restore a semblance of order almost a thousand Jews had died.

Haj Amin modestly accepted the congratulations bestowed on him in secret by the notables among his expanded following. In this, the first countrywide expression of Arab resistance to British imperial betrayal and Zionist colonization, Haj Amin was elevated to the stature of pan-Arab nationalist hero.

The rioting marked the serious beginning of Arab resistance to Zionism in Palestine. The success of Arab violence on so large a scale —there had been previous instances of violence, but always on a local and limited level—gave Haj Amin and his collaborators what they viewed as the vital formula for the nationalization, in Arab terms, of Palestine.

The formula was, of course, violence. Not the spontaneous and random violence that had just occurred, however. Instead, organized violence, in the form of disciplined militia or guerrilla actions overlaid by a strict and carefully orchestrated political program. The result would be an independent Arab-Muslim state of Palestine (Falastin), whose ruler and founding father would be none other than Haj Amin al-Husayni.

In the affairs of Palestine, then, the year 1929 represented a turning point for both Jews and Arabs. For the Zionists it unexpectedly stiffened their resolve to gain the land for themselves; the 1929 slaughter resulted in a rapid increase of Jewish immigrants from Europe. It also organized them in self-defense.

For the Arabs of Palestine it marked the beginnings of their assumption of a separate identity as Palestinians rather than simply as Arabs. Furthermore, it heralded the radicalization of their attempts to block Zionist access to their land, to throw out the British, and to secure for themselves an independent nation.

And, although no one was aware of it, 1929 was a bench mark of another kind. It was in that year—indeed, just about the time the Arab riots were taking place—that Yasir Arafat was born.

PART I

BEFORE ISRAEL

1

Family Tree

Haj Amin al-Husayni never achieved his dream. Frustrated at every turn during the 1930s by the British and then by the rapidly expanding presence and power of the Zionists, he was forced to flee Jerusalem in 1937. He ended up in Nazi Europe during World War II, where he sought and found favor with the Third Reich hierarchy. Had the Axis powers won the war, Haj Amin might well have returned to Jerusalem to preside over a "new order" in the Arab world, sponsored by the Nazis.

As it was, he was never able to return. After the war he took refuge in Paris. But in due time his collaboration with the Nazis became publicized—particularly the blessings he gave to the Germans' "final solution" of the Jewish question—and he had to flee Paris in disguise in order to avoid trial as a war criminal. In 1946 he found sanctuary in Cairo, where the regime of King Farouk had not been unsympathetic to Germany.

Although he was only fifty when he arrived in Cairo, his embrace of Nazi Germany left him with little credibility in the international community as the great powers, through the United Nations, tried to figure out how to settle the problem of Palestine. When in 1948 the United Nations partitioned Palestine and gave the Zionists a state, Haj Amin even lost credit in the Arab world. He had been the leader and spokesman of Palestine Arab resistance for almost thirty years, yet all he had promised, all he had prophesied, had gone unfulfilled. Left to stew in the virulent juices of the anti-Jewish racism he had learned so well in Germany, he became less and less coherent in his pronouncements about Israel. Finally his proclamations began to interfere with and contradict the policy statements and holy-war communiqués of Egypt's President Nasser, who had taken over Arab leadership in the Arab-Israeli conflict. So in the mid-1950s Haj Amin turned to the Muslim Brotherhood.

The Muslim Brotherhood was a clandestine organization of religiously fanatical Egyptians that was soon to be outlawed by Nasser. It had wide influence among Egypt's conservative *fellahin* class, however, and its leaders were constantly plotting the overthrow of Nasser's socialist regime with a view to restructuring Egypt in accordance with the Koranic fundamentals of Islam.

When Haj Amin's collaboration with the feverishly right-wing Brotherhood was discovered, his credibility among politically sophisticated Arabs was totally destroyed. In 1959 he was told to pack up and leave Egypt for good, whereupon he settled in Beirut, Lebanon. There, financed still by his income as Jerusalem's Mufti-in-exile, he settled into a comfortable villa and lived out his days as a lonely, conservative, unlistened-to voice in the rising crescendo of radical rhetoric led, ironically, by his cousin, Yasir Arafat.

There are two things Yasir Arafat does not like to be questioned about at any length. One is the date and place of his birth. The other is his blood relationship to Haj Amin.

It has become the conventional wisdom within the Arab world, and it has been generally accepted elsewhere, that Arafat was born "about 1930 in Jerusalem." Indeed, all press and publicity dispatches emanating from "authoritative" Palestinian sources since 1968 have emphasized Arafat's birthplace as Jerusalem. And to this day Arafat often states with sad, ironic pride that the house in which he was born was only a few houses away from the Jewish Wailing Wall—part of the al-Haram al-Sharif of the Arabs. He concludes his lament with a throw-away line: "Of course, the house is no more. The Jews bulldozed it away in 1967. It was the house I grew up in."

Arafat's claims about his birthplace and the house in which he grew up lend a neat and sympathetic symmetry to his entire life. How could any reasonable man deny the justice of Arafat's devotion to his cause in view of the circumstances of his birth and upbringing? However, the few facts that we know do not coincide with Arafat's claims.

In the Arab tradition generally, and more specifically in the tradition of the Palestine liberation movement, fact is often a malleable commodity, at least from the Western point of view. Whether for benevolent or malevolent purposes, the twisting of fact—indeed, the complete transforming of fact—to suit a particular need is an everyday occurrence, and if it is important enough to a sufficient number of people, a fiction will take on the dimensions of fact and in time become fact itself.

It is most likely, then, that for the Yasir Arafat of today questions concerning his birth—the where and when—have little relevance. To suggest that he has created a lie about his birth, that he is "living a lie," is very much a temptation. But for Arafat it is not a lie. It is a fiction that, through the dynamics of his Arab sensibilities, has become fact.

It is easier to say with certainty, then, where Arafat wasn't born than where he was. Within his own widely scattered family there are two schools of contention among those members who have not got caught up in the passions, politics, and propaganda of the Palestine movement. Both discount Jerusalem. One insists that Arafat was born in Cairo in 1929. The other places his birth in Gaza, a small city along the Mediterranean coast about a hundred miles west of Jerusalem, a year later.

There exists no absolute information on the subject. Official records marking Arafat's birth—whether in Jerusalem, Cairo, Gaza, or elsewhere—seem to have disappeared. One of Arafat's cousins, who subscribes to the Cairo theory, told me that Arafat once boasted of having all official records of his birth in Cairo destroyed in order to underscore his born-in-Jerusalem image. Several other founders of Fatah, the liberation organization that first brought Arafat his worldwide celebrity, are alleged to have done the same so that they too could assume birthrights in the heart of Palestine.

If Arafat was born in Gaza, as one of his uncles and several cousins insist, his self-conceived Palestinian mystique would still retain a certain symmetry, for Gaza is the gateway to the land that was known in New Testament times as Palestine and was so renamed during the formation of the British Mandate following World War I.

But it is the Cairo version of Arafat's birth—as related by two brothers, a sister, and several uncles and cousins on both sides of his family—that makes the most sense. This version has the weight of numbers behind it, and the memories and anecdotes of those who support it are sharper and more definite than those of family members who insist that Arafat was born in Gaza. The following account of the events leading up to Arafat's birth and his early childhood years is reconstructed from the testimony of those family members who seemed best informed and least interested in twisting the question for political or propaganda purposes.

None of this is to suggest that Arafat is without any real connections to Jerusalem. Indeed, his family, or at least part of it, did come from there. His mother, a short, dark, obese woman named Hamida Khalifa al-Husayni, was the daughter of a Jerusalem merchant, Mahmoud al-Husayni, and a cousin (of which there were many) of Mufti Haj Amin.

Family trees are both a preoccupation and a mark of considerable prestige in the Arab Muslim world. This stems from age-old tribal traditions. In ancient Arabian society a man's worth was measured by his connections to his tribe, and more specifically to the clans and families within a tribe. Desert society was highly competitive, and each tribe sought superiority and dominance over its neighbors. For every winner in this perpetual competition there were several losers. The same held true with regard to competition among clans within tribes, and among families within clans. Thus, an individual's pedigree was the primary mark of his worth. If he could prove ancestry from a celebrated tribe or clan, he gained the immediate respect of his peers. If his ancestry was less than noble, he would have to prove himself through his actions before gaining the respect of his peers. If he didn't, then he, along with everyone in his family, became the object of ridicule and disrespect.

This tradition spilled over into the Muslim period, but then it became a matter of how closely one could tie oneself and one's family to an ancestral connection with the Prophet Muhammad, who lived between 571 and 632 A.D.

Through her father, Yasir Arafat's mother was able to prove descent from a man named Muhammad al-Badri, who had settled in Jerusalem in 1380. Before al-Badri's move to Jerusalem, his family had lived for two hundred years in the village of Wadi al-Nusur, just west of the holy city. The family had been brought there from the Arabian peninsula by al-Badri's great-great-great grandfather,

Muhammad ibn Badr, who traced his ancestry on his father's side back to Husayn ibn Ali, who was the second son of Fatima, the daughter of the Prophet.

Although Arabs hungry for ancestral recognition (as most by nature and tradition are) will commonly invent distinguished pedigrees to suit their needs, most scholars of Islamic bloodlines give credence to the claims of the modern al-Husayni family. If true, then Yasir Arafat, at least on his mother's side, has a family tree to be reckoned with.

Such was not the case with regard to Arafat's father, although in pre-Muslim times he might have been thought of as descended from royalty. Born Abdul Rauf al-Qudwa, he was one of many children of Rahman al-Qudwa, the senior member of a wealthy family of merchants, traders, and smugglers who settled in and around Gaza in the late 1700s and became acquainted with European ways when Napoleon tried to colonize the area at the end of the eighteenth century.

The al-Qudwa clan also had its origins in the Arabian peninsula. An offshoot of the famous Qay warrior tribe that was at the forefront of the Islamic conquest of the Middle East in the seventh century, the al-Qudwas split into various families during the post-conquest centuries, some remaining desert fighters, others pursuing the sedentary life as farmers, merchants, and artisans. By the time of the Crusades the branch from which Arafat is descended had settled in Syria. After the Crusaders were expelled from the Fertile Crescent by the Mamluks and Turks, part of the family drifted southward toward Egypt, all the while dividing into further branches. By the eighteenth century one branch was firmly settled and thriving in Gaza. Another, closely related, was established in Cairo.

Mahmoud al-Husayni, although a member of one of Jerusalem's most prestigious families, found his merchandising business suffering as a result of World War I. Coming as he did from a poor-relative branch of the family, he was hard put to it to make ends meet during the wartime restrictions on commerce and trade imposed by the British in Palestine. He was an honest and religious man, and he at first found it difficult to countenance the actions of some of his fellow businessmen and competitors who had taken to smuggling. However, he did have to provide for his wife and four children—the oldest of whom, his daughter Hamida, was approaching marrying age.

Rahman al-Qudwa was doing as well as Mahmoud al-Husayni was doing poorly. Older by a dozen years than Mahmoud, by the end of the war he was one of the wealthiest men in Gaza and one of the largest landowners. As a merchant in both licit and illicit goods, his location in Gaza was auspicious, for it provided easy access to the sea and to the ships that delivered contraband up and down the Levantine coast. The practice was for vessels to stand off the coastline like floating warehouses and to receive visits from enterprising merchants from the coastal cities, who would glide silently out at night in oared barges to stock up on the goods they specialized in.

In the beginning Rahman al-Qudwa had used an oared barge, his sons, among them Abdul Rauf, doing the rowing. But so successful did he become during the war that soon he was able to acquire a larger barge outfitted with a hidden, well-muffled engine. It was not long before he became well known to the merchants of Jerusalem, who frequently traveled to Gaza to make their purchases, as the distributor with the most varied and plentiful merchandise.

In Jerusalem, Mahmoud al-Husayni was finally forced to put expediency before principle. Having heard about Rahman al-Qudwa, he reluctantly journeyed to Gaza one day in 1916 to look over his stocks. He was introduced to al-Qudwa and his sons by another merchant and was surprised to find in him a man as religious as himself. For his part, al-Qudwa was impressed by al-Husayni's family background.

A few weeks later al-Qudwa traveled to Jerusalem with two of his sons to locate a delinquent debtor. While there he visited the home of Mahmoud al-Husayni and met Mahmoud's children, including his daughter Hamida.

No sooner did the two fathers take leave of each other than a scheme was hatched in each of their minds. Rahman al-Qudwa, well-to-do but poorly born, would benefit greatly by an official connection to the eminent al-Husayni family. Mahmoud al-Husayni, wellborn but perennially short of funds, would gain equally by a close tie to the rich al-Qudwas of Gaza.

Chosen to cement the mutually beneficial scheme were Abdul

Rauf, Rahman's son, and Hamida Khalifa, Mahmoud's daughter. The two were married in Jerusalem on May 17, 1917.

The couple settled in Gaza. Abdul Rauf al-Qudwa, now married to an al-Husayni, was given increased responsibilities in his father's various enterprises, while Hamida al-Husayni prepared herself to bear the children who would, in the proud senior al-Qudwa's eyes, infuse into his family the blood of the Prophet.

After several miscarriages a son, Badir Mutar, was born to Abdul and Hamida in Gaza in 1920. Shortly thereafter Rahman al-Qudwa died and Abdul, by dint of his marital credentials, rose above several older brothers to assume the principal mantle of management in the family businesses. In addition to general merchandising, the businesses now included orange groves, shipping and freight, and real estate.

The disturbing events that immediately followed the end of World War I in the Arab world did not go unnoticed by Abdul al-Qudwa in Gaza. Nor could they be ignored by his father-in-law Mahmoud in Jerusalem. Although neither had been particularly political-minded in the Western sense—their politics, as with most Muslims, were contained in their religious consciousness—each was increasingly disturbed by the affront to their Muslim sensibilities of the betrayal of British promises regarding a postwar pan-Arab state and by the British-encouraged immigration of masses of European Jews. Not lost on them, moreover, was the fact that had the pan-Arab state been established as promised, the al-Husayni family would have been foremost among its leadership, acquiring thereby yet more prestige in the Arab world. The credit to both Abdul, an al-Husayni by marriage, and Mahmoud, an al-Husayni by birth, would have been obvious.

Implicit in their feelings, however, was a contradiction. With the ever-expanding wave of Jewish immigration there was much money to be made, especially in Jerusalem and in the burgeoning Jewish coastal settlements. So, while on the one hand paying lip service to the resistance demands being proclaimed by such Palestinian Arab nationalists as Mahmoud's cousin, Haj Amin, on the other they redirected their merchandising energies toward exploiting the new markets being created by the Zionists.

Abdul al-Qudwa financed Mahmoud al-Husayni in a marketing

enterprise designed to appeal exclusively to the Jews: the sale of religious articles. About once a month Abdul would travel from Gaza to Jerusalem to keep tabs on his investment. Occasionally he would take Hamida and their son, Badir, along to visit Mahmoud. On one of these occasions, in 1922, their second child, a girl, was born. They named her Fatima.

The religious-articles business did well, and for the first time in his life Mahmoud al-Husayni was solvent. In his early fifties, he suddenly began to wear his newfound prosperity like a badge, boasting to friends and business acquaintances about the ease with which the incoming Jews could be exploited and singing the praises of his partner and son-in-law.

When word about the sources of Mahmoud's prosperity got back to Haj Amin and other militant members of the al-Husayni family, it did not sit at all well. It was unseemly for one branch of the family to be preaching resistance to the Jewish immigration while another branch sought to profit from it.

At the beginning of 1923 Mahmoud received several warnings through the al-Husayni grapevine to stop doing business with Jews. He ignored them. One morning in July of that year he arrived at his warehouse in Jerusalem to find it vandalized and all his stocks destroyed. An anonymous note was left which promised bodily harm to him and his son-in-law should they attempt to continue to sell to the Jews.

Mahmoud was sufficiently frightened, but Abdul al-Qudwa was merely angered. He replenished the warehouse with fresh goods and ordered his father-in-law to carry on, insisting that his investment be protected.

Mahmoud carried on, but not for long. One evening in November of 1923 a band of enforcers working for the Supreme Muslim Council invaded his house near the al-Haram al-Sharif and, in front of his family, beat him to a bloody pulp.

When they heard of this, Abdul and Hamida rushed to Jerusalem. When Abdul saw Mahmoud, he began to reconsider the wisdom of continuing their business in Jerusalem. And when he went to the warehouse and this time found it burned down, there was no longer any question in his mind about what he should do.

He decided to relocate the business in Jaffa, the old Arab port that was adjacent to the seaside town the Zionists were building called Tel Aviv. There, he thought, he would be beyond the reach of Haj Amin's militants. Mahmoud demurred when Abdul asked him to move to Jaffa. Instead he tried to caution his son-in-law against beginning again.

Abdul al-Qudwa was a stubborn young man, especially when it came to business matters. It was a quality he had inherited from his father, Rahman. One did not become wealthy by being meek or yielding to threats and intimidation. He settled a bit of money on his father-in-law to cover medical bills, then traveled to Jaffa to re-establish the business.

Within a year the enterprise was again prospering, Abdul running it from his headquarters in Gaza while one of his older brothers, Zikim, looked after accounts in Jaffa.

After suffering another miscarriage, Hamida al-Qudwa al-Husayni in 1925 gave birth to her third child, a boy whom Abdul named Zaeed Omar. Shortly thereafter a visit from father-in-law Mahmoud brought disturbing news to Abdul. The Supreme Muslim Council had learned of Abdul's activities in Jaffa, and certain elements within it had expressed their displeasure. Abdul's wife was still, after all, an al-Husayni.

Abdul and Hamida were also disturbed by a strange change that seemed to have taken place in Mahmoud. He spoke glowingly of Haj Amin, a man he had always referred to previously with the kind of contempt that was usually fed by family envy. He praised Haj Amin's leadership of the resistance and even went so far as to chide Abdul for continuing to trade with Jews.

Abdul shrugged off his father-in-law's remarks, unaware that they were really a form of warning. But then, a week later, he received a report from Jaffa: his brother Zikim had been beaten by a gang of Arab thugs and his warehouse ripped apart.

Abdul finally got the message. He brought his brother back to Gaza, closed the warehouse, dismissed his Jaffa salesmen, and liquidated the business. The Jerusalem-Jaffa enterprise had represented only a minor portion of his business conglomerate, and the loss of its income would have little effect on the family fortunes. He would make up the loss by reconcentrating his energies in his purely Arab enterprises.

By the beginning of 1927 Abdul had forgotten all about his Jaffa experiences. But many people living around Gaza hadn't. The militancy and anti-Zionist rhetoric of Haj Amin had spread throughout Palestine by now, and the secret fires of resentment burned in a large portion of the Muslim Arab population. They raged especially fiercely among the youth, many of whom had formed into insurrectionary gangs to do the bidding of Haj Amin's Muslim Council. Raids on Jewish settlements had become common. Beatings were administered, crops burned, shops destroyed. Then the British occupation forces stepped in and began to hunt the Arab gangs and to prosecute and imprison those they caught. This served only to further inflame Arab outrage. Their freedom to raid limited by the British, many of the gangs sought scapegoats among the Arab population.

The area around Gaza had become a center of virulent anti-Zionist feeling. Unlike other parts of Palestine, there were few Christian Arabs living in the Gaza region. Hardly any Jews had settled there either. It was almost exclusively Muslim territory. The nationalist and religious pleadings of Haj Amin in Jerusalem found a particularly intense response in Gaza's singular Muslim outlook. Anti-Zionist sentiment was cultivated chiefly through newspapers and pamphlets published by various groups working under Haj Amin, and it was soon reinforced by secret societies organized to hammer the message home.

The message was that the British represented an occupation force whose sole purpose was to hold the Arab population down until the Jews were able to take over the country. The Jews were out to rule Palestine and to subjugate the Arabs, whose land it was. Hence, any Arab who dealt with the Jews or cooperated with the British was a traitor.

Among the more sophisticated and wealthy Arabs of Gaza, such as the al-Qudwas, the message had at first seemed simplistic and naïve. Many of them were owners of large landholdings up and down the Palestine coast. Much of their land, until the Zionists started to come, had been almost worthless—either arid scrubland or unarable marshland. But the Zionists were willing to pay exorbitant prices for it. What was the harm in selling them worthless land? Or doing business with them in other ways, as had Abdul al-Qudwa and dozens of other Gaza merchants?

Abdul and the others soon found out. Although he had dissolved his Jaffa business and no longer traded with the Jews, Abdul could not escape his past. Somewhat insulated by his wealth from most of Gaza's population, he did not realize that he still enjoyed the dubious reputation of having profited from Zionist settlement.

In March of 1927, during a harvest at one of the al-Qudwa orange groves, a gang of young Arabs attacked a group of pickers and axed down a dozen or so trees. Shortly thereafter a row of shops Abdul owned in Gaza's main *souk* was vandalized. In June another orange grove was vandalized. Then an olive orchard. In August his oldest son, Badir, was stoned in a road near the al-Qudwa home.

Other wealthy Gazans suffered similarly throughout 1927. Those who publicly repented according to the dictates of the minions of Haj Amin and renounced any further dealings with Jews were thereafter left alone. Those who didn't underwent further harassment or else hurriedly sold off their holdings and moved their families away from Gaza.

At first Abdul al-Qudwa refused to be intimidated. He reminded his tormentors, by means of public notices posted all over Gaza, that he had long before closed the business that sold religious articles to Jews. His tactics failed. In September of 1927 he and one of his brothers were attacked and beaten in a Gaza restaurant. While the attack was being carried out, a crude bomb exploded against one of the walls of his house. The conclusion caused Hamida, who was pregnant with her fourth child, to again miscarry.

A month later Abdul, Hamida, and their children were in Cairo, where they were given temporary refuge by relatives of Abdul while he sought a house and a way to salvage some of his Gaza enterprises and transfer them to Egypt.

In November Hamida again became pregnant, and in December the al-Qudwas moved into a modest house on the fringes of Cairo's wealthy Giza district. In August of 1928 the al-Qudwas' fourth child and third son, Nasr Muhammad, was born.

Life for the al-Qudwas in Cairo during those first months was a struggle compared to the halcyon years they had enjoyed in Gaza before their troubles had begun. Abdul still had income from his landholdings in Gaza, but money from the various family merchant and service enterprises had all but dried up. In November of 1928 he returned to Gaza for a brief visit and was surprised to find that his brothers, who had remained there, were completely rehabilitated in the eyes of the local anti-Zionist militants. They had made a public renouncement of their previous dealings with Jews and had been allowed to resume the al-Qudwa business interests safe from harassment.

They urged Abdul to perform a similar penance so that he could return, take over the reins of the family business again, and restore it to its former prosperity. He was tempted. After all he held no brief for the Jews. Indeed, it was because of the Jews that he had got into difficulty in the first place. But, he insisted, he would not lower himself by making a public repentance to those who were his intellectual and social inferiors.

From Gaza he went to Jerusalem to carry out a business commission he had received in Cairo. There he visited Mahmoud al-Husayni, who by then was thoroughly indoctrinated in the resistance philosophy of Haj Amin and was working as a fund raiser for the restoration of the holy mosques. Mahmoud besought Abdul to leave Cairo, make amends with the Gazans, and then move his family to Jerusalem, where he could put his financial acumen to work on behalf of the Supreme Muslim Council. To sweeten the proposal, Mahmoud offered to obtain Haj Amin's personal pardon for Abdul's earlier dealings with the Jews and hinted broadly at the personal fortune he could accumulate in the form of fund-raising commissions. Abdul listened, but remained noncommittal.

He returned to Cairo in January, 1929, to find that Hamida was again pregnant. During the following months he obtained a few more commissions that called for him to travel again to Jerusalem. Arriving there in April, he found the city a hotbed of tension and intrigue. Small riots, fired by the Haj Amin faction's relentless anti-Zionist broadsides, had broken out in various parts of Palestine. British military police patrolled the streets of Jerusalem hoping to keep things quiet there. And, aside from a few scattered incidents, Jerusalem did remain quiet. But only for a while.

Abdul returned to Cairo in June after stopping in Gaza and reconnoitering the situation there. The two months he spent in Jerusalem had finally changed his thinking. Through Mahmoud he had met Haj Amin and was deeply impressed with the Mufti's logic as he expostulated on the Zionist menace to the dream of an Arab state of Palestine. Consequently, on his stopover in Gaza, although he did not publicly recant his sin of having once done business with the Jews, he did make known the fact that he was in thorough accord with the anti-Zionist policies of Haj Amin. Simultaneously word came down from Jerusalem that Abdul had enjoyed a personal audience with the Mufti and appeared to be in his good graces.

Abdul experienced a sudden and pleasing change in the climate of opinion in Gaza. No one said anything specific to him, but people now greeted or smiled at him more readily in the streets and asked after his family. Too, his shops were frequented again. And brokers once more sought him out with orders for his orange and olive crops.

Buoyed by this, Abdul arrived back in Cairo in June feverish with plans to join the interests he had developed there with his and his brothers' Gaza enterprises. He spent the summer working out the details while Hamida grew big with their fifth child.

He was due to travel again to Jerusalem in late August, but the outbreak of rioting there on August 23, triggered by the Jews' attempt to pray at the al-Haram al-Sharif, kept him in Cairo. It was just as well. Hamida was not expected to give birth until the last week of September. In planning his August trip, he had expected to be back in time for the birth.

As it was, Hamida went into labor on August 26. A few hours into the morning of the twenty-seventh she prematurely delivered her fourth boy-child. The next day Abdul went to Cairo's Interior Ministry to register the name of his new son. He called the tiny infant Rahman Abdul Rauf Arafat al-Qudwa al-Husayni. "Rahman" was the name of Abdul's father. "Abdul Rauf" was his own full name. "Arafat" was for the sacred mountain near Mecca where Muhammad the Prophet, according to Islamic belief, had been transformed into the final messenger of God.

The boy would grow up to be Yasir Arafat.

2

Encounter in Jerusalem

Rahman, as Arafat was called by his family, passed the first few years of his life as most Arab children do—generally ignored by his father and totally within his mother's embrace. According to his brother Zaeed, who was four at the time, Rahman, a premature baby, was nursed for three years by Hamida. He was thereafter relegated to the older children's company to fend for himself until he reached the age when it was appropriate for his father to take notice of him.

Like his older siblings, Rahman was dark-complexioned, but unlike them he had the large, watery, slightly protuberant eyes of his mother—al-Husayni eyes. At one year of age his nose was not yet completely formed, but it promised to be broad and bold, like that of his father. He had his mother's full mouth rather than the thin lips of his father, but he inherited his father's finely chiseled ears. He was on the thin side, as his father once had been, but that may have been due more to undernourishment than to genetics.

Once permanently removed from his mother's breast, Rahman did not eat well for more than a year. By the time he was four, he was in stark and slender contrast to his three older brothers, who were still chunky with baby fat. After his fourth birthday, however, he began to pick up weight.

In 1933, when Rahman was still three, his mother gave birth to another child, a boy named Husayn. Shortly afterwards Abdul moved the family into larger quarters, and home for Rahman became a house in an expanding neighborhood of Palestinian émigré families on Cairo's west bank. Next door lived an elderly brother of Hamida's mother who had brought his family to Cairo from Hebron in 1921.

His name was Yusuf Awad al-Akbar, and he was considered a

kind of unofficial mufti for the neighborhood. In the urban Arab world, entire districts were built around the presence of such elderly and sagacious notables as al-Akbar. A devoutly religious man, he was a Koranic scholar and coiner of axioms, but his principal function was to guide the youth of the neighborhood in proper Sunni ways.* Fathers such as Abdul, preoccupied much of the time with commercial matters and often away from their families for weeks at a time, were glad to have elders like Yusuf al-Akbar handy to indoctrinate their young children in the laws of Islam.

Such surrogacy would last until a child, especially a boy-child, was twelve. At that age he was considered sufficiently mature to be worthy of his father's attention, and thereafter his father would assume the responsibility for his religious education. Rahman would find al-Akbar his most powerful early influence.

By 1933 Abdul had successfully welded his Gaza and Cairo interests and was in an almost constant state of travel between the two cities. Three or four times a year he would also trek to Jerusalem, and often on these trips he would take his eldest son, Badir, then thirteen.

After the riots of 1929 Zionist immigration to Palestine stepped up, from the Arabs' point of view, at an alarming rate. As each year more and more Jews poured into the country, the power and influence of the anti-Zionist activists led by Haj Amin expanded. During one of their 1933 journeys to Jerusalem, Abdul and Badir experienced an event that turned the father, and by extension his son, once and for all into thoroughgoing Zionist-haters.

It was a Thursday afternoon in September and they had just come from the Dome of the Rock, where Abdul had been instructing his son on a few of the finer points of the Koran. On their way to the municipality office to keep a business appointment, they came across a large group of young Jews arguing with two Arabs in the middle of al-Zahra Street. The Jews were members of a private security force hired by a shopkeepers' association in the Jewish quarter to prevent Arab vandalism and stealing. They had chased the two

*The al-Qudwas, al-Husaynis, and other related families were Sunni Muslims. Although there are several large Muslim sects and many smaller ones throughout the Islamic world, in the Arab countries the Sunni represent the traditional orthodoxy and are the dominant expression of the religion.

Arabs into al-Zahra Street, now had them surrounded, and were frenziedly accusing them of shoplifting. The Arabs denied the charges. The leader of the Jewish group ordered the Arabs to remove their robes so that the Jews could see the stolen goods they claimed were concealed underneath. The Arabs refused. Thereupon one, then two, then all the Jews pounced on the Arabs, trying to strip their robes away.

The noisy confrontation had attracted a crowd, mostly Arabs. When the Jews attacked the two suspects, the crowd surged forward for a closer look. Suddenly curiosity turned to anger, and out of the crowd dashed a dozen or so Arabs to attack the Jews. A full-scale fight erupted, and scores of additional onlookers swelled the mob. Soon separate fights broke out around the fringes of the crowd, and in a matter of moments al-Zahra Street was a battleground.

Abdul and Badir were caught in the middle of it. Then Abdul realized that he himself was being set upon. Three men, Jews, were raining blows on his head. Another kicked him in the groin. He fell to the street, the Jews on top of him.

When he saw his father fall, Badir threw himself on top of the men, trying to drag them away. Crying hysterically, he pounded his elbow into the back of one of the Jews.

The man turned around and wrestled Badir to his feet. Then he dragged the boy away a distance and began to punch him. He was joined by the other two, who left Abdul bleeding and bent double on the street. Just before he passed out, Abdul saw his son's face soaked in blood.

Abdul came to a few minutes later. British police vehicles were inching their way through the thousands who now filled the street. A platoon of policemen leapt from a lorry and started indiscriminately to pound Arabs with their billies. Abdul, still lying on the ground and trying to collect his senses, himself got a club in the neck.

He watched the police form into twin skirmish lines, divide the mob, and then start to drive each half in opposite directions along the street. A second line of police trailed in the wake of the first. When an Arab managed to break through the first line, the backup policemen were instantly upon him, clubbing him to the pavement and breaking his head open. When an occasional Jew popped through, seeking to escape the mob, he was hustled out of harm's way.

Abdul passed out again. When he awoke, he was being ministered to by Badir, whose face was a smear of tears, dust, sweat, and blood oozing from several wounds. Dozens of people were still milling about, but the din of the mob had moved several blocks away. Abdul struggled to his feet and, though still dazed, managed to get himself and Badir out of al-Zahra Street. Holding a kerchief to his son's wounds, he led him through a series of back alleys to the house of Mahmoud al-Husayni.

Yasir Arafat disclaims any memory of his father and eldest brother's experiences in Jerusalem that day. However, his second eldest brother, Zaeed, who was eight years old at the time, recalls their father's and brother's return to Cairo a few days later. Badir's head, he says, was swathed in bandages, and he was missing two or three teeth. His father had lost a tooth, and his eyes were swollen and blackened.

Zaeed claims also that his father was filled with rage upon his return—rage at the Jews, rage at the British—and that the tale of the beatings he and his son had suffered was narrated frequently during the following years. His brother Rahman could not help but remember the story. Although he was only four, the incident became well entrenched in the family lore. "Rahman excludes it from his memory," says Zaeed, "because to acknowledge it would be to acknowledge his childhood in Cairo."

The story gains further credibility through the recollection of Hasan al-Husayni, a grandson of Mahmoud who was about Badir's age at the time and who claims he was at the al-Husayni house when Abdul and Badir arrived seeking medical attention. "Admittedly my memory is hazy," he said over coffee in Beirut. "But I do recall specifically the blood, and the anger of Badir's father. He was roaring, so much so that it frightened me. There was much talk of revenge that night with my grandfather, and I even recall Badir hissing through his missing teeth and swollen lips about devoting his life to killing Jews."

3

Young Rahman al-Qudwa

By all accounts Rahman al-Qudwa al-Husayni was a quiet, withdrawn child. His sister Halma, younger by five years,* suggests even that there was something wrong with him. Zaeed claims he was merely timid, but Halma insists that there was a certain imbalance in his functioning.

Rahman first appears in Halma's conscious memory at about the time she was four and he was nine. She recalls many instances of Rahman setting himself apart from the other children and engaging in hours-long bouts of silence while staring vacantly, slack-jawed, into space. Such incidents frightened her; she confesses to having grown up always with a sense of fear of her brother.

Nasr, older by a year than Rahman, confirms the odd behavior. Rather than attributing it to some sort of personality dysfunction, however, he ascribes it to a deep instinctive asceticism on Rahman's part. "As far back as I can remember, there was something that made him different from the rest of us. For one thing, as a child he never cried. We would have fights, my brothers and me, childhood tussles. Rahman would always try to avoid them. When he did get caught in one, he would go stiff and cold. If he was hurt, he would not cry out. He would go stiff and stare at us with his mistrusting eyes. Of course we would hit him and taunt him all the more to get a reaction from him. But his eyes would just grow harder. He would lie there, his arms at his side, never attempting to ward off our blows, and just stare us into stopping. Then he would get up and walk away. Soon we gave up trying to get him into our way of things. Most of the time we left him alone. Later we began to understand why he was this way."

*Halma, born in 1934, was the last child born to Abdul and Hamida.

Rahman's seventh year marked the culmination of the efforts of Haj Amin al-Husayni to mobilize the Arabs of Palestine into full-scale resistance to Zionism. His work was not made easier by either the hundreds of thousands of Jews who had immigrated to Palestine since World War I or the British administration.

The year was 1936. Jewish achievement in Palestine since 1918 had been on a scale unprecedented in nation-building. With the help of about a quarter of a billion dollars in foreign (mostly Jewish) capital investment and of the stepped-up immigration of technologically skilled Jews from Europe and the Americas, the new Jewish homeland was in the process of becoming a prosperous shadow state. The Zionists were creating an institutional society on the European model, based on sophisticated socialist-capitalist economic practice. Industry, land reclamation and agriculture, construction, education, health care—all flourished as the Jewish culture settled in and expanded. The Zionists had a new justification for their presence in Palestine: "Look what we are managing to do with this barren land. What are the Arabs complaining about? With them alone here, the land was always unproductive, the society fallow and impoverished. Look how we are transforming it. The Arabs can only benefit from our achievements!"

True, what the Jews were doing constituted an economic and social miracle—for the Jews. Despite the fact that a few Arabs prospered from the Jewish accomplishments, for the general Arab population it was a miracle in reverse. The Jewish economic success brought an influx of poor Arabs from lands around Palestine hoping to find jobs in the hyperactive economy. What they, along with the local Arabs, found was poverty. Zionist labor policy for the most part excluded, or otherwise discriminated against, Arab labor.

The ordinary Arab in Palestine in these years was faced with a steeply escalating cost of living, which was brought about by the Jewish economic "miracle." His resentments were intensified by the spectacle of the handsome new boulevards built in the more desirable parts of the towns and cities by and for the immigrant population, and by the vast tracts of Jewish workingmen's quarters erected by Jewish building societies. Often, too, he had the experience of being driven away from work sites by Jewish pickets, and he resented the fact that when he was allowed to work, the government paid the

Jewish workman double the rate it paid him.

It was in the less populous middle and upper classes of Palestinian Arab society that the transformation had the most profound effect, however. It is true that many Arabs in these classes, especially landowners and merchants, prospered as a result of the Jewish influx. Many families acquired considerable wealth from land sales to the Jews. Others found their shops and businesses increasingly patronized by the immigrants, all to their monetary advantage. Many used the capital so acquired to plant citrus and banana groves. They also used it to educate their sons and daughters. In the course of fifteen years there grew up a generation of young men and, to a lesser extent, young women who had received at least the rudiments of a modern education. Hundreds of them had been sent abroad and had spent a number of years in European schools and universities. This younger generation was brought up on the ideals of the vigorous postwar Arab nationalism that emanated from the broken promises of the European powers; they could not be kept quiet, as the older generation had been, by halfhearted Jewish attempts at conciliation or by such British backing-and-filling maneuvers as the proposal that Palestine be partitioned between Arabs and Jews—with the Jews getting the rich northern coastal plain and the Arabs the dry southern desert region. There thus came about a complete transformation in the nature and intensity of Arab opposition to the Judaization of the country.

By the mid-1930s the Arab population was altogether better educated and more articulate than it had been in 1920. The commonly perceived danger of total Jewish control, moreover, tended to push various segments of the population together. Christian and Muslim Arabs, the large peasant populace and the smaller elite, were acquiring in common a stronger sense of Palestinian identity and a new sense of solidarity. The formation of Palestine into a political entity, symbolized by the passport and customs barriers by which it was now separated from the rest of Syria, accentuated this sense of Palestinian Arab unity while at the same time, through protests over this artificial separation, heightening the notion of Palestinian nationalism.

What was probably most crucial in influencing relations between Arabs and Zionists, however, were the attitudes most of the Jews brought with them. Before the beginning of the twentieth century there were no such people as Zionists in Palestine, only a small native Jewish minority that devoted itself mostly to religious matters. Unlike Jewish communities in the rest of the Arab world, the indigenous Jews of Palestine were unworldly, pious, and seclusive. They were for the most part poor, uneducated (except in religious affairs), and indifferent to the political turmoil around them.

The initial small-scale immigrations from eastern Europe before World War I changed that somewhat, but it was not until after the war that the nature of the Jewish presence really changed. When it did so, it changed radically. As we have seen, with the blessing of the Balfour Declaration in 1917 Zionist immigration accelerated rapidly, reaching a post–World War I peak in the early 1930s. With it came an influx of ethnic attitudes, bigotries, and values which, when concentrated in a crowded tiny land, produced acute antagonisms far beyond political and ideological concerns. To put it more plainly, the Arabs, who were the natives, found much in the attitudes and behavior of the Jews repugnant and detestable.

There were certainly individual Jews who were highly sensitive to the feelings of the Arabs and who strove to soften the impact of this foreign presence. But the majority of Jewish immigrants, heady with the dream of Jewish statehood and convinced that the land was already theirs, were blatantly indifferent to Arab sensibilities.

Haj Amin and his cohorts seized on all these factors to exacerbate tensions and advance their own by now highly structured and extremist brand of nationalism. During the 1920s there had been those among the Arabs who took a more moderate approach to the British and Zionist presence, hoping to turn Palestine into an Arab state through negotiation and political settlement. Some even criticized Haj Amin, claiming that his tactics of militancy and intimidation were actually aiding Zionist nationalist hopes. Their thinking was based on the fact that it was the British who had the real authority in Palestine. It was therefore the British who would determine the ultimate disposition of the land. Test proposals having to do with dividing or partitioning the country between the Jews and the Arabs had already been advanced. The moderates were willing to consider these proposals as a starting point for negotiations. But the Haj Amin faction would have nothing to do with such approaches.

Palestine would be all Arab or it would be nothing.

The moderates were led by the elders of Jerusalem's large Nashashibi family. The Nashashibis were second only to the al-Husaynis as the most prestigious clan in Palestine. Whereas the al-Husaynis had traditionally dominated the high religious positions of Jerusalem, the Nashashibis controlled the civil hierarchy. For instance, the mayoralty of Jerusalem had been in Nashashibi hands for generations.

In the early days of local resistance to the Zionists, many of the Haj Amin–inspired strikes and riots were aimed as much against the authority of the Nashashibis as against the Jews and British. Gradually through the 1920s Haj Amin managed to erode the influence of the moderates and bring more and more of the local population to his side. During the early 1930s the children of the wealthy Palestinian classes began to return home from European universities, having been schooled in nationalist ideas and exposed to the sophisticated techniques of concerted civil and paramilitary action in the pursuit of nationalist goals. To them the extremist philosophy—all or nothing—of Haj Amin had much more appeal than the moderate approach of the older-generation Nashashibis and allied families, even though many of the returning youth came from these families. They naturally gravitated to Haj Amin and by 1935 had swelled the ranks of the militants. Since the future lay with the youth, the moderating influence of the older generation fell into permanent decline.

In 1936, confident of his wide-ranging support, Haj Amin formed the Arab Higher Committee. Its membership consisted of representatives of almost every Arab special-interest group in Palestine, and its design was to move the resistance struggle out of the religious realm, where it had remained anchored through its connection to the Supreme Muslim Council, and onto a political and paramilitary level. Much of the impetus for the new organization came from the returning student-activists, who had persuaded Haj Amin of the virtues of civil action, European style, and of organized partisan and guerrilla warfare as opposed to random rioting and terrorism, which had been the Arab practice.

A few months later the Higher Committee called on the Arab population of Palestine to carry out a general strike against the

British. Even Haj Amin was surprised at the result. The response to the strike call was almost unanimous. All over Palestine daily commerce came to a halt. Stores and businesses shut down. Fields and orchards emptied. The docks and ports grew still.

While the strike was still in its first weeks, cadres of armed youth, organized now into semi-disciplined fighting units, fanned out into the country. They recruited idle shopkeepers and laborers, providing them with arms and some rudimentary training. Suddenly the countrywide strike began to turn into an armed revolt.

The British were hamstrung. At first they had enough forces to contain the revolt but not suppress it. One of the ways they sought to contain it was to rob it of its leadership. The first leader they went after was Haj Amin, ordering his arrest. The Mufti, after hiding out in Jerusalem's al-Aqsa mosque, eventually managed to escape to Lebanon. Thereafter he would join the Palestinian nationalist cause to that of Nazi Germany.

These events had no impact on the reclusive seven-year-old Rahman al-Qudwa in Cairo, except possibly as an awareness he might have gained from hearing his father and other elders in his Palestinian neighborhood discuss them. It was at about this time that Rahman was delivered to the care of his granduncle, Yusuf al-Akbar, for his initial religious training. Al-Akbar conducted daily religious classes for the youngsters of the district, which consisted mostly of readings from the Koran and analyses of the Prophet's revelations. Rahman's older brothers Zaeed and Nasr were already veterans of the classes when Rahman joined, and Zaeed can still vividly recall the effect the old Muslim sage had on Rahman.

"Religious exercises went on in our home all the time," he told me. "Prayers, discussions, fastings, other rituals. Up to a certain time Rahman was considered by my father to be too young to participate in any serious way, although if my father caught his attention wandering, he would clout him. Of course, in religious matters my father was a deliberate man. He went very slowly. What he didn't realize was that when Rahman's attention wandered it was out of boredom with the slowness of my father. But Rahman was afraid of my father, as we all were at that age. He didn't dare reveal that his thoughts and ideas raced ahead of those of my father. We did not discover his religious talents until he began with Yusuf."

Yusuf al-Akbar was at first puzzled by the now chubby, enigmatic Rahman. At times in that first year of instruction it seemed that his grandnephew knew more than he did. At other times it appeared that he was as dull and stupid as a camel. "But then it began to dawn on him," Nasr says. "He had some kind of strange gift. He could not even read yet, but often he would finish a sentence Yusuf was reading aloud from the book. He would suddenly break in and say it aloud before Yusuf could get to it."

Eventually, according to Nasr, Yusuf ceased reprimanding Rahman and began to look at him wonderingly. He went to Abdul al-Qudwa and told him that his son had been specially blessed by Allah. He described what he took to be the nature of the boy's gift—it had something to do with the Koran having been prenatally imprinted in Rahman's mind—and urged Abdul to treat Rahman with deference and sensitivity. "It was as if he was saying that Rahman was wiser than all of us together. This seven-year-old."

Abdul received the news with pride, and immediately cautioned his other children to be gentle in their dealings with their brother. "Then we discovered," says Nasr, "that it was no divine gift at all. It was just that at a very young age Rahman had what you call a photographic memory. He had heard the same lines, the same phrases during our religious periods at home, and when Yusuf read them again he already knew them. His finishing the sentences for Yusuf was simply his way of asserting himself when my father was not around."

The discovery was not made until Rahman was about eleven, however, so for the next three or four years of his life he was handled with care by everyone around him. Particularly attentive was Yusuf al-Akbar. By the time Rahman was eight, he was spending more time in al-Akbar's company than with his family. Al-Akbar, convinced of his grandnephew's inborn connection to the deity, quickly turned the boy into his personal protégé, providing him each day with extra hours of specialized religious instruction while the other boys of the neighborhood were out developing their skills at soccer and other sports.

Rahman seemed happily willing to be immersed in religion. According to Nasr, the lad was ill-coordinated physically and had no taste for sports or for any kind of competitive games. "We would all spend our obligatory two hours with Yusuf," recalls Nasr. "There would always be anywhere from fifteen to twenty boys in the classes. And there would always be a certain amount of impatience to get away after the first hour. Such as giggling and horseplay behind Yusuf's back. When we were finally released each afternoon, we would stampede to get out of Yusuf's house. But not my brother. He would stay, and then we wouldn't see him back in our own home until dark. Yusuf would usually deliver him there, and he would always take my father aside and whisper things about Rahman to him. I believe Yusuf's idea was to groom Rahman to succeed him as the family's religious leader. My father was agreeable to this, and so he continued to punish us whenever he learned that we were taunting Rahman. We all came to resent Rahman for the special treatment he received. However, I must tell you that Rahman was never the one responsible for my father finding out. Rahman would never say anything to cause us trouble. We all resented him for his special treatment. But I think we also envied him for his iron will."

Zaeed recalls an instance of Rahman's will. "One evening he was coming home from Yusuf al-Akbar's alone. He wandered out of his way and was set upon by some boys from another district—Egyptians. He was beaten rather badly, and when he arrived home he was a mess of cuts and bruises and had lost his religious books. My father was enraged. He ordered us to go out and find the attackers the next day, to avenge Rahman. Rahman insisted that we not do it. He demanded that my father reverse his orders to us. He had seen the size of this gang, and he knew that we would have no chance against them. Although the Koran emphasizes revenge, my brother had weighed the need for revenge against the numbers of the gang that had beaten him. He insisted on forgoing revenge in order to spare us a possibly worse beating.

"This was a few years after my father's experience in Jerusalem with Badir. My father had changed a great deal in those years. I was about twelve or thirteen, and I remember my father going from a generally quiet and preoccupied man into a man who was always ranting about the political situation in Palestine, in Gaza. He was still traveling back and forth to Gaza, and each time he returned to our home he would be filled with more stories about the Jews and the British and how terrible they were. He began to have meetings in our home with other men from our district, and they would go long into the night working themselves up about the Jews. At this time Badir was about seventeen, and he would take part in the meetings. The next day he would tell us what was said, and would preach to us about the crimes of the Zionists and about the fact that our people were being robbed of their rightful country. Myself and Nasr, we listened attentively to Badir's lectures. Even little Husayn, who was only five, would absorb the things Badir told us. But Rahman—he must have been about nine then—he paid little attention. He would be off in a corner reading Yusuf al-Akbar's lessons. When Badir demanded that he listen, he would argue with him. He was not at all interested in these political things. He was interested only in Islam."

Zaeed didn't realize it at the time, but his father and his friends, most of whom were Gazans, were meeting to organize and join themselves to a somewhat sinister organization that had begun to form in Egypt at about the time of Rahman's birth.

When World War I broke out in 1914, the Egyptian nationalist movement had spread throughout rural and urban Egypt and had produced an articulate and popular leader, Saad Zaghlul. Although of peasant origin, Zaghlul had become a high official in the Ministry of Education.

Egypt was, theoretically at least, still subject to Ottoman rule at the outbreak of the war. But practically speaking it was under British colonial suzerainty, and since the Ottomans were allied with Germany, Britain unilaterally proclaimed a wartime protectorate over Egypt to ensure the security of the Suez Canal.

Egypt remained relatively quiet during the war years, but the Egyptians themselves, chafing under stricter British military occupation, didn't. They grew restive and more deeply responsive to Zaghlul and his nationalist propaganda. The determination and ardor of the nationalists were in turn intensified by proclamations made by the Allies about guaranteeing the rights of small nations and pursuing the ideals of self-determination for all peoples once victory over the Axis powers was achieved. The Egyptian nationalists became aware toward the end of the war of British commitments to the Arab leaders east of Egypt concerning an independent pan-Arab state. As soon as the war was over, Zaghlul and his followers established an organization called Wafd al-Misri, or the "Egyptian Delegation," to present demands regarding Egyptian independence to the British government and the Paris Peace Conference.

The British were not going to give up Egypt so easily, however; their stake in the land was more economically vital than ever and they had little trust in the Egyptians' ability to protect it independently. They refused to allow the Wafd al-Misri mission to leave the country. When this refusal was met with widespread and violent protest demonstrations, the British detained Zaghlul and three other leading nationalists in Malta. Later, when the United States government assured Britain that it would not support the claims of the Egyptians, Zaghlul and his group were allowed to go to Paris. There the moderators of the peace conference denied them recognition. These events made national heroes out of Zaghlul and his colleagues. In many Egyptian quarters resentment toward England turned into intense hatred.

Agitation increased until finally the British, in 1922, agreed to terminate its protectorate and recognize Egypt as an independent sovereign state. However, the terms of the proposed recognition were such that Egypt would have ended up as nothing but a satellite of Britain. When the nationalist leaders protested, they were seized and once again exiled. The British then declared the protectorate at an end and turned the existing sultan, Fuad, into the nation's king.

These temporary expedients failed to solve the Egyptian problem, however, for British troops remained in Egypt to shore up the new monarchy and guarantee the security of British investment. In 1924, after more nationalist demonstrations, Britain's puppet Egyptian government adopted a constitution under which, in the first country-wide election guaranteed by it, the nationalist Wafd party won a large majority. In 1924 Saad Zaghlul became the first prime minister in a parliamentary government modeled on the English system. But still the problems of Egypt were not over; differences between the British and the new government over the Sudan, along with the continuing presence of British troops on Egyptian soil, conspired to keep matters at an impasse. But at least Egypt had a measure of independence. It was the first Arabic-speaking land to achieve it.

It was, at best, a murky and uncertain beginning. During the many centuries of Turkish-Mamluk rule over Egypt, the Egyptian character had become thoroughly infused with two fundamental values that should have been contradictory in nature but which in fact often complemented one another: spiritual (Islamic) authoritarianism and material corruption. In this the Egyptians—or any other Arab society, for that matter—were not substantially different from most societies that had evolved elsewhere under other religious banners. The impulse to corruption and authoritarianism is certainly not unique to any one culture of the world; it is merely the manner in and degree to which they are pursued that distinguishes them.

As Egypt gained semi-independence in the 1920s, all sorts of internal struggles were born, most of which were generated not so much from a concern for social reform and democratization as from the specifically Egyptian instincts of authoritarianism and corruptibility. Wealth still meant privilege in Egypt, and the customary road to wealth had always been through corruption. Authority meant power as well, and the route to authority had always been through Islam. The nationalist movement that had culminated in Egyptian independence, then, was not a revolution; it represented merely a transfer of wealth and power from one group to another, with the means by which both were attained and sustained remaining more or less the same.

After the death of Zaghlul in 1927, Mustafa Nahas, his successor as leader of the Wafd party, became Premier. The Wafdists consolidated their political power under Nahas and became representatives of the traditional Egyptian establishment as the old corrupt economic and authoritarian religious ruling classes began to back them. Nahas compromised with the British, negotiating in 1936 a twenty-year treaty that enabled Egypt to become a member of the League of Nations in exchange for the British right to maintain a naval base at Alexandria and a military force of ten thousand in the Suez Canal Zone. Otherwise, British military occupation of Egypt was ended. On the surface it seemed that the Anglo-Egyptian Treaty would leave Egypt free to concentrate on the solution of its internal social problems, but by this time the Wafdist leaders had become so preoccupied with extending their authority and lining their pockets that the needs of the Egyptian masses were generally ignored.

The situation following the 1936 treaty was exacerbated by two further elements. One was the succession to the Egyptian throne of the sixteen-year-old King Farouk upon the death of the British-appointed Fuad. At first broadly popular, the adolescent king early on demonstrated a taste for decidedly non-Islamic pursuits.

But even more politically unsettling was the growing strife to the northeast between Arabs and Jews in the Palestine of the British Mandate. Egyptians did not yet identify themselves as Arabs. But they were increasingly cognizant of their Arab heritage. And they *were* Muslims. This sense of religious brotherhood was buttressed by the appeals of a large core of Arab nationalists who had exiled themselves from the British Palestinian and French Syrian mandates in the wake of their failed dream of a post–World War I pan-Arab nation and who constantly reminded the Egyptian masses of their common Arab inheritance. It did not take long for Egyptian emotions to become aroused with regard to the Zionization of Palestine. These feelings were even more inflamed by the fact that it was under British sponsorship that the Zionists were making their inroads. The Egyptians were thus easily persuaded that Palestine was another Muslim land in danger of falling victim to Western Christian (therefore infidel) imperialism and being handed over to infidel Jews.

Out of this mood a new movement had arisen within the religious and reactionary fabric of Egyptian society. Called in Arabic al-Ikhwan al-Muslimin, it came to be known in English as the Muslim Brotherhood. Founded in 1928 by a scholarly and dynamic Egyptian schoolteacher named Hassan Banna as a result of the Anglo-Egyptian Treaty, the movement quickly spread throughout Egypt and rapidly transformed itself into a political organization. Its primary goals were to reform the government of Egypt according to fundamentalist Islamic precepts and to wipe out the ruling-class corruption that infested the country. But its fast-expanding appeal derived from its condemnation of Britain and its demands for true independence from British rule.

Since the British, in the Arab view, were being as treacherous in Palestine as they were in Egypt, the Muslim Brotherhood took up the Palestinian Arab cause as well. In 1937, Haj Amin was forced to flee Palestine as a result of the Arab revolt. With the effective leadership of Arab resistance expelled from Palestine, the resistance movement there began to flounder. The Muslim Brotherhood in Egypt publicly identified the citizenry of Egypt with the Arab populace of Palestine, claiming that they were brothers suffering under a common British oppression. The identification was an effective one, and when it appeared that only the Muslim Brotherhood stood ready to take up the cause of the Palestinians, the Brotherhood gained the sympathy, and later the allegiance, of many of the Palestinians living in and around Cairo. Among them were Abdul al-Qudwa and his friends.

4

Learning the Doctrines of Islam

In August of 1938 Rahman al-Qudwa al-Husayni turned nine. In addition to his daily lessons with Yusuf al-Akbar, he began his formal education in a school run by Palestinian teachers living in Cairo.

At first al-Akbar had tried to dissuade Abdul from sending Rahman to what was for all practical purposes a secular school. The school did have religious instruction as part of its obligatory curriculum, but al-Akbar was more convinced than ever that Rahman had been chosen by Allah for a special mission in life. He argued that ordinary schooling and daily exposure to ordinary pupils and teachers would stain the purity of Rahman's religious gift. "He was quite adamant against it," says Rahman's brother Zaeed today. "In fact, the reason Rahman began school so late—the rest of us started when we were seven—was that Yusuf was able to persuade my father to keep him out. Yusuf used the argument that it would be like putting a pure-blooded horse in a pen full of mules. Rahman would be cheapened by attending an ordinary school."

Abdul had gone along with al-Akbar's wishes, but now, in 1938, he began to suspect the older man's motives. His wife's uncle was an al-Husayni, and the old man was talking more and more about Rahman's gift being the result of his al-Husayni blood. Indeed, al-Akbar had become almost fixated on the subject and had even convinced Hamida that Rahman's religious precocity was a manifestation of their shared ancestral connection to the family of the Prophet.

Hamida had taken to lording it over the other families of the neighborhood because of her ancestry, holding up Rahman as proof of her familial distinction and symbol of her by now well-entrenched conviction that Allah had chosen her for a special role in the Islamic scheme of things. In the process, rather than accumulating respect, she managed to alienate most of the families she was trying to impress.

At the same time Abdul, having become involved in the Muslim Brotherhood, was trying to spread its message among the heads of these families and to form a neighborhood Brotherhood cell in support of Hassan Banna. Despite his reprimands, Hamida continued to advertise the ideas put into her head by her uncle. As a consequence, Abdul finally decided to overrule Yusuf's counsel regarding Rahman's education. Rahman's "specialness" was becoming a liability to Abdul, for it encouraged his wife's snobbery and was beginning to cost him the respect of the men he was trying to win over to the Muslim Brotherhood. Moreover, he had started to perceive Rahman's moody, remote ways less as a divine gift and more as a personal annoyance. He decided that the best way to put an end to all this was to provide the conditions that would turn Rahman into as ordinary a boy as every other. So, Yusuf and Hamida's wishes to the contrary, he enrolled him in the local secular school. The result was the beginning of an intrafamily conflict, with Rahman the pawn, that eventually caused Abdul to give up most of his Cairo business holdings and move his family back to Gaza.

Although Hamida was powerless to reverse her husband's decision, Yusuf al-Akbar felt he was not. The old tutor did everything he could to undermine Abdul. During his first year in school Rahman was still permitted by Abdul to continue his religious studies with al-Akbar. The unhappy boy—Rahman did not, according to his brothers, take well to his school enrollment—resented his father's decision and became acutely susceptible to al-Akbar's designs.

So upset was al-Akbar by Abdul's decision to send Rahman to school, his brothers recall, that after a month or so the old man went to their father and offered, in effect, to buy the boy from him. "Yusuf went among all the families in the neighborhood," says Zaeed, "secretly raising money. He even at one point had one of his relatives in Jerusalem raising money among the al-Husayni clan. The idea was that Rahman was destined to someday bring glory to the al-Husayni name, and it was Yusuf's function to ensure that. . . . Now, that is not as odd as it may sound. In our world the selling or bartering of children was not an unusual occurrence, especially among the poor and the fanatically religious. Of course, my father rejected Yusuf's proposal. He himself was in the process of becoming somewhat of a religious fanatic through his ties to the Ikhwan, but he was not poor."

Abdul's refusal to deliver Rahman into Yusuf's custody, despite the offer of a handsome financial settlement, set the old man on a new course.

During Rahman's first year in the Palestinian school he evinced no change in his withdrawn and often eccentric behavior. He was a natural student, everyone recalls, with a special proclivity for mathematical subjects, but he remained, as usual, aloof from his classmates and spoke only when spoken to. "Yusuf had already instilled in him a strong sense of superiority," Nasr, who was in the same class, remembers. "Naturally the other boys found Rahman strange and gave him more than the usual share of taunting and challenging which boys who are different get. Rahman changed a little from what he was when he was just at home. He started to resist the teasing. He was tentative about it at first. But then he started to push back if someone shoved him, and he would make a retort if someone made a taunting remark at him. At home he would still be completely non-belligerent with us if there was a tussle. But in school he would not idly suffer taunts or manhandling."

Every afternoon after school Rahman would hurry to the house of Yusuf al-Akbar for his studies. Yusuf had given up practically all his other religious concerns to devote himself exclusively to the cultivation of what he perceived as the sacred side of Rahman's nature. But that was not the only goal he had in mind. Unable to persuade Abdul to settle Rahman over into his full-time custody, al-Akbar proceeded to interlard his religious instructions with subtle denigrations of Rahman's father and the entire al-Qudwa family. Although he was an unworldly man with little aptitude for the local political concerns of the day, he decided to utilize the Jewish-Arab question in an attempt to mold Rahman's total allegiance to him. Consequently, he began to slip into his lectures comparisons between the al-Qudwas and the al-Husaynis. He glorified the al-Husayni bloodline, pointing to the numerous religious and cultural dignitaries that had borne it through the centuries, going back to the grandsons of the Prophet himself. The al-Qudwas, on the other hand, possessed little or no distinction within the Islamic ancestral hierarchy. In fact, Yusuf took pains to point out to Rahman, the al-Qudwa line was distinguished by nothing more than common merchants, of whom Rahman's grandfather had been the most notable.

For a boy who had, in the eyes of his brothers, already been brainwashed into believing he had been chosen for a special, higher role in life, al-Akbar's almost daily lessons in the contradictions of his genetic character both confused and impressed Rahman.

"The entire procedure was designed to erode, and finally destroy, his respect for our father," claims Zaeed. "At this time our father, and our brother Badir, were getting deeper into the Ikhwan organization. In fact, you could say our father had become well known in our neighborhood for his promotion of the ideals of Hassan Banna. Many of the Ikhwan's principles were beginning to embrace the ideals of partisan warfare in Egypt. Ikhwan groups were springing up all over Egypt, and many of them were acquiring arms to carry on the fight against the British and the British puppets who ran the Egyptian government. Although the group my father was involved with did not yet have arms in any big way, I remember him coming home one day with an old British rifle. It was the first time we had ever seen a gun up close. My father started to carry it around to his secret meetings. Before long he was well known in the district for his rifle. I'm not even certain it could be fired. He was using it primarily as a symbol for recruiting sympathizers.

"Well, Yusuf used this rifle to work on Rahman. He used it himself as a symbol to prove that our father was not a proper religious man, that he had been seduced by the basic al-Qudwa instinct for thievery and thuggery. Of course this was not the case, but Yusuf's simpleminded teachings made a great impression on Rahman. Rahman began disobeying our father. Before, he would carry out orders silently. Now, if my father told him to do something, he would shake his head or walk away. My father would punish him, beat him, but after a while not even beatings could force my brother to do what my father ordered. Then it began to come out why. It was because Yusuf had told Rahman that our father was not worthy of his respect. When my father discovered this, it drove him crazy. He went to Yusuf and swore to kill him if he didn't stop. Yusuf was frightened, and he repented."

Al-Akbar's repentance was short-lived. Once over his initial fright, he took a new tack with Rahman. According to both Zaeed and Nasr, he began to draw the boy's attention to the fact that their father had been driven out of Gaza because of "his dealings with the Zionist Jews who were intent on conquering the al-Husayni Palestine nation."

It was the first time Rahman had heard anything, other than in passing, about the Jews. "It was a very effective tactic on Yusuf's part," says Zaeed. "There had always been talk around our home about the Zionists. Also, all of us knew my father had come from Gaza, but except for Badir none of us really had thought about why we were living in Cairo. The fact that my father had been forced to leave over this business with the Jews was never talked about, although we heard rumors once in a while. In any event, all the talk and all the rumors had always passed by Rahman's ears. I'm sure he knew there were such people as Jews, and that they were doing something that was objected to. But he had never shown a bit of interest. Then Yusuf began to work on him, putting this question of the Jews together with his claims about my father and his shame. It had a devastating effect on Rahman. I remember that for about a year the issue of Rahman and what to do with him became a great and constant thorn in my father's side."

Shame is to the psychology of the Arab Muslim as guilt is to that of the Western Christian. Al-Akbar, a man whose own sense of shame was highly developed as a result of his lifelong immersion in the precepts of Islam, knew well how to manipulate the dynamics of shame in others. Whether consciously or unconsciously, in his desperation to preserve the mind and soul of his grandnephew for the service of Allah and the glorification of the al-Husayni name, al-Akbar sought to shame Rahman into permanent allegiance to his designs.

"He gave up unfavorably comparing the al-Qudwas to the al-Husaynis, as he had promised my father during their confrontation," says Nasr. "Instead he secretly started to work on the identification of my father with the Jews. You must understand, because of all that had gone before, and because of the influence of my mother, Rahman had grown almost umbilically attached to Yusuf. It was as if he was under his spell. At this time in his life Rahman was fat, soft, ungainly, and completely unimpressive. He had a very high voice, and was beginning to suffer from comparisons to girls which were made by the other boys. Even my father had started to curse him out in such terms, and he would often shout at my mother for wishing for a daughter before Rahman was born. He blamed my mother for much of what he thought was wrong with Rahman, saying that her dreaming of a girl had caused Rahman to be born more like a girl than a boy. The only one who showed any sympathy for Rahman was Yusuf. Therefore, anything Yusuf said to him, no matter how outrageously false, Rahman believed without question."

Yusuf, in all his religious instructions to Rahman, had never before in any way related the evolution of Islam to anything having to do with Judaism. The fact was that in the seventh century the man known as Muhammad had been deeply impressed by the religious lore of the well-entrenched Jewish population of the Hejaz—the province of the Arabian peninsula that had been for ages the center of Arab pagan religions. Muhammad, an ascetic and otherworldly individual, had sought to bring the Jews' single-God message to the dozens of tribes of the Hejaz that worshiped a variety of gods. At first he tried to do this with the cooperation of the Jews. But the Jews of the Hejaz, by tradition exclusivists and lacking proselytizing instincts, saw little profit to themselves in cooperating with Muhammad. From their viewpoint he was superfluous. If it was their message he was seeking to disseminate, why did they need him? They were quite capable of performing the task on their own, and had, for a long time before the advent of this self-appointed Arabian prophet, been doing precisely that.

Muhammad persisted in his efforts to enlist the Jews in his cause. He went so far as to incorporate a great deal of Jewish ritual into the schema of his embryonic religion, even decreeing to his small but expanding group of followers that they turn toward Jerusalem when praying. Despite his efforts, the Jews declined to join in his venture to convert the Arab tribes to the worship of a single God. Indeed, their rejection turned to scorn. Muhammad had modeled his message on that of the Hebrew scriptures, but was forced to confess, when questioned closely by some of the Jewish elders he had sought to convince, that he had never actually read them and had only become acquainted with their theology through word of mouth. In the scholarly Jews' eyes, then, Muhammad was perceived as being wholly untrained in the very serious matters of Jewish law and lore. His audacity in presuming to call himself an Arab messenger or prophet of their God was deserving only of contempt.

In the Jewish scriptures and ritual law, however—or at least in his adaptations of them—Muhammad had found a convenient framework upon which to construct his own theological edifice. Thus, despite his failure to ally the Jews to his vision, he clung to his Arabian version of the Judaic message and swiftly concluded that the Jews' error in rejecting him lay not in his own ideas but in the Jewish tradition. He thereupon developed and preached the view that the Jews had corrupted the original message of the One God and that he had been chosen by the Almighty, and given the power, to reverse the corruption.

Once this notion was thoroughly embedded in his mind, Muhammad turned away from the Jews altogether. Eventually, for Islam, Judaism became an infidel religion and all Jews, like others who "rejected" the messages of the Prophet, became themselves the objects of Islamic scorn. The Jews, however, having been the original rejecters of Muhammad, became the objects of a special and more highly developed scorn.

Yusuf al-Akbar seized upon the seventh-century Jewish rejection of Muhammad to introduce into the awareness of young Rahman his first notion of Jews and Judaism. He spent many weeks of lessons in early 1939 underlining in Rahman's mind the "infidelity" of the Arabian Jews and the supposed treachery and corruptness of Judaism in general, without at all pointing out the debts in dogma and doctrine Islam owed to Judaism. He traced for Rahman a false and bizarre history of the rise and spread of Islam, always, according to his version, in the face of Jewish perfidy. Finally, he brought his conception of Judaism to bear on the matter of Palestine and Zionism, thus providing Rahman with his first exposure to one of the burning issues of the day in the Arab world. Not even his teachers in the Palestinian school, where the subjects taught to those of Rahman's age were mainly numbers and grammar, had yet broached the subjects of Arab history or current events.

The purpose of al-Akbar's machinations was not simply to instill in Rahman a visceral hatred of Jews. Indeed, that was only to build the foundation for the achievement of his real purpose, which was to further undermine the boy's father in Rahman's eyes.

To this end he then began to drop hints about Abdul's shame, tossing in veiled references to Gaza and Jerusalem and relating in roundabout ways stories about how Rahman's father had brought dishonor upon the al-Husayni name by "enticing" Mahmoud, Rahman's maternal grandfather, into setting up a business that sold religious articles to Jews.

Zaeed says it was a classic case of mental seduction. "The more hinting Yusuf did, the more curious Rahman became. Yusuf simply led Rahman on, feeding his questions with half-answers that only provoked more specific and insistent questions. Yusuf later insisted that it was all Rahman's doing—that Rahman had learned all this independently and had then prevailed upon him, since he knew the family history, to tell him the whole story. He pleaded old age, feebleness, his inability to resist Rahman's storm of questions. Why, in the end he even went so far as to insist that he was hopelessly senile and didn't know what he was doing. But there can be no doubt what the truth was. Rahman was not a naturally curious boy, as we knew him. Even with Yusuf, his mentor, he was timid and obedient. He would not have had the mental wherewithal to come up with all these questions on his own initiative. It was Yusuf who cleverly provoked them."

Rahman's education with Yusuf continued into the spring and early summer of 1939. After implanting in his consciousness the vague idea that Rahman's father had been treasonous to his Arab heritage and had brought shame upon the al-Husaynis, Yusuf proceeded to become more specific. He told Rahman of the Gaza episodes, embellishing here and there, and of how Abdul was forced to leave Gaza in shame. He attributed the Jerusalem beatings Abdul and Badir had received to Abdul's continuing collaboration with the Zionists. Then, as if to apply the coup de grâce, he invented the story that in their Ikhwan activities both Abdul and Badir, putting their basic al-Qudwa monetary greed over the high principles of the al-Husaynis, were in reality acting as secret agents of the Zionists. They continued to betray the high moral principles of the exiled Haj Amin

—an al-Husayni, after all—and by their actions heaped deepening shame upon Rahman's mother, upon Yusuf, indeed upon Rahman himself. Only by devoting himself to his benevolent granduncle, and by following the sanctified path the old man had been appointed by Allah to blaze for him, would the shame and dishonor created by Abdul be exorcised from Rahman's being.

The soon-to-be ten-year-old absorbed all this information with increasing wonder and seriousness, according to Nasr. "Then—it was sometime in the summer and our father was away, but Badir, our first brother, was there—Rahman came home from one of his visits to Yusuf. Badir ordered him to do something. Rahman refused. Badir, acting in my father's place, reprimanded him."

The reprimand unleashed a torrent of hysterical abuse and accusation from Rahman. Like a programmed machine having had the proper button pushed, the boy poured out a litany of charges against his nineteen-year-old brother, repeating by rote the worst of the insinuations and innuendoes of Yusuf which he had digested as fact.

A few days later Abdul returned and was informed by Badir of the incident. Abdul thereupon confronted Rahman, only to hear a similar litany, although this time delivered in cold, measured tones. The father was at once astonished and enraged. He slapped Rahman several times, then charged about the house looking for a strap with which to inflict more lasting punishment. While he did so, Rahman fled into the street.

It was not long before Abdul and Badir found him. He had taken refuge in Yusuf al-Akbar's house, and when the old man learned what Rahman had done, he feared for his own safety. When Abdul and Badir crashed in, Rahman clung to al-Akbar's robes, pleading with him to protect him from his father's wrath, begging his father to allow him to become Yusuf's son. This merely enraged Abdul more. He seized Rahman and handed him over to Badir, ordering him to take the boy home and await his arrival. Then he turned to face Yusuf.

"What my father said I cannot tell you," Nasr al-Qudwa says today. "Over the years we have heard many versions. I do know that someone in Yusuf's family heard him pleading for mercy, putting all the blame on the fact that Rahman was precocious. In any event, there was a meeting that night between my father and some of his

Ikhwan friends. It lasted until late in the night. The next morning Yusuf was found dead. He had been garroted and his body hung by the neck from his doorway. I remember seeing him there, his eyes bulging with panic. He was growing stiff when he was found, and he was left to hang there all day. By the time he was cut down, his arms and legs were standing stiff in front of him. Badir took us to see him. Rahman was taken too. I don't remember his reaction, because at that time I wasn't aware of all the things that were happening. If he had had any particular reaction, I think I would be able to recall it. Since I can't recall it, I suppose he showed no particular emotion. Perhaps he did his usual thing. One thing, however. That was the end of our days in Cairo."

5

The Muslim Brotherhood

Shortly after Yusuf's body was cut down and buried, Abdul al-Qudwa received a visit from a detachment of Cairo police. They were interested not so much in the actual murder of the old man as in its method. The garrote-and-hang technique was becoming an increasingly common sight about Cairo, and the police had identified it as an Ikhwan trademark. Since the Ikhwan had begun to preach, among other things, the overthrow of the Wafd government and to advocate terrorism, the police were very curious about the death of Yusuf al-Akbar. They had theretofore been able to learn very little about the Ikhwan. Thus they questioned Yusuf's family closely.

Out of their interrogations came the hint that Abdul al-Qudwa, a distant relative, had had a personal grievance against the victim over matters pertaining to one of al-Qudwa's sons. When the police approached Abdul about this, he conceded the fact but heatedly denied any involvement in Yusuf's death.

The police left, but only to return a few days later with further questions, this time about any knowledge Abdul might have of the Ikhwan. It was by now a well-entrenched tradition within the Brotherhood that anyone, member or not, who betrayed the secret society to the authorities signed his own death sentence. Abdul, although frightened by the questions, trod carefully in answering them. He managed to persuade the police that he was innocent of any useful knowledge.

Indeed, he made up the novel story that Yusuf's murder had in fact been carried out as a warning to him. He claimed that he had been approached several times during the previous year by men who said they represented the Ikhwan. Since he was a fairly prominent businessman who traveled often between Cairo and Gaza, he said, they insisted he join the Ikhwan for the purpose of smuggling arms into Egypt from Gaza. He had consistently refused, he told the police, because he was a peace-loving man, had a large family and many responsibilities, and enjoyed the hospitality of the Egyptian government. He had been told that if he didn't join the Ikhwan his family would suffer. Since Yusuf al-Akbar was the most respected member of the family living in Cairo, it was Abdul's theory that the Ikhwan had killed him to intimidate him into changing his mind. Could Abdul identify any of the men who approached him? asked the police. No, they always approached him on the street after dark, he replied.

The police seemed to buy the explanation, and when they left, Abdul thought he was done with them. But a week later one of them returned with a proposal that was as novel as Abdul's story. The officer suggested that since Abdul had been approached to join the Ikhwan on several occasions, and al-Akbar's murder had, as Abdul claimed, been committed to pressure him into joining, he should do so. He should allow himself to be recruited into the Brotherhood and then, once well established as a member, should become an informer for the police.

Abdul politely demurred, skillfully covering his astonishment at the suggestion. But he would be well compensated, said the police officer. Yes, replied Abdul, but he was a peaceful man and it would be irresponsible of him to expose his wife and children to the dangers of such an activity. No amount of compensation could justify it.

The police officer turned tough, shouting at Abdul that he had all along suspected him of lying, claiming that he knew Abdul was responsible for Yusuf's murder and that if he didn't cooperate with the police in becoming an informer he, the officer, would hound Abdul until the truth came out. With that he departed, giving Abdul a few days to think over his proposition.

That night Abdul reported the policeman's demand to a meeting of his Ikhwan cell. He was trapped in a dilemma, he complained, and he besought the society to help him find a way out. He was told to remain calm, that a solution would be found.

The solution came two days later. The police officer who had approached Abdul was found murdered. He had been garroted and hung.

At first it hardly seemed a solution in Abdul's favor, for the police were back on his doorstep a few hours later with a host of new questions. But evidently the dead policeman had not told his colleagues of his hopes of turning Abdul into an Ikhwan informer; an ambitious young officer, he had planned to present his accomplishment to his superiors only after the fact, anticipating a promotion as his reward for penetrating the secret Brotherhood. Nevertheless, the police were struck by the coincidence of having one of their men murdered Ikhwan-style while pursuing an investigation that involved Abdul. They therefore put some hard questions to him, and came away convinced they had not received entirely consistent answers.

However, it was August of 1939. Europe was suddenly plunged into war by the ambitious actions of Adolf Hitler. Following the outbreak of European hostilities the British, aware of Hitler's designs on the oil resources of the Middle East, put Egypt and the other lands they controlled there on a wartime footing. Suddenly the Cairo police had more tasks than they could handle, and their investigation of the murder of the police officer faded into limbo.

The start of the war in Europe and the diversion of Cairo's police to other preoccupations provided additional benefits to both Abdul and the Ikhwan. With Egypt placed on permanent military alert, with military arms beginning to pour into the country for its possible defense by the British, and with the police authorities involved in other tasks, Hassan Banna and the leadership of the Ikhwan saw an easy opportunity to expand their influence and, at the same time, through the inevitable black market in weapons and munitions that would develop, increase the Ikhwan's arms supplies and guerrilla activity. This they proceeded to do, writing secret expansionary plans and forming committees to implement them. Their goal was to wrest power, through terrorism and other tactics, from the incumbent civil administration. At war's end, went their thinking, they would be in control; they would expel whatever foreign power (British or German) remained and would reform Egyptian society according to fundamental Koranic principles. In the bargain, should they receive the cooperation of the Arab nationalists in Palestine, they would help them rid their land of European and Zionist control and restore Palestine to purely Arab sovereignty.

Abdul al-Qudwa had come to the notice of Hassan Banna as a

result of his adventures with the Cairo police. Banna was impressed by Abdul's willingness to resist police pressure and inform the Brotherhood of their attempt to infiltrate it, although he thought the Palestinian cell's assassination of the policeman a bit precipitate. In fact, had Banna been consulted on the matter before the policeman's death, he would have countermanded the action, met with Abdul al-Qudwa, and worked out a scheme whereby Abdul would appear to accede to the policeman's proposal that he become a spy. It would have been very useful to Banna and the Brotherhood to have a double agent working for them.

That opportunity was lost, at least for now. However, Abdul al-Qudwa had other uses. Banna had founded the Ikhwan in Port Said, which was about halfway between Cairo and Gaza. Thus far, however, the Brotherhood had not established itself solidly in the Gaza area. This was because the operatives of the departed Haj Amin's Palestinian nationalists were still powerful there. In Banna, a fanatical religious fundamentalist, the followers of the more worldly and political Mufti perceived a threat. Although their causes were more or less common, the leaders of Haj Amin's Arab Higher Committee and Supreme Council had ignored overtures of alliance from Banna and the Brotherhood. The Ikhwanites were too fanatical even for the Haj Aminists—this despite the fact that the Brotherhood had espoused Palestinian Arab aspirations and had found a wide following among Palestinians living in Egypt, Palestinians such as Abdul al-Qudwa.

In September, Abdul was brought before Hassan Banna at a secret meeting place in Qalyub, a suburb of Cairo. He was surprised to discover that the guiding light of the Ikhwan knew so much about him. He was further pleased to learn, during the conversation they had, that Banna's religious and social impulses were akin to his own.

At the meeting neither Banna nor Abdul knew that the Cairo police had been diverted from their investigation; Abdul was still walking on eggshells. Banna proposed a means by which Abdul could remove himself from police harassment—return with his family to Gaza, where he and his family name were respected (Banna was unaware of Abdul's unpleasant experiences in Gaza twelve years earlier), and devote much of his time and influence to establishing the Brotherhood there. Banna told Abdul that he knew of his family's connection to the al-Husayni clan and that he thought Abdul could exploit that tie to still the fears of Gaza's Haj Amin followers and to effect an alliance between the Ikhwan and the Palestinian resistance.

Abdul, often a preening man, said nothing to disabuse Banna of the notion that he could win over the Haj Aminists of Gaza. Although he had been back to Gaza many times since 1927 and had been well received as a visitor by the general populace, he was uncertain of the reception he would receive among the anti-Zionist militants should he and his family return for good. Nevertheless, he was grateful for Banna's proposal and pledge of support, for it gave him a reason to leave Cairo. He thought also of the benefits of removing Rahman, his recalcitrant son, from the place in which he had been so evilly influenced, and placing him in an environment in which he would have more control over him.

He therefore accepted Hassan Banna's commission. To the police he would explain, if asked, that the Ikhwan was still threatening him and that he had decided to move his family to Gaza for safety's sake. To make the story even more convincing, Banna proposed to arrange another murder—that of Hamida's cousin, Khouri al-Husayni, who was visiting from Jerusalem. Abdul argued that that was unnecessary. If he was to recruit the al-Husayni–inspired nationalists of Gaza to the Ikhwan, it would not do to have it known that another member of the al-Husayni clan was killed by the Ikhwan.

Banna and Abdul then went on to discuss the more specific functions of Abdul's assignment in Gaza, such as arms procurement, recruitment and the formation of Ikhwan cells, fund raising among the citizens, liaison with the Arab Higher Committee, and, eventually, the mounting of guerrilla raids against British and Jewish installations. Terror and destruction were the ultimate goal, claimed Banna, for only through its deeds would the Brotherhood be taken seriously by the Palestinians.

These points settled, Abdul left with a special blessing from Hassan Banna and returned to Cairo. A few days later he packed family and belongings together and set out for Gaza.

6

Majid Halaby

Gaza in 1939 consisted of a narrow strip of land along the Mediterranean coastline that blended in the south into Sinai and Egypt and in the north into Palestine. Although included as part of Palestine under the British Mandate, because of its centuries of commercial intercourse with Egypt it was almost as much Egyptian in character as Palestinian (or South Syrian, to use the designation that preceded World War I). A combination of desert inland and citrus and olive plantations along the coast, its principal municipality was the city of Gaza, where the British maintained an administrative force but where parochial Arab affairs were run by an Arab civil service with its own parliament or municipal council. Through Gaza ran a railway line linking Egypt to the lands to the north and along which much of the city's produce and import goods were freighted.

The city was built around a large main plaza called Falastin Square and was completely Arab in style and architecture. The main street leading off the square was Omar al-Mukhtar Avenue. Parallel to it ran al-Wahda Street. Separating the two was a large cemetery which fronted on the square. At the rear of the cemetery, between the two thoroughfares, ran a connecting street with no particular name. It was in a house on this street that Abdul al-Qudwa settled himself and his family upon their arrival in Gaza in early October, 1939. His son Rahman was just two months past his tenth birthday.

It was after the move to Gaza, Zaeed al-Qudwa recalls, that it began to become apparent to the family that Rahman's genius was not an innate religious inspiration but a gift of memory. "No doubt the fact that Yusuf was gone had something to do with it. Also getting out of the neighborhood in Cairo. Once we were all in Gaza, Rahman seemed to lose his devotion to religious studies. I suppose the reason he had kept it up for so long in Cairo was because of

Yusuf. Yusuf coddled him, praised him, almost mothered him. He was the only source of pleasure and security Rahman had. Rahman played the good little religious student in order to keep Yusuf interested in him. Once Yusuf disappeared, Rahman had no need to continue with the game."

Brother Nasr, however, claims that Rahman did not give up the game all that quickly. "Zaeed is right, but it took about a year before Rahman began to change. When we first arrived in Gaza he remained his usual self. He was immediately sent to school, like the rest of us, but he still stayed apart, always with his nose buried in a religious book. In my opinion he was hoping for someone else like Yusuf to come along and take notice of him, to take up where Yusuf left off."

No one took notice except to remark on Rahman's strange behavior. The teachers at the Zeitoun secondary school where Nasr, Rahman, and his younger brother, Husayn, were enrolled permitted Rahman to go his lonely way, making no demands on him in the classroom and looking the other way when his classmates made fun of him.

One of his classmates was Muhammad al-Alami, a son of one of Gaza's leading politicians, who remembers Rahman as "a fat, moody boy who managed to frighten everyone a little. He was not like most fat boys, who tend to be buffoonish and always eager to be everyone's friend. These were the kind of boys it was always easy to be cruel to. But Rahman was not like that. He played up to no one. He was shy, of course, and was always ill at ease. But if you came up to him and did something or said something nasty, he would just look right through you with his eyes. His eyes were hypnotic, and they could stop you cold."

Toward the end of his first school year, however, things began to change for Rahman. A new teacher came into the school, a young man from southern Lebanon, still in his twenties, named Majid Halaby. Halaby had been born in Tyre, but most of his family on his mother's side came from Haifa in Palestine. Wellborn (his father owned a large amount of land in the Galilean hills of northern Palestine, as well as along the coast between Haifa and Acre), he was also well-educated and had, a few years before, taken a degree in mathematics at the Sorbonne in Paris. He had returned to Tyre in

1937 with a view to assuming the accounting responsibilities in his father's property business, but certain convictions he had formed while a student in Paris created difficulties for him.

Following World War I and the failure of the Arab nationalist movement to achieve a pan-Arab state, many nationalist leaders and activists had been forced into exile. They gravitated to the Paris of the 1920s, Europe's most liberal and hyperactive city and a magnet for just about every political ideology extant. There they came in contact with Arabic-speaking nationalists from the French colonies of Morocco, Tunisia, and Algeria. A natural symbiosis developed between Eastern and Western Arab, and by the 1930s Paris was the principal European outpost of the Arabist movement. As the movement took shape, it spread into the universities and became intermixed with various European socialist ideals. As noted, many wealthy Palestinian and Lebanese families had sent their most promising male offspring to Europe to receive their higher education after World War I. Most of them became caught up in the Arab socialist-nationalist groups at the schools they attended there and returned to their homelands in the late 1920s and 1930s to impose new and more sophisticated ideas on the native nationalist movements (the movement led by Haj Amin being a case in point).

Majid Halaby was one of these. He returned to Tyre not only expecting to take over the accounting tasks of his father's prosperous property business but also intending to use his position in the business to establish himself politically. France still controlled Lebanon; fired as he was with notions of Arab independence of European suzerainty, he dreamed of one day leading Lebanon to independence.

His aspirations were short-circuited almost immediately. Once placed in a training position in his father's land enterprises, he was astonished to discover how much of his family's fortunes derived from the sale of land in Palestine to the Zionists. Although he had nothing in particular against Jews as such ("After all," he was fond of saying, "Karl Marx was himself a Jew"), Zionist Jews were for the most part Europeans. In his view, which was the accepted Arab nationalist one, the Zionists were just another manifestation of European colonialism, another tool employed by European imperialism to maintain its hold over the Arab world. To cooperate with them by selling them land in Palestine was tantamount to encouraging further capitalist European exploitation and the further repression of the right of Arab self-determination.

Majid tried hard to persuade his father to discontinue his land sales, marshaling all the arguments he had absorbed in Paris about colonialism and imperialism. But his father was an old-fashioned man, a merchant and trader who had little interest in political matters. He was perfectly content with life the way it was, and no amount of appeals by Majid could dissuade him.

A rift between the two quickly grew. One day his father discovered that Majid had sabotaged the sale of a tract of land in Galilee to a group of Jews who had hoped to turn it into a communal farm. He summarily expelled Majid from the business, cutting off his income, and even banished him from Tyre.

Without a home, but even more impassioned by his father's intransigence, Majid drifted down to Haifa, where he made friends with several young layabouts who frequented a local coffeehouse. With his Parisian education and his name, he found himself looked up to. He used the respect he enjoyed to organize his friends into a political action group. At first his intention was merely to employ the group to exercise revenge on his father. To that end he sent them out on missions to vandalize various properties owned by the elder Halaby in Haifa. From there the group graduated to terrorizing Jews and desecrating synagogues.

Although Majid enjoyed the feeling of power he was accumulating in his role as leader of the group, he soon grew bored with its limited achievements. He was an intelligent young man, and once the initial thrill of danger in the group's activities wore off he realized that he was involved with nothing more than a collection of thugs. Try as he did, he was unable to interest them in any political ideas. The violence they were committing was merely, in the end, gratuitous.

The violence did not go unnoticed, however—either by the British police or by the Haifa representatives of the Arab Higher Committee. One evening several members of Majid's group were caught trying to set fire to a Jewish carpet shop near the Haifa waterfront. Arrested, they were brought to a British police outpost and questioned, whereupon they disclosed Majid's identity as their leader. Majid was arrested and imprisoned for several weeks. Then, without any hard evidence against him, he was released with a warning to leave Haifa.

While in jail Majid came into contact with several terrorists who had been caught while operating under the auspices of a Haj Aminist group. Their leader was a Jerusalemite named Yasir al-Birah, a descendant of the clan that had founded the Arab town of Birah, between Ramallah and Jerusalem.

Several of the Haj Aminist terrorists were released before Majid Halaby. When he was released, he found a reception committee awaiting him a few steps from the prison. He was ordered to accompany them to the secret headquarters of Yasir al-Birah.

Al-Birah questioned Majid intensively, challenging him to explain what he and his gang had been up to. Majid poured out his ideological dreams and confessed his frustration at being able to lead only a band of uncommitted thugs. The two talked into the night, and by the next morning Majid had been recruited into al-Birah's group, which called itself the Sacred Society for the Recovery of Palestine.

"We are all *fedayeen,*" al-Birah is remembered as having said to Majid by Aziz Ghawazi, an old man now, who claims to have been there. *Fedayeen* was a word derived from the root Arabic word for "sacrifice." It referred to those who sacrifice themselves or embark on suicidal missions. Historically, the name was first used in the twelfth century to designate warriors selected by the Isma'ili sect of Islam to assassinate its enemies.

According to Ghawazi, who now lives quietly in Lebanon, it was the first time he had heard the word used in connection with the Palestinian resistance. "Yasir and Majid talked and argued all night. At first they didn't trust each other. Majid was well-spoken and vaguely elegant in his manner. Besides that, he was half Christian. Yasir al-Birah was poorly educated and, you would say, coarse in manner. But he was a devoutly religious Muslim and a great disciple of the Mufti, even though Haj Amin had been gone from Jerusalem for a long time. Finally Yasir challenged Majid Halaby to join our society. Majid accepted right away. It was then that al-Birah said, 'We are all *fedayeen.*' Majid did not understand. So al-Birah explained. To be a member of our society meant to die sooner or later in the service of a free Palestine. To be in our society meant to be a *fedayeen.* To be a *fedayeen* meant to sacrifice oneself for the cause. Majid said he understood."

It was the beginning of 1939, and the British Mandate authorities were already preparing Palestine for the coming war in Europe. As did the Ikhwanites of Hassan Banna in Cairo, the Haj Aminists of Palestine perceived in the wartime conditions of their land an opportunity to increase their armed strength. They were now totally committed to violence as the only means of rescuing their country from the Europeans and the Zionists. Consequently, they made contacts with diplomatic and intelligence representatives of Nazi Germany who were posted in Lebanon. They offered themselves as a potential German fifth column in Palestine and Lebanon in exchange for weapons and munitions. Soon the matériel began to flow clandestinely into Palestine. One of the principal ports of entry was Gaza, the traditional smugglers' haven.

Majid Halaby, after being initiated into the secret *fedayeen* society of Haifa, remained for a year with Yasir al-Birah. Al-Birah appointed Majid as a kind of political officer of the society. His primary function was to lecture al-Birah and his mainly unlettered lieutenants on the finer points of modern political theory and ideologies. Al-Birah was about forty-five years old and a thoroughgoing homosexual, as were most of his cohorts. (This was not unusual among devout Muslims; indeed, it was totally accepted practice, having its precedents both in ancient tribal tradition, when men spent weeks and often months alone together in the lonely wastes of the desert, and in the Koran, which sanctioned and even encouraged sexual relations between men through its strictures on women.) Majid was no stranger to homosexuality, but had up to then preferred a heterosexual existence. However, to demonstrate his fealty to al-Birah and the Sacred Society, he gave himself to the pleasure of the others and was soon taking his own pleasure from them. Majid quickly came to idolize Yasir al-Birah for his terrorist exploits against the British and Jews around Haifa, and felt, according to Aziz Ghawazi, that much of Yasir's reckless and awesome physical courage would be transfused into him through sexual union.

On an early morning in December of 1939, al-Birah's recklessness proved ill-advised, at least for him. He, Majid, and a party of cohorts put ashore just above Haifa after sailing all night from Saida in Lebanon with a boatload of German automatic rifles. The landing spot was supposed to have been secured and sealed off from any surprises by members of the society who had been left behind for that purpose. The stay-behinds had been picked up the night before in a general British roundup of resistance groups, however, and al-Birah and his small band came ashore on a totally unprotected beach. Al-Birah leaped from the boat and made his way up through a cut in the bluff, looking for his people. Quickly sensing that something had gone wrong, he started back for the boat, where he had left the others, when he chanced upon a British shore patrol. They ordered him to halt. Al-Birah shouted to the men in the boat to pull it away from the beach. Aziz Ghawazi was at the helm.

"We backed off," he recalls today, "leaving Yasir about a hundred meters up the beach. He diverted the attention of the two British beach scouts by running away from them. We could see them chasing him. He led them for more than a kilometer down the beach, south, while we set a course north, back to Lebanon. Majid was frantic, he wanted to go back and help Yasir. But we had our orders. Soon we heard gunfire. It wasn't the sound of the Sten, more the pop-pop of Yasir's pistol. We were far away now, we could only see vague tiny figures on the beach, we couldn't see what was really happening. Then there was more gunfire—this time the sound of the Sten. We feared the worst."

Ghawazi managed to get the boat back to Lebanese waters where he, Majid, and the others abandoned it on a deserted beach near Tyre and hiked overland back to Haifa. When they arrived, they discovered that Yasir al-Birah had been killed.

"Majid was crushed," says Ghawazi. "The society was crippled. Yasir was dead. Many of the others were in jail. But Yasir had given me a secret note a few months before. I was to give it to Majid if Yasir ever got killed or arrested. It was an instruction to Majid. It said: 'If you have loved me, carry on my name. Carry on my cause. Go to Jerusalem and seek out Abdelqadir al-Husayni. Do with him as I would.' "

Abdelqadir al-Husayni was a young nephew of Haj Amin who had been especially groomed by the Mufti to act as a liaison between the older generation resistance leaders and the more youthful European-educated ideologues who were joining the movement. Despite the shared goals of the various elements within the resistance, family rivalries, ideological hairsplitting, individual egos, and personal idiosyncrasies all combined to produce a high degree of factionalism within the movement. Once Haj Amin was forced to flee Palestine in the aftermath of the 1936 riots, the factionalism intensified, breaking down into two general categories: the conservative radicals, who were faithful to Haj Amin but who had developed no clear-cut Arab political vision or program for Palestine once their goals were achieved; and the extremist radicals, who sought to revolutionize Palestinian life in socialist European terms, and through such revolution gain statehood and purge the land of its European and Zionist character.

With the departure of Haj Amin, it fell largely to Abdelqadir al-Husayni to hold the resistance together. Those who remember Abdelqadir recall a young man of officious mien, fierce temperament, and consummate courage. In Arab resistance mythology he has been elevated to the first position, above that of even Haj Amin himself. The al-Husaynis generally tended to be short and squat, but Abdelqadir was a tall and impressive man. Perhaps even more imposing than his physical presence were his intellectual acuity, his gifts as an orator, and his personal bravery.

This, according to Kemal Sanduqa, once an aide to Haj Amin, was the Abdelqadir al-Husayni whom Majid Halaby came to Jerusalem to see. "I remember Halaby, because he was the one who brought the news of Yasir al-Birah's death in Haifa. He was a young man, very handsome, about the same age as Abdelqadir. I recall that we were all impressed that he spoke French so fluently and could also speak some German. He came as a volunteer to the cause, vowing that his most sacred desire was to continue the work of Yasir al-Birah. This was just after the war had begun between the Germans and the British. We were having difficulties obtaining the weapons we were expecting. The British and French had closed off the ports to German shipping. About two weeks earlier a German submarine had tried to deliver a few boxes of land mines to our emissaries in Gaza, but no one there understood German. Thus the radio messages went unheeded. The German submarine crew floated the crates of mines on a raft about a mile off Gaza, expecting our people to go out and tow them in to shore. But not having understood the German message about the time and the date of the rendezvous, we did not get the mines. So Abdelqadir accepted Halaby's offer and ordered him to go and settle in Gaza, find employment as a cover from the British, and be in charge of radio communications with German craft that were delivering arms. Unfortunately, Halaby became too ambitious and eventually exceeded his assignment from Abdelqadir."

Halaby arrived in Gaza in the spring of 1940 and in due course managed to obtain a job teaching elementary mathematics to the youngsters of the Zeitoun school. There he came across the junior members of the al-Qudwa family—Nasr, who was somewhat of a happy-go-lucky lad of twelve; Husayn, who at eight had just begun school; and Rahman, the strange, withdrawn eleven-year-old who, when he looked at someone, seemed to peer into his deepest interior recesses.

Majid was intrigued by Rahman. It was immediately apparent to him that the boy had a superior gift for things mathematical. Mathematics was the only subject he had been doing well in and was the only subject that seemed to interest him. His previous teacher had been competent but unimaginative, in Majid's opinion, content to leave Rahman to his own musings rather than draw him out. The teacher had told Majid, when passing over the class to him, that Rahman was able to remember algebraic formulae after only a brief glance at them and that he was by far the most advanced student in the class, but that he was eccentric and unreachable. Majid confirmed this after his first classroom encounter with Rahman. He resolved to make some sort of contact with the boy.

Majid's resolve was sparked, however, not by Rahman's aloofness or by his clear mathematical talents, but by the resemblance he bore to the late Yasir al-Birah. Rahman could have been Yasir's son, Majid at first thought. No, the resemblance was even more uncanny than that, he then decided—young Rahman al-Qudwa al-Husayni looked exactly as Yasir al-Birah must have looked as a boy.

In addition to his fascination with Rahman, Majid was curious about the fact that he and his brothers carried the al-Husayni name. In his interviews with Abdelqadir and other al-Husaynis in Jerusalem he had been told nothing about al-Husaynis living in Gaza. He made some discreet inquiries and was surprised to learn that Abdul al-Qudwa, Rahman's father, was married to an al-Husayni woman and that Rahman and his brothers were third cousins of Abdelqadir, as well as distant nephews of Haj Amin. His surprise was compounded when he discovered that Rahman's father was secretly involved in the resistance.

Upon his return to Gaza the year before, Abdul al-Qudwa had found the political climate considerably changed in his favor. That his business continued to prosper was an indication that the past had been forgotten and that he was welcome there again. He immediately set out to perform the commission bestowed on him by Hassan Banna in Cairo—to establish a cell of the Ikhwan in Gaza and to link it up to the Palestinian liberationists now led from Jerusalem by Abdelqadir al-Husayni.

The first part of his task was easier than the second. As in the rest of Palestine, the resistance had established itself in Gaza in a variety of factions, most more or less allegiant to the Haj Aminists, but a few leaning toward the smaller and more politically radical branch of the movement which was taking most of its cues from a left-wing group emerging in Syria called the Baathists.

The Baathists were a socialist revolutionary group founded by two young Paris-educated Syrians, Michel Aflaq and Salah Bitar. Their goal was to use European revolutionary methods to liberate Syria from French domination and deliver the country to its people as a free and independent Arab socialist state. Their philosophy was formed in Paris during the 1930s and grew out of their deep immersion in the ideological socialist literature of European nationalism. They felt they had discovered the deficiencies that were at the heart of the failure of the independence struggle in the Arab world. The impulse to national sovereignty could not be based on religious tenets, as it had theretofore been, with religious leaders such as Haj Amin in Jerusalem dictating policy, but must have a cultural-sociological-ethnic base.

By virtue of the fact that Syria was a discordant conglomeration of vying religious sects, Muslim and non-Muslim, the basing of a nationalist liberation movement on religious principles would inevitably produce disunity and failure. Revolutionary socialism on the European model had won its successes through the encouragement of political unity by means of appeals to ethnic and cultural identity and solidarity, appeals that overrode religious differences.

The application of this principle, insisted Aflaq and Bitar, would be the key to the success of Syrian national self-determination. And the key to Syrian political identity was not the diverse religious character of the people but their shared "Arabness." The Syrian nationalist movement would have to be transformed from a congeries of religious impulses into a unity of ethnic identity—an Arab identity. From this sense of unity would flow a powerful political entity that would nourish itself on a belief in Arab political rather than Muslim religious destiny, and would be able thereby to work out its goals of nationhood.

Upon their return to Syria in 1940, Aflaq and Bitar taught for a short time in Damascus but then shifted their activities to the American University in Beirut, a gathering place of left-wing Arab intellectuals that had developed into a nursery of Arab nationalist ideas. There they indoctrinated Arab students in their Baathist principles. As World War II progressed, their infant nationalist movement evolved into an organized party.

Since Palestine had for a long time been considered an integral part of Syria and since many Palestinian Arabs still thought of themselves basically as Syrians, the Baathist philosophy found great favor among the increasing numbers of political intellectuals returning to Palestine from abroad. To them the Baathist analysis of the failure of Arab self-determination, and its solution, made sense. If the Baathist scenario was capable of working in Syria, it could work as well in Palestine in the struggle to loosen the Zionist grip on the land and win Arab sovereignty there.

But a commitment to Baathism, or to similar rationales, required an abandonment of allegiance to religion in Arab life. This in turn would erode the authority of Haj Amin, and other religious leaders. Such a commitment went against centuries of deeply ingrained Arab attitudes and instincts. Consequently, in Palestine, enthusiasm for the socialist approach to liberation grew slowly. Nevertheless, the Haj Aminists were determined to see that it did not grow at all. Thus they spent almost as much time during the early 1940s endeavoring to counter the Arab socialist threat to their religious authority as fighting the Zionists and the British. In Gaza especially they clamped down on the introduction of socialist aspirations. Gaza therefore remained a fertile area for nationalist dreams based on purely religious principles.

On his return to Gaza, Abdul al-Qudwa had found the city and its environs well and tightly organized into Haj Aminist groups. Some were civil action groups, others were paramilitary and guerrilla organizations, but most were still loyal to the Arab Higher Committee and the Supreme Muslim Council. Membership in the Haj Aminist movement had become a matter of status and honor among most of the leading citizens of Gaza. But there were those who always remained on the outside, in most cases because in their view the Haj Aminists were not religiously fundamental enough. It was among these citizens that Abdul conducted his initial Ikhwan recruiting. Before long he had formed an organization of thirty or so men who subscribed to the ideals of Hassan Banna. Most of their time, however, was spent in convoluted discussion; they achieved little in the way of action.

This was not because of a lack of desire. It was due to an absence of even rudimentary arms. Weapons promised from Egypt had not arrived but had been intercepted by British authorities along the way. Finally Abdul decided to appeal to the Haj Aminists for weapons. He would use the opportunity to establish a link as well; he envisioned himself as the engine of Haj Aminist—Ikhwan cooperation and joint action.

Abdul traveled to Jerusalem, sought out his father-in-law, Mahmoud, and through him got an interview with Abdelqadir. Mainly because he was interested in learning more about the Ikhwan, Abdelqadir listened to Abdul's proposition in the company of several of his elderly counselors.

At the end of Abdul's presentation the counselors mulled over the proposal. One reminded Abdelqadir of Abdul's dealings with the Jews in the late 1920s. Abdul protested. It was a mistake on his part and he had paid for it, he said; besides, Haj Amin had absolved him seven years before.

Another counselor brought up the question of Yusuf al-Akbar's murder in Cairo. Still another inquired if Hassan Banna and his Ikhwan philosophy were not too fanatical. A fourth suggested that the Ikhwan might be a cover for radical socialists seeking to gain a stronger foothold in Gaza and thus diminish Haj Aminist authority there.

Abdul had a difficult time handling these objections. Abdelqadir gazed at him imperiously for a time, then reached his decision. He told Abdul that he did not trust him, in spite of Haj Amin's earlier absolution. Nevertheless, he would see that Haj Amin (who was then in Iraq and secretly negotiating with the Nazis) received word of his request. Should the Mufti approve, then he, Abdelqadir, would cooperate with Abdul. Pending such approval, however, Abdul was to disband his Ikhwan cell and join his recruits to one of the Haj Aminist organizations in Gaza.

Abdul refused; to accede to Abdelqadir's command would have meant a great loss of face before Hassan Banna and the men he had already recruited to the Ikhwan in Gaza. He returned to Gaza empty-handed and soon began to spread the word that Abdelqadir al-Husayni was an incompetent trustee of the principles of Haj Amin.

What he didn't know was that Abdelqadir was aware of Haj Amin's dealings with the Nazis and did not entirely approve of them. Having gained a great deal of authority over the resistance movement in Haj Amin's absence, Abdelqadir was intent on keeping the Palestinians free of any open identification with the Nazis. He had learned of the Nazis' anti-Jewish pogroms in Europe and realized that to ally the Palestinian case against the Zionists, which was basically political, to the Nazi "final solution," which was racial—at least until the probable outcome of the war in Europe was clearer—would severely damage the Arab cause and create sympathy for the Zionists.

Abdul continued to recruit for the Ikhwan, his son Badir acting as his right-hand man. At the beginning of 1941, using his criticisms of Abdelqadir as a device for winning over members to the Brotherhood, he managed to convert an entire group of Haj Aminists who were also displeased with Abdelqadir's leadership. When word of this got back to Jerusalem, Abdul was visited by a special emissary of Abdelqadir.

7

Becoming Yasir

The emissary was Majid Halaby, the mathematics teacher and secret Haj Aminist radio operator.

Majid had been in Gaza for a year, but he was growing bored with his radio assignment. He had made no contacts with German vessels delivering arms to the resistance movement. The Germans had concentrated all their energies and matériel in North Africa and in oil-rich Iraq, where Haj Amin was trying to bring about the overthrow of the British-sponsored government and the installation of a regime aligned with Berlin.

Majid had gone to Jerusalem seeking another assignment from the Haj Aminists. During his discussions with one of Abdelqadir's lieutenants, also an al-Husayni, he casually revealed that he was the teacher of several al-Husayni boys in Gaza and inquired as to the nature of the relationship of these boys to the Jerusalem al-Husaynis. It was not long before the lieutenant figured out who Majid was talking about. Word had recently reached Jerusalem that Abdul al-Qudwa had not only been disobeying Abdelqadir's orders by failing to disband his Ikhwan group, but had managed to conscript a group of previously loyal Haj Aminists to the Muslim Brotherhood. The al-Husayni lieutenant immediately passed the information about Majid being the teacher of al-Qudwa's sons to Abdelqadir, who thereupon summoned Majid. He instructed him to return to Gaza and call upon al-Qudwa with a warning that if Abdul did not instantly abandon his efforts to bring Haj Aminist groups into the Ikhwan—indeed, if he did not disband his Brotherhood organization—he would be killed. Majid was assigned not only the task of delivering the warning but of ensuring that it was enforced. He was to take over Abdul's group and reintegrate it into the resistance along Haj Aminist lines.

Returning to Gaza in May of 1941, Majid arranged to visit Abdul in his offices near Falastin Square on the pretext of discussing Rahman's school performance. In the year that he had been Rahman's teacher Majid had managed to open the boy up a bit. After having first encountered him the year before, he had begun to think of him privately as "little Yasir." The name became implanted in his mind, and one day, when asking Rahman in class to answer a question, he called him "little Yasir." According to Nasr, "Rahman was confused, he didn't realize the teacher meant him. Then it happened a few more times, this 'little Yasir' business. The other boys were delighted, for it gave them something new to tease Rahman about, and they all started calling him 'Little Yasir, Little Yasir.' Of course they did it in a mocking way, and of course Rahman hated the name —so much so that when Majid continued to use it, Rahman would turn around and stare out the window."

When Majid learned that Rahman's classmates were using the name to taunt him, he interrupted the class one day to reprimand them. He did not wish to reveal his connections to the resistance movement (who could know which of the boys might have a father working for the British?), so he told them that he had been calling Rahman "Little Yasir" because of the boy's striking resemblance to "a great Arab hero, Yasir al-Birah, who you will all learn about when you are older." He had seen pictures of al-Birah, Majid went on—not assigning the "great Arab hero" to any particular era—and was certain that Rahman al-Qudwa al-Husayni would grow up to look just like him. With looks such as Yasir al-Birah's, he added, Rahman must himself be destined for greatness when he grew up. Using that logic, Majid scolded the class for its teasing of Rahman and demanded that the boys look upon him in a new light. "Our great heroes are always lonely, aloof men," Nasr remembers him as saying. "But we do not revere them any the less for that. Muhammad himself was a remote man. If the boy Muhammad was a member of this class, you would all probably tease him too—simply because he was not like the rest of you."

The analogy impressed the class, and Rahman was thereafter treated with more deference by his classmates. But no one was more affected by the comparison than Rahman himself. Having from an early age been immersed by Yusuf al-Akbar in the lore and legend of the Prophet, he began to respond to Majid and to enjoy being referred to as "Little Yasir." He did not even mind it when his classmates, being about the same height as he was, dropped the "little" and took regularly to calling him "Yasir" instead of Rahman. Nor did he object when on other occasions they called him "Muhammad." The nicknames were now being spoken more in respect then in derision. For this Rahman—or Yasir, as we shall now begin to call him—realized he had only Majid, his teacher, to thank.

When Majid returned from Jerusalem to Gaza to deliver Abdelqadir's warning to Abdul al-Qudwa, he had already gained Yasir's devotion. Shortly before, Abdul, interested to know why his son was being called Yasir by his brothers and classmates, inquired of Zaeed. "I was the one who told my father the story about Rahman's teacher calling him Yasir because of the great Arab hero Yasir al-Birah," Zaeed says today. "My father was befuddled. He said he had never heard of such an Arab hero."

Abdul *had* heard of Yasir al-Birah, the Haj Aminist resistance leader in Haifa, however. Thus he awaited with some curiosity the visit from his sons' teacher. When Majid arrived, the two politely exchanged pleasantries. Majid complimented Abdul on his sons, praising Rahman (he was careful to use the boy's given name before his father) particularly for his mathematical talents. He explained that Rahman seemed to have a photographic memory but that, alas, his fortunate gift, as it often did as children grew older, appeared to be in the process of fading. In explaining to Abdul what a photographic memory was, Majid unwittingly exposed him to the realization that Rahman's earlier "religious genius" might have been attributable to nothing more than his feats of memory.

Abdul raised the question of Rahman's new nickname. He had been told that it was bestowed on him by Majid and that it had something to do with one Yasir al-Birah, a supposedly great Arab historical figure.

Majid could tell by Abdul's tone that he didn't approve of the nickname, and that he also suspected the veracity of what Majid had told his class. However, he was there to do the business of Abdelqadir al-Husayni and there was no point in concealing from Abdul his reasons for having told the story of Yasir al-Birah as he did.

"Then you are a member of the liberation movement," concluded Abdul, measuring Majid as a potential member of his Ikhwan cell.

The teacher nodded, explaining that it was in connection with movement business that he had really come to see Abdul.

Oh? said Abdul.

Majid went on to explain that it was his unpleasant task to convey the warning from Abdelqadir about Abdul's activities.

Abdul grew angry and loudly condemned Abdelqadir as a traitor to the spirit of Haj Amin.

Majid shrugged. It was not his place to make such judgments. He was a Haj Aminist and was acting under orders. If Haj Amin had entrusted the movement to Abdelqadir, then he was duty bound to follow the latter's instructions. It was far from his desire, he continued, to see any personal harm come to Abdul, especially in view of the fact that he was the father of his most prized student. However, obedience to the movement came first.

Abdul countered by flattering Majid. According to Zaeed, his father perceived a weakness in the young teacher. He sensed that in spite of Abdelqadir's assignment, Majid was more a follower than a leader, and that he could be seduced away from the distant Abdelqadir by charm and salesmanship, which Zaeed claims his father possessed in abundance.

Look, Abdul in effect argued, you are a misguided young man. Even the memory of your hero, Yasir al-Birah, has been betrayed by the Abdelqadirists. Here on the one hand is Haj Amin in Iraq, helping the Germans. The Germans are our best friends, for they have taught us best the nature of the Jews and how to deal with them. Here on the other hand is Abdelqadir in Jerusalem, refusing to acknowledge Haj Amin's pronouncements that we must support the Germans. So the Germans refuse to send any of us arms, because they think Abdelqadir represents all of us. Yasir al-Birah was a disciple of Haj Amin. I can even tell you that al-Birah was betrayed by Abdelqadir. I know how he died, and I can tell you that his colleagues were prevented from securing that beach at which he landed because they were secretly turned in to the British by informers working under Abdelqadir's orders in Haifa. Abdelqadir wanted al-Birah killed or captured because he was a threat to Abdelqadir, because he was complaining about the way Abdelqadir has corrupted the ideals of Haj Amin. I am proud that you think of my son in terms of Yasir al-Birah. But I am proud only if you understand that al-Birah was a Haj Aminist, and that he was against Abdelqadir. If you continue to put your faith in Abdelqadir, however, then I cannot permit you to call my son Yasir, for it is clear that you are a stupid man and cannot see that you corrupt the memory of Yasir al-Birah.

How did Abdul know all this? Majid wanted to know. After all, he was close to Yasir al-Birah, he was at the beach that day when al-Birah was killed. He still had the note al-Birah had left for him. Majid pulled the carefully preserved note from his pocket. He carried it with him wherever he went, he told Abdul. There, look, see what it says, he demanded: "... Carry on my cause. Go to Jerusalem and seek out Abdelqadir al-Husayni. Do with him as I would."

Abdul perused the note, then looked at Majid with an expression of pity. He accused Majid of being blind, lamented that the teacher had duped himself. The note was not a command to go to Jerusalem and join Abdelqadir, it was a command to prevent Abdelqadir from further destroying the Haj Aminist cause, of which Yasir al-Birah had been so loyal an advocate. If it wasn't, why had Abdelqadir not sent Majid back to Haifa to revive al-Birah's organization? Why had he instead dispatched him to Gaza to sit by a radio doing nothing? To get him out of the way, of course. And then why had Abdelqadir chosen Majid to be the bearer of this warning to Abdul and the Ikhwan? The answer was simple, claimed Abdul. Because Abdelqadir knew that the bearer of such an impertinent warning would be killed by the Ikhwan. Thus the entire affair was a device on Abdelqadir's part to get rid of Majid.

According to Ibrahim Rashidiyah, today an elderly Gazan but then a member of Abdul al-Qudwa's Ikhwan cell, Majid succumbed to the passion of Abdul's argument and to the force of his logic. "Majid was an impressionable young man," Rashidiyah recollects, "and Abdul very cleverly played on his imagination. He put all types of alternate possibilities in Majid's mind. He showed him that the Abdelqadirists were not interested in using him directly for the cause but were only using him to carry out their internal politics. He proved with his arguing that Majid was considered useful not for fighting the Zionists but only for fighting other Arabs who did not agree with Abdelqadir. Abdul convinced Majid of the insult this was to him. Once he did this, it was easy for him to win Majid over to the Ikhwan."

Abdul painted for Majid a glorious picture of Ikhwan plans. A large supply of weapons would soon be forthcoming from Egypt, he claimed. (Whether he was lying or not is uncertain; Rashidiyah says that he thinks Abdul had made a trip back to Cairo and had extracted from Hassan Banna the promise of another attempt to send arms to the Gazans.) Once properly armed, the small Ikhwan group would be in a position to embark on two elementary tasks. One would be to expand its membership—Gazans who had so far resisted joining the Ikhwan because they found its religious fundamentalism unattractive would flock to join when it was seen how well armed the Brotherhood was.

And once properly armed, the other task—to conduct concentrated guerrilla operations against the Zionists. This would also help to expand membership. Since the beginning of the war all the other resistance groups had grown quiet. Guerrilla action had dwindled to practically nothing. This, Abdul insisted, was a consequence of a secret agreement between Abdelqadir and the British to mute Arab resistance in Palestine for the duration of the war so that the British would be free to concentrate on defending their Middle Eastern possessions against the Axis. The British, he told Majid, had promised that in exchange Palestine would be given independence at the conclusion of the war, with Abdelqadir named ruler.

"This was a common belief," says Ibrahim Rashidiyah today. "We had heard about this agreement from several of the people who had defected to us earlier from an Abdelqadir group near Khan Yunis. One of them had an uncle who was close to Abdelqadir's circle in Jerusalem, and he told them he had heard about it there. I can say that Abdul believed it wholeheartedly. He had become quite a fanatic about the Zionists, and would believe anything about Abdelqadir that was negative."

Abdul explained to Majid that it was the Ikhwan's solemn duty to carry on the cause of Haj Amin in the face of the treachery of Abdelqadir. Abdelqadir was seeking political rewards from the British. But British promises to Arabs were famous for being broken—witness 1917. Britain's real design, he argued, was to put a lid on

Arab resistance so that the Zionists could use the war to become more solidly entrenched in Palestine. Then, at the conclusion of the war, Palestine would be handed over to the Jews. The only way to prevent this was for the Ikhwan to overcome Abdelqadir's perfidy and carry on a *jihad,* a holy war, against the Jews. By so doing, the apathy that had fallen over the general resistance as a result of Abdelqadir's machinations would be transformed back into the passion of sacrificial struggle that had been its main feature during the years Haj Amin was at its helm.

Abdul's campaign of persuasion took several days, remembers Ibrahim Rashidiyah. However, although Majid had come to believe Abdul's contentions about the Abdelqadirists, he was still doubtful about the wisdom of allowing himself to be enlisted into Abdul's Ikhwan group. "He had by then betrayed his instructions from Jerusalem," says Rashidiyah. "He knew that his actions would cause him difficulty with Abdelqadir, that once word of what he had done reached Jerusalem an order might come back to someone else in Gaza to seek him out and kill him in retribution. Of course, he could simply return to Jerusalem and report that he had been unable to force Abdul to disband, that the Ikhwan was already too well organized and powerful for him to combat on his own. I know he considered this, hoping that the Abdelqadirists would give him some other job far away from Gaza. But Abdul convinced him that this would be foolhardy. He said that if Majid joined the Ikhwan he would be protected. And then he cemented his hold over him by appealing to his instincts for combat. He told him that a man who had served so closely at the side of the great freedom fighter Yasir al-Birah should not be forced to allow his experience and desire to go fallow. So Abdul promised Majid to make him commander of the Ikhwan guerrilla forces once the arms came from Egypt. He said that Majid would organize an Ikhwan fighting force along the lines of that of Yasir al-Birah, would train this force, and then would become its leader. In that way Majid could protect himself from the Abdelqadirists. Once our movement was powerful enough in Gaza, we would publicly denounce Abdelqadir, assassinate him if necessary, and carry on the fight against the Jews until the return of the Mufti."

Majid finally succumbed to Abdul's cajolery and in June of 1941 was secretly inducted into the Ikhwan cell. There remained, however, the question of what duties he would perform until the arrival of arms from Egypt. Abdul's answer was quick in coming. It was vital, he explained, that the Gaza Brotherhood's guerrilla force, when the time came to organize and train it, have available to it the services of the youth of the area. Most of the Ikhwan membership was made up of men in their forties and fifties, men too old to endure the rigors of prolonged guerrilla warfare. The only young men then participating in the Brotherhood were Abdul's son Badir and a handful of his friends, all in their early twenties. These boys would form the nucleus of Majid's guerrillas. What was important now was to gather into the Ikhwan more young men, teen-agers from the schools of Gaza, who would expand the guerrilla ranks when it came time to launch operations. With their natural endurance and daring, they should be indoctrinated in the idea of being the Ikhwan's front-line soldiers against the Zionists. "We must get them before the Abdelqadirists get them and turn them into docile pawns," Abdul exclaimed.

To illustrate his conviction as forcefully as he could, Abdul told Majid to start with his own sons. Zaeed was sixteen and, although he had begun to show interest in his father's secret pursuits, he was basically lazy and lacked the personal motivation of his older brother, Badir. Nasr was fourteen, very courageous, but a happy-go-lucky boy with little awareness of the seriousness of the future should the Jews take over the country. Rahman, "Little Yasir," was about to turn twelve and was a continuing source of worry to his father. His mind had been polluted in Cairo by the senile al-Akbar, an al-Husayni, Abdul explained. Ever since, the boy had been a trial to him—disrespectful, aloof, effeminate.

"Abdul practically begged Majid to devote special attention to Rahman," Rashidiyah recalls. "He gave Majid the job of converting all his sons, even little Husayn, to the Ikhwan cause. At the same time he was to use his position and influence as a teacher at the school to indoctrinate other boys as well, even boys whose fathers still remained faithful to the Abdelqadir faction."

8

Ambush in Gaza

It was Majid Halaby's decision to join the Ikhwan and carry out Abdul al-Qudwa's wishes that brought the Muslim Brotherhood to stage center of the Arab resistance movement in Gaza. What is more significant is that the decision was in many ways responsible for the creation of the Yasir Arafat of today.

Majid took Abdul's plea about recruiting the boys of the Zeitoun school seriously, and he pursued the task assiduously until one day in the fall of 1941 he learned that word of what he was doing had got back to Jerusalem through the father of one of his students and that his life was in peril. With Abdul's blessing he immediately resigned his position at the school, leaving everyone with the impression that he had fled Gaza. Instead of leaving Gaza, however, he was secretly set up by Abdul in one of his houses on the outskirts of town. Paid a small stipend by Abdul, he was told to remain hidden there until the by now long-awaited shipment of arms arrived from Cairo. In the meantime he would work with Abdul's sons each day after school. His job was to turn them into faithful Ikhwanites, models for the youth who would flock to the Brotherhood once its guerrilla force was organized.

Majid, though now himself a full-fledged Ikhwanite, was only cursorily interested in the religious aspects of the Brotherhood. What captivated him, according to Zaeed, was its combat potential, along with the romance and justice of its militant political rationale.

"Once the threats on his life became an actuality for him," says Ibrahim Rashidiyah, "he became in many ways even more fanatical than Abdul. But his fanaticism was in the military realm rather than the religious. He took to reading all the historical literature of the Islamic conquest of a thousand years earlier. He spent long hours studying the great Arab military battles. Soon he was an expert on ancient Arab warfare. I know because I was the one who was always ordered to search out the books for him. He vowed to me one day that as soon as he could organize an Ikhwan armed force he intended to model his group on the ancient armies of Arabia, of Abu Muslim, of Khalid, of Amr, and then drive the Jews and the British out of Palestine."

Each day after school, Zaeed, Nasr, Yasir, and even eight-year-old Husayn arrived at Majid's hideout for tutoring in the Ikhwan guerrilla mystique. Their first instruction was on the absolute necessity for secrecy, and Majid was frank with the boys. He told them that his life was now in constant danger and that if any one of them revealed his whereabouts, inadvertently or otherwise, he would probably be killed. They must discuss their after-school activities with no one but their father. Not even their mother was to know.

To seal his pact with the boys, he assigned himself a code name. From then on, whenever the boys talked about him, they were to refer to him only by his code name; as well, whenever they addressed him, they were always to call him by his new name.

The name he chose was Abu Khalid. "Abu" in Arabic meant "father of." He explained that those who joined the secret guerrilla force of the Ikhwan would have to discard their previous identities and take on the names of great heroes of Muslim history. The use of "Abu" was a custom of the desert tribes which had conquered the Middle East. Men and boys were not known by their given names. Instead, a boy would be known as "Ibn Rashid," or "son of Rashid." Similarly, a man would be called "Abu Abdullah," or "father of Abdullah"—Abdullah being the man's oldest son. This traditional method of identifying people became, for the Arab armies that drove the Crusaders out of the Middle East, a system of code names for the armies' leaders. The founders of the Ikhwan in Egypt revived the practice in the 1930s not only to provide code names for members of the secret society but also to symbolize the traditional religious nature of their struggle.

Being more interested in the military potential than in the religious aspects of the Ikhwan, Majid chose the name Abu Khalid to symbolize his devotion to what he viewed as the forthcoming armed struggle. "Khalid" was for Khalid ibn al-Walid, the legendary Arabian warrior whom Muhammad had converted to Islam at the time the new religion was beginning to establish itself in Mecca and who subsequently played a pivotal role in spreading the religion beyond the borders of the Arabian peninsula.

The al-Qudwa boys were duly impressed with the sense of urgency and conspiracy Majid imparted, and none more so than Rahman-Yasir. Yasir had already formed an emotional attachment to Majid following Majid's earlier defense of him at school. Possessed of a much deeper grounding in Muslim history than his brothers, Yasir responded with particular enthusiasm to Majid's daily lectures on Zionism, British imperialism, and the need for young Arab boys to prepare themselves to be the nucleus of the forces that would one day expel these twin evils forever from Palestine. As a result of Yasir's eager interest, Majid assigned him the responsibility of ensuring that his brothers kept the secrets they had all entered into.

Although Majid at first tried to conduct his lectures in the conventional pedagogical way, Yasir's mounting enthusiasm for the project soon turned them into something more resembling seminars. When Majid would occasionally misstate a historical fact when rhapsodizing on the achievement of some Arab general a thousand years before, Yasir, drawing on the knowledge he had gained through his earlier tutelage under Yusuf al-Akbar, would immediately correct him. "They would argue endlessly over points of history," Nasr says today. "Majid enjoyed the way Yasir would leap right in to question him on something, or make a point Majid hadn't thought of. It grew boring to Zaeed and me. Husayn usually sat there quietly, soaking it all up. As time went on, Zaeed and I would just let our thoughts wander while Majid and Yasir had this back-and-forth discussion. We only got interested and joined in when the talk turned to the future, to discussions of plans to go on secret raids, that sort of thing. We all admired Majid greatly, and I believe Zaeed and I were jealous of Yasir for occupying so much of his attention. But Yasir would not let up. You could see in the way he looked at Majid the extent to which he hero-worshiped him. He would start these arguments or discussions just to gain Majid's attention."

Adds Zaeed, "After about three or four months of these meetings, Yasir began to change in his attitude to our father. He was no longer always so sullen. Majid often lectured us on how vital the work of our father was. And Badir, who was our father's alter ego. So after a while Yasir began to look at our father with a different eye. He still didn't know the details of what our father was doing. All he knew was that somehow what he was doing had something to do with what Majid was doing. Of course, Majid was all along giving us the impression he was doing more than he was. He would even hint at secret missions in the night into the Zionist areas, promising us that one day we would be allowed to go on such missions. It excited us all very much, but I suspect that at that time he was actually doing less than he boasted of. It was the same with our father. There was always a great deal of talk, but I can remember no signs of any action yet. In fact, except for the big secrecy business concerning Majid, we all lived pretty normal lives. Yet Yasir—somehow he changed during this period. He retained his intensity, of course. But he became more open, less timid, less withdrawn. He was beginning to model himself on Majid, I'm sure. We all were to a certain extent, but Yasir much more so. Majid was an outgoing man who laughed easily. He was very handsome and had a very interesting charm, almost boyish. In retrospect I see that he was not a natural leader. In many ways he was playing a game, living a fantasy of himself as a leader, a warrior. But his charm was not in strength, it was basically in his weakness. He attracted people to him not because he was strong or commanding or austere but because he was basically weak and helpless. But to us boys the impression he gave at that time, through the ferocity of his lectures on the Jews and so on, was one of strength. So, as I say, Yasir modeled himself on Majid, and because Majid spoke well of our father, Yasir began to relate to him in a better way. That made our father happy, and it made life for the rest of us a bit easier."

Majid Halaby, alias Abu Khalid, was again growing restless, however. Six months had passed since he had gone into hiding, and the arms promised by Abdul had yet to materialize. With each passing day as spring turned into summer in 1942, Majid complained more strenuously to Abdul. Abdul was running out of excuses. Then, one day in July, according to Ibrahim Rashidiyah, Majid ventured out of his hideout behind the disguise of a newly grown beard and presented himself at a meeting of Abdul's Ikhwanites. Word had reached him, he said, of a cache of German-made rifles, pistols, ammunition, and hand grenades hidden by an Abdelqadirist group in a cave south of Jerusalem.

Abdul and his colleagues were surprised at the news. How had Majid come upon such information?

Majid explained that for the past several weeks he had been slipping out of his hiding place at night to test his new disguise in the coffeehouses of Gaza. He had befriended a local activist who, not knowing who he was, had tried to get him to join the Abdelqadirists. He had led his new friend along, he said, and just the night before he had gone home with him and permitted himself to be seduced. Afterwards, in a kind of post-coital glow, the fellow had spoken freely in answer to Majid's questions. The man told him that in a few days' time he and several cohorts, disguised as Bedouin, were to leave with a train of camels for the cave. There they would load the arms onto the camels and then make their way back to Gaza. They still needed one or two more men to make the trip, and that was why he had approached Majid. With his beard, Majid could easily pass for a Bedouin.

Majid was in a state of high excitement. "At first, Abdul and the rest of us reacted angrily," recalls Rashidiyah. "We thought Majid had come to tell us he was leaving us to rejoin the Abdelquadirists. But then his real intentions became clear."

Majid proposed that he join the camel caravan—his Abdelqadirist friend had even offered to see that he got paid for making the trip. Then, once the arms were loaded and the group had progressed a certain distance back across the desert toward Gaza, Abdul and a party of Ikhwanites, also disguised as Bedouin, should stage an ambush. They should tie up the Abdelqadirists—including himself so as to make it appear that he too was a victim—and abscond with the camels. The arms could be hidden at one of Abdul's properties until Majid was able to make his way back to Gaza, at which time he would organize the Ikhwan's long-awaited guerrilla force.

"We were all quite startled by Majid's plan," says Rashidiyah, "and at first no one knew what to say. We looked to Abdul, but even he was mute. It was clear, however, what we felt. This was our first call to action, and it made us all fearful. It was only Badir, Abdul's son, who finally provoked a response. He was wildly enthusiastic about the plan, and he insisted that it be carried out. His father mulled it over reluctantly, but then he agreed. So then it became a question of the details, and who among us was to go on the mission."

That was not all. In its broad outline Majid's plan was resourceful, but it possessed a clear hazard. The four or five Abdelqadirists whom Majid would be joining would surely be armed with personal weapons. How could the Ikhwanites, without weapons of their own, expect to ambush and disarm the column?

"So Majid revised the plan," Rashidiyah remembers. "He calculated that the entire trip to and from the caves would take six days and nights. On the fifth day after he left Gaza our group would be waiting at a predetermined place along the trail, about fifteen kilometers outside the city. As the Abdelqadirists approached, Majid would suddenly train his weapon on them and disarm them. He would shoot any who resisted. Then we would descend upon the train and seize the Abdelqadirists' weapons. Majid, of course, would be revealed as the betrayer. We would therefore be forced to kill the Abdelqadirists so that no one would know who made away with the shipment of arms."

Abdul objected to this revision on the grounds that the Ikhwan's mission was to kill Jews, not Arabs. Majid countered with an impassioned plea to the other members. The time had long since passed when the Ikhwan could make such distinctions, he insisted. If it is necessary to kill a few Arabs in order to carry out the Brotherhood's mission, so be it. The group had spent too much time already in talk. They were now presented with the opportunity to act. They could no longer use the lack of arms as an excuse for their inaction. The war between the Europeans was progressing and nothing had yet been done about the Zionists. It was Abdelqadir who was responsible for that situation by his collaboration with the British in Palestine. Thus the Abdelqadirists were in their own way as much an enemy of the Ikhwan as the British and the Jews. The death of a few Abdelqadirists should not be allowed to stand in the way of the Ikhwan and its higher, more sacred goals.

The assemblage nodded its agreement and looked back at Abdul for confirmation. But Abdul was still reluctant—now not only over the question of killing Arabs, but because he sensed in Majid's speech a criticism of and challenge to his leadership of the group. He looked at Majid darkly, silently wishing that he had not allowed his sons' teacher to be exposed to his fellow Ikhwanites.

It was again Badir who forced the issue, speaking up on behalf of Majid's rationale. He too was growing impatient with Ikhwanite inaction. Abdul knew that if he now vetoed Majid's plan, he would lose face with his eldest son. So he agreed to put the entire operation in Majid's hands.

A group to conduct the ambush was chosen. It consisted of Badir, two of his youthful cohorts, the thirty-year-old Ibrahim Rashidiyah, and three other members of the cell, all of whom were in their forties. Majid then contacted his Abdelqadirist friend and, using the name Khalid Fawzi, volunteered to make the caravan journey to the caves. He was given the date of departure—a few days thence—and the planned itinerary. He then met with his fellow Ikhwanites to work out the final details of the ambush plan.

"Four days after Majid left," recalls Rashidiyah, "we were taken in a truck belonging to the Palestine Citrus Company to an orchard on the outskirts of Gaza. From there we walked another ten kilometers along the caravan trail, dressed as Bedouin. We reached the agreed-upon place, about three hundred meters from a watering hole, and pitched a camp off the trail, but in sight of it. As it turned out, we had to wait there for three days instead of one. But sure enough, on the afternoon of the third day along came Majid's camel train. They stopped at the watering hole, and we watched from a distance. The plan was for Majid to disarm his companions when they stopped, provided that there were no other Bedouin about, and then fire a shot in the air to summon us. The place was empty. We waited for the shot, but it never came. We were astonished to see the caravan start out again, heading for Gaza. We followed at a distance, always staying out of sight. Finally, after another three or four kilometers, as it was growing dark, we heard a shot from ahead. We did not know what to make of it, it was not according to the plan. We stayed where we were, not daring to show ourselves. As night descended there was another shot, and then another, and another. Six or seven in all, from the same distance. The caravan had not moved. We peered over a dune to observe what had happened, but by then it was too dark to see. We stayed frozen there for the night, thinking that all the shots we had heard were the others killing Majid. We agreed that they must have found him out. With the first light of dawn we looked again. There in the distance the camels were standing haphazardly all about the trail. There was no sign of anyone. We decided to approach. When we got close, we saw the bodies of the others lying about. Then Majid appeared from behind cover, cursing us. He explained that he had not disarmed the men at the watering hole because we had not given the prearranged signal he had been waiting to see, telling him we were there. That was Badir's fault. Badir was supposed to have passed through the watering hole like a lone Bedouin, but had forgotten that part of the plan. When Majid had not seen the signal, he thought we must have grown tired of waiting and returned to Gaza. He finally disarmed the others farther up the trail as darkness was coming on, because if he didn't do it then the caravan would reach Gaza by morning. Then he realized he would not be able to keep the others under guard at night all by himself. One or two might have escaped back to Gaza. So he shot them. He accomplished the entire ambush on his own. He didn't even need us. All we did was bury the bodies away from the trail."

9

World War II

Majid's exploit, once news of it got around among the fifty or so members of Abdul's Ikhwan cell, turned him into a local hero. The Gaza Brotherhood had finally obtained its long-awaited arms, and when an inventory was taken it turned out to be a formidable arsenal indeed—close to a hundred automatic rifles, twenty Luger pistols, two hundred boxes of ammunition, six crates of hand grenades, and a dozen land mines. But in the end the very success of the enterprise brought about a delay in putting the arms to use.

Majid, flushed with the success of his venture and basking in the almost awestruck admiration he was receiving, grew careless about his security. Instead of maintaining a low profile around Gaza, he began to appear freely on the streets, a German Luger concealed in his robes. At the same time, the news of his accomplishment spread beyond the Ikhwan membership; so proud was one of the Ikhwanites about the group's acquisition that he boasted about it to a relative, who mentioned it to a friend, who passed it on to another friend. Eventually, the people for whom the shipment of arms was originally intended got wind of the story.

One night Majid, returning to the al-Qudwa house from a tour of Gaza's coffeehouses, was waylaid by a gang of Abdelqadirists. He was beaten unconscious, then hauled off to a hiding place. The next day Abdul received a note from the Abdelqadirists announcing that they held Majid captive and demanding the return of their arms for his release. Along with the note they sent one of Majid's fingers.

The kidnaping produced a crisis among the Ikhwanites. As founder and leader of the group, Abdul's first impulse was to ignore the demand. Secretly, thinks Ibrahim Rashidiyah, he was glad to be rid of Majid, for he disapproved of the way the other members of the cell had suddenly begun to look upon him. His son Badir, nursing resentment for the way Majid had belittled him in front of his father for forgetting to provide the crucial signal at the time of the ambush, concurred. "Badir argued that we had the arms now, what did we need Majid for? He, Badir, would take over the organization and leadership of the guerrilla force. If we gave back the arms and recovered Majid, we would be back where we had been before the raid. And even at that, giving back the arms was no guarantee we would recover Majid alive. Majid, he said, would want it this way. The paramount thing was that we had the arms. With the arms, we could proceed with our program against the Zionists. With Majid but without the arms, we could not proceed."

The meeting at which the discussions about Majid's fate took place was held at Abdul's house, Rashidiyah recalls. "There were about thirty of us there, all crowded into the main room. A few of us argued against abandoning Majid, but Abdul and Badir hardened their position, claiming that it had been Majid's fault for being captured in the first place. He had become too reckless, they said, and had exposed the Brotherhood to discovery and danger. Who knew what torture he had suffered at the hands of his captors, and what information he had revealed about us? So it was decided. Majid would have to fend for himself. If he was killed, we would name our group for him in honor of the things he had done for us. But we would not trade with the Abdelqadirists. We would simply send a message back saying we knew nothing of their demands, and nothing of Majid.

"Rahman—Yasir—he must have been eavesdropping at the door. When he heard his father's decision, he burst into the room shouting that we could not do it. It was a terrible scene. He threw himself at his father, punching him upon the chest and shoulders, crying out accusations of betrayal. Abdul threw him off and gave him a severe beating in front of all of us. It was the first time I had ever seen Yasir show any feelings. No one there had realized the depth of his attachment to Majid. Abdul was embarrassed but outraged. To show such disrespect to a father, especially in public, was a disgraceful thing. He beat Yasir, then ordered Badir to remove him. Then he affirmed the decision about Majid, and a note was written to be delivered to the Abdelqadirists the next day."

Unbeknown to anyone at the meeting, however, Majid was

managing to escape his captors that very night. With his hand in agony from the infection that had set in through the amputation of his finger, he managed to slip out of the warehouse in which he was being held and make his way back to his sanctuary. The next night, his hand swollen and red, he appeared at the home of Abdul al-Qudwa. The only ones there at the time were Yasir, recovering from his beating, his sisters, his younger brother, Husayn, and their mother, Hamida, who was nursing Yasir.

Majid was as surprised to see Yasir, his face bruised and blackened, as the boy was to see him. While Hamida tried to treat Majid's hand, Yasir spilled out the story of the night before, telling Majid bitterly about how his father and brother had declared him expendable. Majid consoled Yasir, but defended Abdul's actions, resurrecting the words of Yasir al-Birah. "We are all *fedayeen,*" he said. "We all must be prepared to die for the cause. The cause is more important than any man." Inside, however, he was furious with Abdul, for he knew that that had not been the reasoning behind Yasir's father's decision if what the boy had told him was true.

Later that night, when Yasir's father returned, Majid confronted him on the question. Abdul, once recovered from his surprise at seeing Majid alive, was solicitous and repentant. He denied Yasir's version of the meeting and claimed that the Ikhwan had decided only to wait a day or so to see how things developed. "Majid accepted the explanation," says Rashidiyah, "but he made it clear that he believed Yasir, not Abdul. From that moment on he made it clear also that he would no longer trust Abdul. In fact, from that moment on he started to treat Abdul with less and less respect."

Majid's hand needed medical attention. Abdul, in an effort to show how concerned he was over Majid's misfortune, insisted that he remain. He arranged for a doctor to come to repair and disinfect the wound. It would take several weeks for the infection to clear up, so Majid was given a bed in Abdul's home. During his recovery period he and Abdul could work out on paper the establishment of the Ikhwan guerrilla force.

"With Majid a full-time resident," says Ibrahim Rashidiyah, "Little Yasir became his constant companion, bringing him coffee, running errands for him. Majid remained there for a period of two or three months, and during that time Yasir became like a worshipful servant. The older boys remained fairly indifferent to Majid, and Badir, the oldest, grew to despise him. But Yasir was always in his room, always at his side. Whenever one of the older boys would say something unfavorable about Majid, Yasir would fly into a fury in his defense. And the youngest boy, Husayn—he was closest in age to Yasir and he more or less followed him—mimicked him."

Majid was eager to get on with his guerrilla ambitions. He began to draw up tables of organization, orders of battle, and rosters of fighters, demanding that Abdul implement his plans and gather the necessary people together so that he could lead the first raid as soon as his hand was recovered.

Abdul was more cautious. He insisted on a less impetuous and more considered approach to organizing the Ikhwan fighting force. His reasoning was based on the pronouncements by Haj Amin then emanating from Berlin.

After failing in his attempt to engineer the ouster of the British in Iraq, Haj Amin had fled Baghdad and, via Iran and then Rome, and with the aid of Axis agents, had made his way to Berlin. He was publicly welcomed by the Nazis upon his arrival in November, 1941, and was given political asylum and the use of a comfortable villa in a suburb of the German capital.

Throughout the early months of 1942 the Mufti assiduously cultivated the Nazi leadership. Hitler had decided earlier to extend his global ambitions to western Asia and the vast petroleum resources of the Persian Gulf. Consequently, he unilaterally broke the German-Soviet peace pact of 1939, invaded Russia, and spread tendrils of German armed might down through the Balkans of southeast Europe and into North Africa. His strategy was to mount a huge pincer movement that would close in on the Middle East from two directions: from the north, through Russia, and from the west, through North Africa and Egypt.

Before World War I Italy, as a result of the trading and securing of colonial spheres of influence then common among the European big powers, had colonized the old Ottoman North African provinces of Tripolitania and Cyrenaica, west of Egypt, and formed them into a single entity which it named Libya. After the war Italy further developed Libya and thereafter sought to gain control of Ethiopia. Hence, at the beginning of World War II there was a considerable

Italian presence in North Africa. In their designs on the oil fields of the Middle East, the Germans decided to augment the presence of their Italian allies with their own forces and, with Italian support, achieve a successful penetration eastward through Egypt, Palestine, and Syria to Iraq, while at the same time dropping southward out of Russia to win Iran.

Toward this end a large German force headed by General Erwin Rommel was landed in North Africa. With the collaboration of the Vichy government of France, the Germans secured much of French North Africa, and then, accompanied by the Italians, proceeded to drive through the Libyan desert toward the heartland of British-controlled Egypt.

Initially, it appeared that the Germans would be able to slice across Egypt, Palestine, and Syria as easily as a knife through butter. It was this very anticipation that motivated the exiled Mufti of Jerusalem in his dealings with his Nazi hosts. On the Germans' part, it was the Mufti's notability as an Arab leader that compelled them to entertain him; once they conquered the northern Arab world, Haj Amin would be very useful to them in representing German aspirations there.

Acting as the "spokesman" for the Arab people and for the theretofore unrealized ideals of Arab nationalism, Haj Amin spent the early months of 1942 assiduously lobbying among the Nazi hierarchy in Berlin for Arab independence once the Germans ran the British and French out of the Middle East. The Nazis, and particularly Heinrich Himmler, responded with sympathy. In order to dig himself in deeper in German favor, Haj Amin went so far as to publicly endorse the German approach to the "Jewish problem." In gratitude, the Germans provided him with radio facilities by which to send back to the Arab world the news of the German advance on Egypt and his prophecies of the coming liberation of the entire Arab world from British and French control by the "benevolent" Nazis, who he claimed were the "true brothers" of the Arabs in their struggle for self-determination. Throughout the spring of 1942 he broadcast appeals to all the liberationist groups within the various countries of the Arab world to begin mobilizing so that they could join with their German liberators as they swept across the Middle East.

The highlight of the Mufti's efforts in Germany, and the highlight of his broadcasting career as well, came at the end of April, 1942, when he received a joint German-Italian diplomatic letter sent to him in response to his demands that the Axis powers take a public stand on the Palestine question. The letter, delivered over the signature of Count Ciano of Italy and dated April 28, 1942, read in part:

> EMINENCE,
>
> . . . In confirmation of the conversations with you, I have the honour to communicate the following:
>
> The Italian Government fully appreciates the confidence placed by the Arab people in the Axis Powers and in their objectives, as well as their intention of participating in the fight against the common enemy until final victory is achieved. This is in accord with the national aspirations, as conveyed by you, of the Arab countries of the Near East at present oppressed by the British. I have the honour to assure you, in full agreement with the German government, that the independence and freedom of the Arab countries, now suffering under British oppression, are also the objectives of the Axis governments.
>
> The Axis Powers are therefore ready to grant to the Arab countries, now suffering under British oppression, every possible aid in their fight for liberation; to recognize their sovereignty and independence; to agree to their federation if this is desired by the interested parties; as well as to the abolition of the Jewish National Homeland in Palestine. . . .

The letter was supposed to have been kept a secret, but the ebullient Mufti could not resist hinting at its contents in his subsequent broadcasts. Soon excerpts from the letter began to appear in print in the Arabic newspapers of Palestine, and soon after that circulars and broadsides carrying varying versions of it were being circulated, along with calls for mobilization, throughout the Arab world.

During the summer and early fall of 1942 other Arab propagandists picked up the Mufti's messages as they came over the airwaves from Germany. The Axis armies were at the doorstep of Cairo, went the theme. Within weeks they will be pouring through on their way to the east, sweeping ahead of them every vestige of British and Jewish presence in Palestine. The time was approaching to prepare the Arab militia to join with the Germans and Italians in ridding the Arab world of British and Zionist oppression.

The Mufti's broadcasts were listened to with rising anticipation by nationalist groups all over the Arab world, and nowhere with more excitement than in Palestine. Abdelqadir al-Husayni and his cohorts in Jerusalem, finally convinced that a German victory was inevitable, abandoned their caution and began to surreptitiously distribute arms to the nationalist groups that had remained loyal to them from secret caches throughout Palestine. (It was at this time that Majid hatched his plot to hijack the shipment to Gaza.)

The broadcasts were also listened to by Hassan Banna and other Ikhwan leaders in Egypt. They were considerably less enthusiastic about the Mufti's appeals to aid the advancing Germans. In the first place, in their view a German-Italian presence in Egypt would simply be a replacement of the British presence.

Second, King Farouk and the Wafd government of Egypt had been caught by the British making secret overtures to Germany. The British had immediately clamped down on Egypt. If the corrupt Farouk and the Wafdists—the very people the Ikhwan was bent on ousting from power—were eager to embrace the Germans, the Germans thereby came ill-recommended in Ikhwan eyes.

And third, the Ikhwan had little trust in the Haj Amin version of Arab nationalism. Although Hassan Banna had earlier sought to ally the Ikhwan to the Haj Aminists in Palestine, he had been dismayed by Abdelqadir al-Husayni's temperate direction of the Haj Aminists following the Mufti's departure from Palestine in 1937. And although he still perceived certain beneficial expediencies in such an alliance—for instance, the sharing of arms—he was distressed by Abdelqadir's resistance to the establishment of active Ikhwan cells in Palestine. He and his associates in Cairo had all but shelved their ambitions for Palestine. Except for the cell in Gaza headed by Abdul al-Qudwa, there was little Ikhwan activity there. And even the Gaza cell had not expanded as Banna had hoped. He was even prepared to abandon the Gaza operation altogether and concentrate the Ikhwan's efforts on dealing with the Germans in Egypt. He therefore put out a directive to all Ikhwan cells to proceed slowly in response to the urgings of the Mufti in Berlin.

In Gaza, Abdul al-Qudwa found himself in another dilemma as a result of these events. On the one hand, he too had been listening to the broadcasts of the Mufti and had been stirred to action. On the other, he had received Hassan Banna's directive concerning restraint with regard to mobilizing. Banna was an Egyptian, Haj Amin a Palestinian. Banna operated primarily from religious impulses, the Mufti from political ones. There could be little doubt: Abdul's first and most fundamental loyalty should be to Haj Amin, particularly in view of the way the Abdelqadirists had distorted his movement. But Haj Amin was thousands of miles distant, whereas Hassan Banna was nearby.

It was the fall of 1942. As Abdul fretted over which direction he should point the Ikhwan, Majid Halaby, recovered from his kidnapping experience, agitated for immediate mobilization. There were long arguments between the two at the almost nightly gatherings of the Gaza cell.

Another member of the group, one of Badir's contemporaries named Ismael Dewan, today recalls that "Majid had most of us on his side, at least the younger members. The older men were more hesitant about organizing ourselves into a guerrilla group—despite the fact that Majid had taken such risks to obtain the arms. Yasir, although he was only thirteen or fourteen, was now at these meetings all the time, always at the side of Majid. He never said much, of course, but he was always there like Majid's mascot. There was a great deal of trouble between Abdul and Majid because of this. Majid was trying to persuade the group to immediately start raids on British outposts and supply centers, and on the Zionist places. Abdul said no, we had to follow orders from Cairo. Majid would answer that our allegiance was not to Cairo but to Palestine. Abdul would agree but say Hassan Banna was right, it was too early yet to commit ourselves to a single course of action, we were not strong enough. 'But look what Abdelqadir and his people are doing,' Majid would argue back, 'they are mobilizing!' 'Yes,' Abdul would answer, 'but the Abdelqadirists are traitors.' If the Germans came and drove the British out, the Mufti would return and discover Abdelqadir's treachery. He would disown the Abdelqadirist faction and would then make an alliance with the Ikhwan. 'Aha!' would shout Majid. 'You are wrong, you are stupid. You can hear with your own ears from Haj Amin that we all must mobilize.' Abdul would grow angry. 'No, it is you who are stupid, Majid,' he would say. 'The Mufti does not know what is going on here. Hassan Banna does know what is going on. We will obey Hassan Banna until the Mufti returns and can see for himself what has happened in Palestine.'

"These arguments went on week after week. Majid would be shouting all the time at Abdul. It made Abdul angry for his sons to see him shouted at. Then Majid began to accuse Abdul of cowardice. I was believing that too. So was Badir and the other young men. Finally Abdul ordered Majid to leave his house, to go back to the other house. He also would not permit Majid to come to any more meetings. So Majid began to call his own meetings. Many of us would go to these. It was clear that he was trying to take the cell away from Abdul. We wanted action, and we didn't care who was the leader so long as he got some action going. The Abdelqadirists had already started doing things—blowing up railroad lines, ambushing lorries and buses, things like that. We felt left out and ashamed. So we went with Majid. And do you know who would always still be with him? Yasir. Little Yasir was always there, always doing things for Majid. I thought it was strange. The older boys, even my friend Badir, were afraid to disobey their father. He had forbidden them to go to these meetings. He had forbidden Yasir also. But Yasir was always there. I don't think any of us realized it, but Yasir had run away from his father's house. He was living with Majid."

Ibrahim Rashidiyah realized it. "There was a great confrontation between Abdul and Majid one night over Yasir. This was after Abdul had ordered Majid out of his house. Majid began to have secret meetings of his own to organize a guerrilla operation. When Abdul discovered this, and discovered that Yasir was all the time at these meetings, he broke in one night and tried to drag the boy home. Yasir resisted, and his father struck him. Majid then struck Abdul and ordered him never to strike Yasir again. Abdul was in a rage. He threatened to have Majid killed for interfering in his family affairs. Yasir then burst in and shouted that if Majid was killed he —Yasir—would have to be killed as well. 'What do you mean by that?' Abdul said. That's when Yasir told him that he was not going back to his father's home. He announced that from then on he would live in the house of Majid."

10

Guerrilla Beginnings

The war years in Palestine were an intense confusion of contrasting events. In 1939, in the wake of the earlier Mufti-inspired Arab riots and in an effort to placate the remaining Arab Higher Committee leadership, Britain had imposed restrictions on Jewish immigration, limiting the number of Jews who could enter Palestine to 15,000 a year for the next five years. A few months later Britain forbade Jews to buy land, except in certain areas.

These measures mollified the Arab leadership somewhat but brought a violent reaction from the Zionists. Coming at a time when tens of thousands of Jews were trying to escape Nazi-controlled Europe, the immigration restrictions were a virtual death sentence for them. During the 1920s the Jews already in Palestine began to form their own local paramilitary defense groups, mainly to counter increasing Arab terrorism. Eventually these groups were organized into a single force under the auspices of the Jewish Agency, which was a kind of local Jewish government established in the early days of the Mandate to operate in conjunction with the British administration for the purpose of dealing with purely Jewish affairs. This armed group came to be known as Haganah (from the word meaning "defense" in Hebrew), and when Britain announced its immigration restrictions in 1939 it was rapidly transformed into a force whose mission was to resist the British.

Soon several smaller groups within the Haganah grew impatient with its progress. The resistance it represented was basically moderate. At a time when Jews in Europe were being slaughtered in increasing numbers and forbidden sanctuary in Palestine, moderation in dealing with the British was viewed as collaboration in the slaughter. These dissident groups therefore splintered off from the Haganah and formed into two vying extremist factions that became known as the Irgun and the Stern Group (later called the Stern Gang). With arms easily available to them, and with their cause striking to the core of every Jewish emotion about genocide, they gained a wide and respected following and quickly initiated a program of militant and often violent resistance to British immigration restrictions.

As anti-British Jewish terrorism increased during the early 1940s, the pace of Arab terrorism momentarily slackened. But when it became clear to the Arab nationalists that the British immigration restrictions were being successfully overridden by the Haganah and its extremist offshoots, the Arabs resumed their war on the Jews. By the autumn of 1942 the British were besieged on all sides, not only in Palestine but in the great North African desert to the west, where the forces of General Rommel were making ready for a final thrust into the heart of the Arab Middle East.

As noted in the last chapter, with the exception of the Ikhwan, militant Arab nationalists were mobilizing all over Palestine in response to Haj Amin's long-distance predictions about the coming German sweep. There was only one thing wrong with the Mufti's prophecies: the Germans never made it. Unexpectedly defeated in a great tank battle at El Alamein by an Allied force under British Field Marshal Montgomery, the Germans had to renounce their ambition to take over the Arab world.

News of the German defeat came as a serious blow to the Arab militants; thereafter, and until the end of the war, they wallowed about in confusion, apathy, and internal squabbling. No one was more directly involved in and affected by this strife than Majid Halaby, who by then was generally known among everyone in the Gaza Ikhwan by his nom de guerre, Abu Khalid.

"Abu Khalid had won several of us away from Abdul al-Qudwa's Ikhwan," says Halib Mansour, one of the young men who had earlier come over to Abdul from Gaza's Abdelqadir faction. "It was after El Alamein, the beginning of 1943, I believe. Abdul was going around saying that he and Hassan Banna were right all along. The Germans were not going to liberate us. It was proof that the Mufti was out of touch with things. Some of the Brothers tried to get a reconciliation between Abdul and Abu Khalid, but by then there was a deeply personal antagonism between them. Much of it revolved around Yasir, who was still living all the time with Abu Khalid."

Fouad Assaf was another Ikhwanite who had begun to attend meetings organized by Abu Khalid. "After El Alamein there was a terrible letdown. Abdul al-Qudwa was insufferable. He kept saying 'I told you so,' and many of us began to dislike him, to be repelled by him. He had the elders of the Brotherhood on his side still, but most of the younger men wanted none of his attitude. He kept comparing himself to Abu Khalid, saying that caution was the pearl of wisdom, while impetuousness was the cancer of ignorance and failure. Of course, he represented wisdom, while Abu Khalid was supposed to be ignorance. Well, we thought little of such aphorisms. Our morale was down for several months after El Alamein, but Abu Khalid rallied us. We began to meet again. There were thirty or forty of us now with him. We devised our force. We called it *Asifah* [Arabic for "the storm"], and we all were assigned ranks. It was to be a guerrilla force. Abu Khalid took the rank of colonel, he was the leader. There were several majors, several captains, many lieutenants. It was done basically on an age basis. I was twenty-six in 1943, so I became a captain. Even Little Yasir was given the rank of lieutenant. Of course, that was the trouble. We were all officers. There were no soldiers."

Raghib al-Masri was another lieutenant in the group. "Abu Khalid had got hold of a British army training manual," he says today. "He started to train us in the military disciplines. We would assemble in some out-of-the-way place, and he would train us in marching, close-order drill, things like that. Then we graduated to infiltration tactics, night marches. We were supposed to be guerrilla fighters, but he had us training like regular army people. It was a novelty for a while, but then the novelty wore off. We were accomplishing nothing. Abu Khalid started to become imperious, as well, acting like some pompous British subaltern. By the summer of 1943 he had lost many of us. That is when I dropped out. It seemed to me that he was merely using us to show how much better a leader he was than Yasir's father. Also, he had Yasir under his wing. He would treat Yasir with great favoritism. Of course, he was still a young boy, but nevertheless . . . Yasir was basically a complainer, a whiner. During these exercises he would always try to find a way to avoid them. There were two or three other boys who were Yasir's age, but only Yasir was exempted. If the others complained, they would be slapped by Abu Khalid. In my opinion he gave Yasir special treatment because Yasir was his pawn in the battle he was having with Abdul al-Qudwa. He thought that if everyone in Abdul's group saw how fervently Yasir believed in him, they would throw Abdul out and invite him to take over the Ikhwan. In that way he would gain access to the arms he had obtained the year before in his raid on the Abdelqadirists. Abdul and the Ikhwan Brothers had the arms hidden, and would not give them to Abu Khalid."

Musallah Said was yet another early follower of Abu Khalid. Nineteen at the time, he did not leave the Asifah group, but he agrees with Raghib al-Masri about Abu Khalid's motivations regarding Yasir. And he adds an ingredient to the formula of the relationship. "Abu Khalid was a strange man. After his finger was cut off, he would use the stump as a symbol of the mystique he tried to build about himself. He talked of trusting no one, of living the ascetic, sacrificial life with no comforts, no pleasures. His pleasure would only be warfare or preparing for warfare. He worked very hard at this image. Most of us understood that the whole idea was inspired by his experiences with Yasir al-Birah in Haifa. He was modeling himself on al-Birah, and as time passed he became more and more fanatical. When anyone was curious about his background, his family, he would refuse to reveal anything. He would say he had no past. He would call Yasir al-Birah his spiritual father, and then point to Yasir al-Qudwa, this little, rather sad, and not very impressive boy, and say that he was al-Birah's spiritual grandson. He did not do these things in any wild, hysterical way, however. He was always very quiet, but firm, absolute. His eyes would shine when he spoke of al-Birah, and when he looked at Yasir his eyes would then glisten. He would tell us how much Yasir looked like al-Birah. The two—Abu Khalid and Yasir—were suited to each other, even though Abu Khalid was twenty years older. . . . Abu Khalid had turned into a remote man after losing the finger. Remote and stern, but commanding. His demeanor, I would say, impressed many of us, as did his talk of future battles and the way he led our training. What mystified us was his almost slavish devotion to Little Yasir, and Yasir's to him. This commanding man and this fat boy who complained all the time.

Certainly Abu Khalid was using Yasir as a hostage, in a way, to Yasir's father. But then we discovered another reason. Abu Khalid was truly modeling himself on al-Birah. We went one night on a training exercise, about twenty of us. We were camped in a citrus grove near Gaza, in tents. There was an emergency of some kind, I don't recall exactly what, explosions in the distance, I believe. Several of us ran to Abu Khalid's tent to find out what we should do. There we discovered Abu Khalid and Yasir giving themselves pleasure—or should I say Yasir was giving Abu Khalid pleasure? After that, Abu Khalid was quite open about what he did with Yasir. In fact, he encouraged all of us to participate in such activities. He said it should be a part of the guerrilla way of life, to give pleasure to your Arab brother under arms. It created a closer bond among us. Most of us sooner or later were doing it as a regular thing. Some of us even gave pleasure to Abu Khalid, and him to us. But he would never let us touch Yasir. Yasir was his special province."

Ahmed Nabulsi, also a member of Abu Khalid's arms-less Asifah during 1943, corroborates Said. Still active after thirty-five years in the Palestine liberation movement (although not in an extremist fashion), he lives in Saudi Arabia today and works, like many Palestinians, in the Saudi diplomatic service.

"Abu Khalid, in my opinion, resorted to all his bizarre techniques solely to impress and hold on to his followers. After all, he was a Lebanese, not a Palestinian. Plus the fact that after he broke off with the Ikhwan, he had no chance to get the arms he had so daringly obtained. He used to wave his hand in our faces to prove that his amputated finger was greater proof of his loyalty to the liberation cause than anything we could show. As time went on and he was able to produce nothing in the way of arms or action, he began to lose followers. He became a bit deranged. He started this homosexual business, this principle of a sexual bond between guerrilla brothers, solely because everyone was bored and he thought this would renew their interest. It went on for about a year, nothing but meetings at which everyone ended up smoking water pipes and fondling one another. This became Abu Khalid's guerrilla group. But rather than cement bonds, all it did was create jealousies. And apathy. Everyone was having so much pleasure that no one could have been rallied to fight, even if we had been able to acquire arms. I left at about the middle, and later on a lot of the others simply drifted away. By 1944 Abu Khalid's group was down to six or seven people, mostly boys like Yasir al-Qudwa. Then Abu Khalid did the most stupid thing of his life."

What the desperate and, according to all observers, deranged Abu Khalid did was to seek a reconciliation with Abdelqadir in Jerusalem. In March of 1944 he set out with his dwindled band of seven youths—Yasir al-Qudwa at fourteen still the youngest among them—for Jerusalem. Aziz Gazal, then eighteen and today a Jordanian civil servant, was a member of the party.

"Abu Khalid had got a lorry from somewhere," he recounts. "Yasir came round to our houses in the middle of the night to round us up. We started off at dawn for Jerusalem, Abu Khalid driving, Yasir sitting next to him up front, the rest of us in the lorry bed. We got as far as Hebron, then the lorry broke down. We stayed two days and nights in Hebron while Abu Khalid had the lorry repaired.

"What we didn't know was that our fathers would be waiting for us in Jerusalem. One of us had a brother who was supposed to have gone with us. He backed out at the last moment the night Yasir rounded us up. He was supposed to keep our journey a secret, but when his father discovered that his brother was missing, he beat the secret out of him. The father was a member of the Ikhwan, as were all our fathers. He went to Abdul al-Qudwa and told him that Abu Khalid had taken us, Yasir included, to Jerusalem to join the forces of Abdelqadir al-Husayni. Abu Khalid's idea was to offer himself and us to the Abdelqadirists in exchange for weapons and mines. We would then go out and live in the hills and conduct hit-and-run raids on the Zionist areas.

"Abdul al-Qudwa, we found out later, immediately called all the fathers together. The fathers were furious that their sons had been taken by Abu Khalid. They felt it was a kidnaping, although we all went willingly. The fathers decided all to go to Jerusalem immediately to take us back to Gaza. They decided to do something about Abu Khalid, too. They wanted to have him killed. The only trouble with that was Yasir. The rest of us, we admired and followed Abu Khalid, but we were in it more for the adventure than anything else. We could easily be removed from Abu Khalid's influence. But Yasir, he worshiped Abu Khalid, and I later learned there was a great debate among our fathers about having Abu Khalid killed. Abdul al-Qudwa was afraid that Abu Khalid's hold on Yasir was so great that Yasir would try to protect Abu Khalid and be killed himself. He was also afraid that if Abu Khalid knew he was going to die, he would kill Yasir first as a kind of advance retribution."

Ibrahim Rashidiyah remembers the debate: "The fathers of the boys were outraged that Abu Khalid had secretly taken them to Jerusalem. They decided to go to Jerusalem themselves and force a confrontation with Abu Khalid. They all wanted to kill him. But Abdul objected. He told them that Abu Khalid had once threatened to kill Yasir if Abdul or the Ikhwan tried to interfere with him. This just aroused the others more. They began to blame Abdul for having lost control of Yasir. They said that if Yasir had not turned into such a slave of Abu Khalid, their own sons would not have fallen under his influence. Finally, after much arguing, Abdul said that his father-in-law Mahmoud had good connections to Abdelqadir. They would go to Jerusalem and discuss the problem with Mahmoud al-Husayni. Perhaps Mahmoud could arrange with Abdelqadir to have Abu Khalid killed so it would appear that the Brotherhood had nothing to do with it."

According to Aziz Gazal, "Once the lorry was repaired, we made our way to Jerusalem. None of us had been there before, so when we arrived Abu Khalid took us to a mosque for prayers. Then he left the rest of us with the lorry while he took Yasir away with him to try to make contact with the Abdelqadirists."

Abdul and the other fathers had arrived in Jerusalem the day before. Not knowing that Abu Khalid and their sons had been delayed in Hebron, several of them combed the city looking for the youths. Abdul and Rashidiyah, in the meantime, went to see Mahmoud al-Husayni to seek his help.

"Mahmoud was at first very contemptuous of Abdul," recalls Rashidiyah. "He belittled him for having failed to obey Abdelqadir's instructions about disbanding the Ikhwan, and he conveyed the impression that Abdelqadir would do nothing to help him. Abdul argued that this crazy Abu Khalid was a greater enemy to Abdelqadir than himself and the other members of the Ikhwan. Then he divulged the secret of Abu Khalid. He told Mahmoud that it was Abu Khalid who had arranged for the ambush of the Abdelqadirist arms shipment to Gaza. He claimed that Abu Khalid had done this without any authorization from the members of the Ikhwan. He said that the Ikhwan had taken the arms away from Abu Khalid and had them safely hidden away in Gaza. He said that it was because the Ikhwan would not give Abu Khalid access to the arms that he had come to Jerusalem with Yasir and the other boys. He then promised Mahmoud that if the old man could persuade Abdelqadir to have Abu Khalid killed, the Ikhwan would immediately return the stolen arms.

"Mahmoud softened, more, I think, because of his concern over Yasir than out of sympathy with Abdul and the rest of us. He finally agreed to contact the headquarters of Abdelqadir and see what he could do."

That night Mahmoud obtained an interview with one of Abdelqadir's aides. After explaining the situation much as Abdul had related it to him, he asked the aide to pass on to Abdelqadir Abdul's request and promise. He then returned to his home to wait with Abdul and the other Ikhwanites for an answer.

The next day passed without a response. In the meantime Abu Khalid and his tiny band arrived from Hebron. After their visit to the mosque Abu Khalid, with Yasir in tow, set out to gain his own audience with Abdelqadir and present his proposal. That night he was able to track down someone he knew who had an entrée to Abdelqadir. Over cups of coffee he told his friend of his desire to join his band of "guerrillas" to the forces of Abdelqadir and demanded an immediate meeting with the nationalist leader.

Abu Khalid's acquaintance, promising to see what he could do, left. An hour or so later he returned with the news that Abdelqadir would see him in the morning. He was to drive his lorry to an intersection behind St. George's Cathedral, a few hundred yards north of the Old City. There he should wait with his youthful companions until some men came along and made contact. From there he would be taken, alone, to one of Abdelqadir's secret meeting places in the Old City. His companions would remain under guard in the lorry until the meeting was concluded.

Abu Khalid protested, saying that he wished to present his entire band of warriors for Abdelqadir's inspection. His acquaintance shrugged and said it was impossible, that he must follow instructions exactly if he wished to meet with Abdelqadir. He explained that there had been several recent attempts on Abdelqadir's life and that security was extremely strict.

Abu Khalid insisted that he at least be permitted to bring Yasir with him. The boy was an al-Husayni. Certainly Abdelqadir would be impressed to see that one of his young relatives from Gaza stood ready to join the resistance struggle.

He was again denied. Abdelqadir would meet with him only if he came alone. Finally, Abu Khalid agreed.

During the night Abdul al-Qudwa and his fellow Ikhwanites, still waiting at Mahmoud al-Husayni's house, were notified that Abu Khalid had made his approach to Abdelqadir and that a meeting had been arranged between the two for the following morning. Before that meeting, Mahmoud was to bring Abdul and the others to Abdelqadir for a discussion of Abdul's promises.

"We were taken before Abdelqadir at about ten the next morning," says Ibrahim Rashidiyah. "He was encamped in a villa just outside Herod's Gate with about a dozen bodyguards and advisers. He was very uncompromising with us. He announced that if we wished to be rid of Abu Khalid and to have our sons back, we would have to do precisely as he said. His conditions were that we not only return the arms we had hidden in Gaza, but that we all then and there renounce allegiance to the Ikhwan and pledge our allegiance to the Palestine Arab party, which he was directing in the absence of Jamal al-Husayni, another relative of the Mufti's whom the British had sent into exile.

"Abdul as our leader immediately agreed, and he received no argument from the others. He promised to convert the Gaza Brotherhood into a branch of the Palestine Arab party and to accept orders from Abdelqadir's people, who would be sent to Gaza to take over the branch. Everyone agreed to this in front of Abdelqadir and his entourage. Then we were dismissed. We were told to return to Gaza, do as instructed, and await the return of our sons."

Half an hour after the delegation from Gaza left Abdelqadir's villa, four men approached the truck of Abu Khalid behind St. George's Cathedral. Two of them remained with Yasir and the other boys while two departed with Abu Khalid, walking in the direction of Herod's Gate and the Old City's Muslim quarter. It was the last anyone was to see of Majid Halaby–Abu Khalid.

11

Deception in Jerusalem

Abdelqadir al-Husayni was the son of Musa Kazim al-Husayni. Musa Kazim had been mayor of Jerusalem before the British Mandate, but had been ousted from office by the British during the 1920 Arab-Jewish disturbances for his vocal support of the Arab extremists led by his nephew Haj Amin. In his place the British had appointed Raghib Nashashibi, thereby exacerbating a decades-old feud between the two leading families of the area.

Raghib Nashashibi remained mayor of Jerusalem until 1934, and around him there grew a cadre of politicians and other notables who eventually formed into the National Defense party. Their program vis-à-vis the British and Zionists was basically one of moderation, negotiation, and, to a certain degree, collaboration.

Musa Kazim al-Husayni, in the tradition of clan competition in Arab society, was compelled to form a separate political party to advance the more extremist al-Husayni position. This became the Palestine Arab party, and when the elderly Musa Kazim died, also in 1934, its leadership passed into the hands of his close nephew, Jamal al-Husayni, who allied it with the Arab Higher Committee formed in 1936 by Haj Amin. When Haj Amin was forced to flee Palestine in 1937 after orchestrating the Arab riots and strikes, Jamal became the pre-eminent al-Husayni in Jerusalem and the keeper of the extremist flame. As well as heading the Palestine Arab party, he also was charged with keeping alive the militant movement of Haj Amin. In this he was assisted by his cousin, the son of Musa Kazim, the young Abdelqadir al-Husayni.

Despite increasingly harsh punitive measures imposed by the British, the Arab rebellion, begun in 1936, dragged on into 1938. It reached its climax in the early fall of that year, when the commanding general of the British Mandate forces reported to the War Office in London that "the situation [in September, 1938] was such that civil administration and control of the country was, to all practical purposes, non-existent."*

The Arab revolt was not just a struggle against the British; it was also a manifestation of the rift between the al-Husayni and Nashashibi clans that had been intensifying during the 1920s and early 1930s. The Nashashibi National Defense party had proposed that, by way of a solution to the strife, Palestine be joined to the neighboring British mandate, Transjordan, to form an independent confederated Arab state. This was anathema to the Palestine Arab party of the al-Husaynis. Transjordan was ruled by King Abdallah, the son of the Grand Sharif of Mecca, Husayn ibn Ali, and the brother of Husayn's eldest son Feisal. Husayn and Feisal had cooperated with the British during World War I by staging their revolt in Arabia in order to divert the Turkish army and enable Britain and France to displace the Arab world from the Ottoman Empire. For their efforts the British had promised them an independent pan-Arab state following the war—a state that would take in the Ottoman provinces of Syria (including Palestine and Transjordan), Mesopotamia (Iraq), and the entire Arabian peninsula.

The British, as we have seen, defaulted on their promise after the war. As a sop to the Hashemites (as the royal family headed by Husayn ibn Ali were known), they installed Feisal as a provisional king first in Syria and then, when they turned Syria over to the French, Iraq; they recognized Husayn ibn Ali as ruler of the Hejaz (the northwestern Arabian province that contained the holy cities of Mecca and Medina); and they established Husayn's younger son, Abdallah, as provisional king of Transjordan, which, like Palestine, had been carved out of southern Syria and placed under British mandatory control.

The al-Husaynis of Palestine, and especially Haj Amin, had since the early 1920s held the Hashemites to blame for the fact that Britain reneged on its commitment to establish a pan-Arab state. Having thought of themselves for centuries as Syrians, the al-Husaynis viewed the Hashemite acceptance of their various kingdoms as a sellout to the treachery of the British. Thus the Hashemites, al-

*General Haining, General Officer Commanding, Report to War Office, November 30, 1938, par. 14; from Private Papers Collection, St. Antony's College, Oxford University, Oxford, England.

though by tradition the most royal family in the Arab world, were viewed by the al-Husaynis as traitors to the Arab nationalist cause. The Nashashibi proposals for a national alliance with King Abdallah's Transjordan therefore struck an already inflamed nerve in the al-Husayni faction and provoked a war within a war between them and the Nashashibis during the later stages of the Arab rebellion against the British.

It was during this time that Abdelqadir al-Husayni came to prominence as an extremist nationalist leader. With his father, Musa Kazim, dead, with Haj Amin orchestrating policy from abroad, and with Jamal al-Husayni held in forced exile in Southern Rhodesia by the British during the early stages of World War II, responsibility for the conduct of the extremist nationalist movement within Palestine fell to Abdelqadir. He did not, as was rumored among dissidents at the time, enter into a secret agreement with the British to put a lid on anti-British and anti-Zionist guerrillaism. The diminution of Arab terrorism was caused instead by the further factionalization within the nationalist movement provoked by the internal al-Husayni–Nashashibi war that had spilled over from the latter days of the Arab rebellion into the early World War II years. Abdelqadir was forced to spend most of the war years attempting to snuff out factions that were not fully aligned with the Palestine Arab party and the general Haj Aminist movement. The factionalism was compounded by the German defeat in 1942 at El Alamein; the failure of Haj Amin's predictions severely discredited the Mufti in the eyes of nationalists who were only marginally loyal to him.

The murder of Majid Halaby was only one in a long series of assassinations carried out by the Abdelqadirists to keep the spirit and inspiration of Haj Amin at the core of the nationalist movement. Nashashibi sympathizers were eliminated in scores, and other aspirants to nationalist leadership, whether political or military, disappeared as quickly as they surfaced. It is quite likely that Abdul al-Qudwa, the organizer of the Gaza Ikhwan, notwithstanding his connection to the al-Husayni clan, was spared only because the impulses emanating from the Ikhwanist philosophy were religious rather than political or military.

Abdelqadir's ruthlessness as leader of the nationalist movement was well known to Abdul when he and his fellow Ikhwanites petitioned for the elimination of Majid Halaby. Abdelqadir's ruthlessness was an acquired trait, something he had sharpened to a fine edge during the years between his first meeting with Abdul and his second one. After the first meeting Abdul had ignored his instructions about breaking up his Ikhwan organization in Gaza. He knew that he could not disobey the second order. Thus, upon learning that Majid Halaby had been taken care of, he returned with his cohorts to await the return of his recalcitrant son and to prepare to re-form his organization in an Abdelqadirist mold and turn it over to the representative Abdelqadir had promised to send from Jerusalem. Little did Abdul imagine who that representative would be.

After watching Abu Khalid disappear toward Jerusalem's Muslim quarter for his meeting with Abdelqadir, Yasir al-Qudwa, Aziz Gazal, and the five other boys from Gaza lazed about the lorry behind St. George's awaiting his return. With them waited the two Abdelqadirists who had stayed behind when Abu Khalid was led toward Herod's Gate.

"We must have been there for five or six hours," remembers Gazal. "All through the afternoon we stayed there, guarded by these two men. Then the other two returned, but without Abu Khalid. We asked about him, and the men said that he was still meeting with Abdelqadir. They had come back, they said, because Abdelqadir now wanted to see us. They were to take us to him.

"They got into the lorry and drove us around for some time, away around to the other side of the city and back, until it became dark. Then they parked near St. Stephen's Gate and we walked into the Old City. We did not know the city, so we did not know where we were being taken, but the four of them led us up and down streets and alleys until we were totally disoriented. Finally they brought us into an old building. Later that night we were ushered into a room, and there was Abdelqadir.

"We had been told about him by Abu Khalid, but we were surprised just the same. He was a handsome man with a thick moustache and a scraggly beard. His eyes in the candlelight were piercing, like black knives. He looked us over, and then said, 'Which one is Rahman al-Qudwa?' Yasir stood up and said he was Yasir al-Qudwa, he did not wish to be called Rahman. Abdelqadir laughed. 'Yasir, eh?' he said. 'Why Yasir, little one?' Yasir said because that was his name. 'But your father named you Rahman,' said Abdelqadir. 'Who has named you Yasir?' 'Abu Khalid has named me Yasir,' he answered. 'And who is Abu Khalid?' Abdelqadir wanted to know. 'He is the one who has brought us to see you,' Yasir said. 'He is also known as Majid Halaby.' 'Aha,' said Abdelqadir, 'Majid Halaby. So that is why he calls you Yasir. Yasir al-Birah from Haifa. The follower of al-Qassam.* Yes, I see the resemblance.'

"The rest of us were silent. Abdelqadir then went on to give us a lecture about how important it was for Arab boys to learn to be warriors in the war against the Jews. We had already heard much of what he said from Abu Khalid, and Yasir announced that that was why we had come to Jerusalem. I must say, though Yasir was at least two or three years younger than the rest of us, he had no hesitancy in speaking out to Abdelqadir. The rest of us were, in many ways, totally awestruck by Abdelqadir. We were too frightened to say a word. But Yasir, he just naturally acted as though he was the leader of the group. Abdelqadir seemed amused by him. He said, 'You are an impertinent boy, aren't you? But I suppose this is because you are an al-Husayni.' And Yasir said, 'I am ashamed to be an al-Husayni. Abu Khalid tells us that the al-Husaynis have collaborated with the British and have failed to cleanse the land of Allah of its Zionist stain.'

"Now, Yasir had begun to talk like that. It was an imitation of Abu Khalid. And as with Abu Khalid, with him everything was black and white. He had no notion of the factionalism within the liberation movement, he had no awareness of the blow to Arab morale brought about by the German failure to invade the Arab countries, he had no appreciation for the political realities of the region. Like Abu Khalid, he was a fanatic, but in a juvenile way. He had never fired a shot or even handled a weapon, but all he could talk about was killing Jews and Britons.

"The rest of us were angry with his forwardness to Abdelqadir,

*Abdelqadir's reference was to Sheikh Izzaddin al-Qassam, who had been the founder, in the 1920s, of the Haj Aminist guerrilla group Yasir al-Birah had succeeded to the leadership of when Majid Halaby joined it in 1939. Sheikh al-Qassam and his group had conducted anti-Jewish terrorist attacks throughout northern Palestine during the early 1930s. In 1935 they took to the hills hoping to organize a peasant revolt, but al-Qassam was soon killed in a skirmish with British police. Al-Birah took over the group, and his first action was to assassinate the British district commissioner for Galilee.

frightened that he would punish us. But perhaps he saw in Yasir a kindred spirit, for he tolerated his impertinence. He brushed aside Yasir's statement about the al-Husaynis and instead lectured us on the achievements of the family. He pointed to all the al-Husaynis either in exile or in prison. He explained how the mission of the al-Husaynis had been hindered by the Nashashibis and other dissidents of true Arab self-determination. He explained how the battle for complete Arab sovereignty in Palestine could not be won until all groups united under one banner behind a single leader. Through the night he went on and on about the virtues of al-Husayni ideals and actions. He said the war in Europe would be over soon, and then the real battle for the Arabs would begin. But before we could fight the battle we must become united. It would do no good to have the Ikhwan here, Nashashibis there, other groups elsewhere, each fighting its own battle for supremacy within the liberation struggle. All must join together under the banner of the al-Husaynis, whom history had proved to be the most zealous defenders of Arab sovereignty in Palestine.

"At some point during the night Yasir inquired as to the whereabouts of Abu Khalid. Abdelqadir told us that after meeting with Abu Khalid earlier in the day he had sent him on a mission into Syria to make contact with the famous Syrian guerrilla Fawzi al-Qawuqji. He said Abu Khalid was going to form a band of experienced fighters from al-Qawuqji's Syrian group and then return with them and a supply of arms to Gaza to start guerrilla operations there under the al-Husayni banner.

"We all believed the story without question. Yasir, however, was extremely upset that Abu Khalid had gone to Syria without him. Abdelqadir soothed him by saying he was too young to go on such a mission, that Abu Khalid had agreed that having Yasir along would slow his progress. Then he produced a note which he said Abu Khalid had left behind for us. It was addressed to Yasir, and it appeared to be perfectly legitimate. It told Yasir that he—all of us—must follow the dictates of Abdelqadir while Abu Khalid was in Syria. We were to do whatever Abdelqadir commanded us to do, and if anything happened to him before he got back to Gaza, we were to continue as followers of Haj Amin and Abdelqadir.

"Yasir looked at Abdelqadir for a very long time before saying anything. Then he nodded. Abdelqadir gazed at each one of us, and each of us nodded in turn. 'You are now members of the Palestine Arab party,' he said. 'Do you know what that means?' None of us did, really. So he said, 'It means that you will be unswervingly loyal to the principles of Haj Amin and myself. You will do whatever you are commanded to do in the name of our struggle.' And so on. Then he told us we were to return to Gaza to await the arrival of Abu Khalid and his group. He said that when they came they would train us and that we would become guerrillas.

"And then the amazing thing! He told us that he was appointing Yasir to be his personal representative in Gaza with Abdul's Ikhwan group. He explained that he had ordered Abdul to abolish the group's Ikhwan identity and to re-indoctrinate it in the principles of the Palestine Arab party. Yasir's job was to see that his father did this to his—Abdelqadir's—satisfaction, and to report to him any deviation. His job was also to convey any orders he might send to the group. The rest of us, we were to be Yasir's lieutenants in the task. We were all ordered to recruit as many young men into the group as we could who were not already affiliated with other Abdelqadirist organizations in Gaza, so that when Abu Khalid returned from Syria with his querrillas we would have a large pool of potential fighters.

"Of course, none of us knew that Abu Khalid would not return from Syria. That he had never been sent to Syria. We only learned later that he had been tortured that morning into writing the note to Yasir, and then killed."

12

Abu Khalid's Legacy

Yasir was delivered back to his father in Gaza by Salah Tuqan and Hamdi Rasoul, aides of Abdelqadir. Tuqan was killed a few years later by the Haganah, but Rasoul has survived three decades of bloodshed and lives today in northern Lebanon. He says that he and Tuqan were instructed to see that Abdul al-Qudwa had begun disbanding the Ikhwan cell and to inform him that Abdelqadir had appointed Yasir as his liaison to the group to ensure that it was re-formed according to the principles of the Palestine Arab party.

"Abdelqadir cared little about the Gaza Ikhwan," Rasoul says. "Otherwise he would not have entrusted such a mission to a fifteen-year-old boy. The Ikhwanites were no threat to the Abdelqadirists, they were mostly old men. But Abdelqadir saw something in the boy. He felt he would be of great use to the liberation movement once he became a little older. It was the boy's way of speaking. He was daring, provocative, even hypnotic in a way. But very calculating, as if everything he said was designed to produce a certain response. He had little of the traditional Arab boy's respect for his elders, and would always say what was on his mind, no matter who he was addressing.

"Tuqan and I stayed in the home of Abdul al-Qudwa for two or three weeks. We presided over meetings of Abdul's society until all these things were hammered out. The men agreed to detach themselves from the Ikhwan, to join the party and work solely for Abdelqadir, to donate their money to Jerusalem. We told them that Yasir must become a member of the executive committee of the society, as he was to report to Abdelqadir, carry money and reports to Jerusalem every three months, bring back messages and orders. The men were taken aback by this. The prospect of being ordered about by this brash boy did not appeal to them at all, but we informed them that they would be in extreme difficulties if they did not comply with Abdelqadir's wishes.

"While staying in the house, we witnessed great tension between Abdul and Yasir, also between Yasir and the oldest son. Abdul wanted Yasir to return to school. Yasir said he did not want to, that he had more important things to do. Finally Abdul approached us. He asked us to talk to Abdelqadir upon our return to Jerusalem, to propose to him a deal. He said that if Yasir learned that his hero Abu Khalid had been killed by us, he would renounce his new allegiance to Abdelqadir. We knew this to be true, for Yasir spoke endlessly of Abu Khalid, of how he would be returning shortly to Gaza with a force of guerrilla fighters, of how he would lead all of Gaza in the coming war against the Zionists. Abdul told us to tell Abdelqadir that he would make sure that Yasir found out that Abu Khalid had been eliminated by Abdelqadir unless Abdelqadir ordered Yasir to return to school. After spending three weeks listening to Yasir talk about Abu Khalid, we felt we understood his attachment to him better than Abdelqadir did. So we agreed to tell him of Abdul's threat."

The two men returned to Jerusalem and, after assuring Abdelqadir that Abdul's Ikhwan group had been made over, conveyed Abdul's message. "Abdelqadir was angry at first. He had a quick temper and did not take kindly to threats. But we pointed out the wisdom of going along with Abdul. We convinced him that Abdul felt that he had lost all control over Yasir. Also, Abdelqadir's elevating Yasir over him in authority had meant a great loss of face to Abdul, not just with his peers but with his other sons. We explained that Yasir had taken Abdelqadir's assignment to heart, and that he was playing the role of the great boss with his father and brothers. We convinced Abdelqadir that Abdul felt he had nothing to lose by telling Yasir about Abu Khalid's death and how it had happened. We said that if he did so, Yasir was headstrong enough not only to renounce Abdelqadir but to become a dangerous enemy as well, who would himself have to be killed. We told Abdelqadir of Yasir's great devotion to Abu Khalid. He did not understand this, saying that Abu Khalid had been merely a self-deluded adventurer. 'That may be so,' we said, 'but these are the facts. If you wish someday to employ Yasir to greater benefit, it would be unwise to alienate him, even though he is only a boy. The thing you must do is replace Abu Khalid in his heart. So long as he is expecting Abu Khalid to return, you cannot do this, for Yasir only follows you now because he thinks Abu Khalid has ordered it.' "

Abdelqadir was due to make a secret journey to Rafah, a village in southern Gaza, to negotiate the acquisition of a load of German mortars, mines, and other arms that had been scavenged in Libya by Bedouin after the German defeat at El Alamein two years earlier. On the way he would pass near Gaza city. Rasoul says that he and Tuqan persuaded him to pay a visit to the town. Abdelqadir agreed.

The visit, in November of 1944, was a signal event for Gaza. Although Abdelqadir's journey itself was made largely in secret, once he was in Gaza word spread of his presence, and the two days he spent there took on the air of a general inspecting his troops. The leaders of Gaza's various Haj Aminist groups paid court to him at his secret hideaway, while British authorities, alerted to his presence, vainly tried to track him down. Midway through his stay he summoned Abdul al-Qudwa and Yasir.

According to Ibrahim Rashidiyah, who accompanied the two, Abdelqadir saw Abdul first. "Abdelqadir congratulated Abdul for siring such an intrepid al-Husayni son and said he saw great things ahead for Yasir. This did not particularly impress Abdul, for Yasir had become the least favorite of his children. He disagreed with Abdelqadir, saying that Yasir was an al-Qudwa first, and only then an al-Husayni. He complained that Yasir had done many things to blemish the al-Qudwa name. Abdelqadir became angry and insulting. He cut Abdul off, saying that the al-Qudwa name was as an ant to a horse in comparison to the al-Husayni name. He warned Abdul not to fill Yasir's head with his al-Qudwa demands but to let him develop as a true al-Husayni. In exchange for this, he said, he would see that Yasir returned to school. And that he would show ordinary respect to Abdul on all matters that were purely personal between father and son. There was no mention made of Abdul's threat to tell Yasir about what had happened to Abu Khalid."

Abdul grudgingly agreed. Then Yasir was called into the room. "Abdelqadir looked upon Yasir with a sympathetic expression. His eyes moistened, his face saddened. He said, 'Yasir, I have bad news for you. It pains me very deeply to have to tell you that your beloved

Abu Khalid has been called by Allah. He was on his way here by boat from Latakia [in Syria] with arms and a squad of commandos. They were chased ashore near Netanya by a British patrol boat. Some of them escaped, but others were murdered by a gang of Jews. Abu Khalid was among them. He fought valiantly, and his efforts allowed the others to escape. He has martyred himself for our cause.' "

Yasir was stunned and confused. "He gazed blankly at Abdelqadir," says Rashidiyah, "and then his body started to tremble. But he did not break down. He swallowed a few sobs and then collected himself. Abdelqadir went on. 'Yasir,' he said, 'one of the men who escaped reached Jerusalem last week. He came to me. He told me that Abu Khalid, just before he took the fatal bullet, had ordered whoever managed to get away to seek me out and pass his last message on to you. The message was that you must avenge his death. But you must do it as an Arab freedom fighter. You must from here on work under the direction and guidance of Abdelqadir to free our land of foreign oppression. Do you understand?'

"Yasir nodded. Abdelqadir asked him if he was willing to do whatever he said. Yasir nodded again. 'Then,' said Abdelqadir, 'I have these instructions for you. First, you will return to your school and finish your education there. While you are there, you will organize your schoolmates into a secret society. You will call it the Martyr Abu Khalid Society. And you will prepare it for the future so that it will be united and ready in mind and body to embark on our war against the British and the Jews.'

" 'Second,' he said, 'you will be respectful and obedient to your father and mother at all times, except if they attempt to interfere with your mission. If that happens, you are to invoke my orders.' Abdelqadir looked at Abdul. Abdul nodded. Yasir looked at Abdul, then back to Abdelqadir. 'Your father understands,' Abdelqadir said to him. 'Do you understand as well?' Yasir said he did. Abdelqadir then made Yasir embrace Abdul and Abdul embrace Yasir. He told them to make a covenant of mutual respect and honor, which they did.

"Later that night Abdelqadir came to Abdul's home. All the family was there. He made all the members of the family embrace and make a covenant among themselves. He said that even though their father was an al-Qudwa, they were all al-Husaynis and that he would expect them to devote themselves to al-Husayni ideals. It was very solemn. Abdelqadir was a very forceful man, and when he left there was an air of peace and reconciliation in the house."

13

The Martyr Abu Khalid Society

As early as 1937 concrete proposals for the partition of Palestine into separate Jewish and Arab states had been made by the British, who were growing weary of the difficulties of maintaining peace between Arabs and Zionists. In July of that year the Peel Commission, sent by the British government after the start of the Arab revolt to study ways of bringing peace to the Mandate, issued a proposal that would have given much of northern and coastal Palestine to the Jews and most of central and all of southern Palestine to the Arabs. A corridor leading from Jerusalem to the Mediterranean coast at Jaffa, which adjoined the new Jewish city of Tel Aviv to the south, would remain as a kind of international neutral zone controlled by Britain.

Although under this plan the Arabs would have received the lion's share of the land area, most of it consisted of the barren and infertile Negev desert. But this was not the reason the Arabs rejected it. They rejected it out of shock that it had even been advanced in the first place. To them it was another instance of British perfidy; that the British would unilaterally dare to split up their land and give part of it away to a foreign people was, in the context of every Arab and Muslim tradition, unthinkable. Instead of cooling the flame of the Arab rebellion, the Peel plan merely added fuel to it.

The Zionists, under their principal leader, Chaim Weizmann, were amenable to the idea of partition but maneuvered behind the scenes with the British to obtain a plan more favorable to them than the Peel scheme. When Arab leaders learned of this, they simply became more resolute in their resistance.

Notwithstanding Arab objections, the British continued to issue amended plans for partition until early 1939, when they finally yielded to the increasing pressures of Arab insurrection by doing an about-face and placing restrictions on Jewish immigration and land purchases. This, of course, aroused Zionist ire while it only briefly soothed the Arabs.

The British had invited Zionist and Arab leaders—Arabs from both Palestine and other countries—to a conference in London. The outcome of this conference was the British White Paper of 1939, which imposed the aforementioned Jewish immigration limitations and was in most other ways favorable to the Arabs, specifically in its promise to establish an independent Arab state throughout all of Palestine ten years hence should the Arabs behave themselves and cooperate with Britain.

Many of the more moderate of the Palestinian Arabs felt privately that they should accept the White Paper, for it came close to realizing their nationalist objectives, albeit at some distance in time. Acting under orders from the exiled Haj Amin, however, the powerful al-Husayni element rejected it, principally because it did not offer a guaranteed time limit for Palestinian statehood, but also because the White Paper expressly forbade the return of Haj Amin to Palestine. The al-Husaynis made it clear that anyone who publicly favored acceptance of the White Paper would, in effect, be publicly rejecting the primacy of the Mufti.

By rejecting the White Paper, the Palestinian Arab nationalists unwittingly threw away any chance they might have had of fulfilling their aspirations of Arab sovereignty over all of Palestine. The Nazi persecution of European Jewry during World War II—and particularly the knowledge of its monumental dimensions, which began to become known as the war drew to a close in 1945—galvanized world public opinion in such a way that it became inevitable that Zionist demands for a permanent Jewish sanctuary or homeland in Palestine would be supported and eventually sanctioned.

As the war drew to a close, the Arabs of Palestine and other Middle Eastern countries began to realize this. They were helpless, however, to stop it. During the war the Jewish community of Palestine had become too strong and too mobilized to be contained. Enormous sums of money had been raised by the Zionists, principally in the United States. Much of this money was spent to clandestinely purchase arms and munitions from sympathetic sources and to pay for pro-Zionist propaganda. Moreover, the Zionists had sent a Jewish brigade to fight with the British against the Axis. Now, at war's end, many members of the brigade had returned to Palestine as highly skilled soldiers, trained in the use of sophisticated arms and military tactics.

Furthermore, as the conclusion of the war in Europe approached, Britain began to drop hints of its desire to relinquish its mandate over Palestine. When they became aware of this, the Zionists redoubled their efforts to ensure themselves security in Palestine. Their dream of a Jewish homeland there had long before transformed itself into an ambition for a sovereign Jewish state, and it was to this end that most Zionist propaganda and international political maneuvering were directed.

The more the Jews of Palestine united behind the idea of an independent state, the more disunited became the Palestinian Arab nationalists. Many realized their mistake in rejecting the 1939 White Paper; had they accepted it they might now be in the position of other Arab countries which were about to obtain independence from Britain and France. Their rejection of it had been at the insistence of Haj Amin. Their regret about it provoked in many minds a diminution in their reverence for, or fear of, the Mufti.

Haj Amin had lost even more credibility as a result of his friendship with the Nazis. With world opinion revulsed by revelations of the horrors the Germans had visited upon the Jews, and with the Zionist propaganda machine underlining the Mufti's oft-expressed approval of the German philosophy of *Judenrein,* any Arab leader who now publicly supported Haj Amin would hardly find himself taken seriously in the world. Consequently, the Haj Aminist faction of the nationalist movement suffered a considerable loss of prestige, both within Palestine and without.

Haj Amin had fled Germany for Paris, where he was placed in detention for eventual judicial action to determine whether or not he qualified as a war criminal. Without his voice and direction, Haj Aminist influence eroded further.

Evidence of this became apparent in July of 1945, when the major Arab countries formed the League of Arab States (the Arab League) with a view to presenting a unified front in postwar negotiations with the Allies over Arab independence in the Middle East. Since the League was meant to symbolize Arab nationalism and common interest, the Palestinians were invited to send a representative. Had the League been formed a year or so earlier, there would have been no question but that an al-Husayni appointee, possibly Abdelqadir himself, would have been sent. Now, however, no agreement could be reached about who should represent the Palestinians. Finally, the Syrian leader Jamil Mardan stepped in and imposed his own choice on the Palestinians—Musa al-Alami, a lawyer who had no particular affiliations.

Al-Alami immediately attempted to dissociate Palestinian nationalism from the extremist point of view, thereby causing further rifts within the movement. Then Mardan, ambitious to be the sole spokesman for the Palestinians (who, he and many others still claimed, were really Syrians), organized a new Arab Higher Committee and installed it in Jerusalem over the objections of the al-Husaynis.

Mardan's committee seemed to be making some headway in unifying the nationalist movement, although it was forced to function in the face of mounting dissidence on the part of those still loyal to the al-Husaynis. Abdelqadir, although an astute militarist, found his political authority waning because of his relationship to Haj Amin. Early in 1946 Jamal al-Husayni returned to Jerusalem from his years of British detention in Southern Rhodesia to find the Haj Aminist movement and the Palestine Arab party a shambles.

Jamal, more of a politician than Abdelqadir, rallied the demoralized Haj Aminists and managed to reorganize Mardan's Arab Higher Committee along lines once again favorable to them. His efforts were aided enormously when, a few months later, having escaped from his captivity in Paris, Haj Amin arrived in Cairo.

The Mufti's sudden reappearance in the Arab world served to restore much of the leadership credit he had lost during the wartime years. He was still, after all, the Mufti, and so deserved deference and respect. The leaders of the other Arab countries appreciated this; consequently the Arab League intervened to restore Haj Amin as the sole spokesman of the Arabs of Palestine, with Jamal and Abdelqadir al-Husayni his chief representatives there. The League put its imprimatur on the reascension of Haj Amin to the leadership of the Arab Higher Committee, provided funds for its activities, and placed Musa al-Alami, the Syrian-appointed Palestinian representative to the League, under Haj Amin's direction. Haj Amin himself, however, was not permitted to return to Palestine.

Until the arrival of Haj Amin in Cairo, the foregoing events went largely unnoticed by sixteen-year-old Yasir al-Qudwa in Gaza. During the year and a half between his encounter with Abdelqadir and Haj Amin's return to Cairo, he attended school faithfully, maintained a reasonably obedient relationship with his father, and spent practically all his spare time organizing schoolmates into the group he called the Martyr Abu Khalid Society. In so doing he experienced his first taste of the demands of leadership. According to many who knew him, the experience wrought a sharp change in his personality.

"No one was terribly impressed when Yasir returned to school and started to pass notices around calling for meetings to organize a youth group," says Zuhayr Zarur, who was a student in the school. "Most of us knew that he had been involved with Majid Halaby for the previous few years. Though we all liked Majid, when he disappeared from the scene we went back to thinking of Yasir as we had before, as an object of humor, I suppose. But then he managed to get four or five boys together and start this Abu Khalid club. The boys he attracted at first were like himself—the outcasts of the school, the boys who always stayed apart, who never joined in any normal activities.

"None of the rest of us paid any attention to Yasir and his club at first. But then it became known that this Abu Khalid was really Majid Halaby. Stories got around about how he had really been a secret freedom fighter and how he'd been killed by the Zionists, and how Yasir had been chosen by Abdelqadir al-Husayni to organize a youth group in his memory. So some of us attended a few meetings of Yasir's group. We heard all this talk about guerrilla action against the Jews, about becoming an elite force under the command of Abdelqadir. It was all a bit on the childish side, but we were impressed. Especially so because the talk was coming from Yasir. He had picked up many of the mannerisms of Majid Halaby, bulging his eyes when he talked, cocking his head to the side when making an important point, using his hands in sweeping gestures, all very animated. This was a different Yasir from the timid, sullen boy we were accustomed to. We were amused, but impressed."

Hadar Talhuni, today a shopkeeper in Beirut, was another of Yasir's schoolmates. "I had an older brother who was killed by the Jewish Irgun in 1942," he recalls, "so I was very interested in anything having to do with action against the Zionists. In fact, I even tried to organize a group, but it amounted to nothing. When I learned what Yasir was doing, I began to go to his meetings. I didn't expect much, because I had never thought much of Yasir or any of the al-Qudwa boys. But I was surprised. He was very commanding, very knowledgeable, very articulate. He had pamphlets he said were given to him by Abdelqadir. He had us read them, and then we would discuss them. They were legal pamphlets—all about how the British Mandate had been illegal under international law, about how the Balfour Declaration had no legality, about how the treatment of Palestine was a violation of the League of Nations covenant, about how Zionist immigration and settlement without Arab concurrence was illegal. Yasir lectured us on all these things. Then he would tell us how we must take the law into our own hands to overcome these illegalities. We had received some of this instruction in our classrooms, but it was usually given by elderly teachers who would always say that eventually Allah would set things right. Yasir never talked about Allah. He talked about guns and fighting. He talked about how the Arabs had driven out the Crusaders, and about how we must do the same with the Jews. Because of my brother, this appealed to me very much. I became a full-fledged member of the Martyr Abu Khalid society.

"The first few months there were only half a dozen of us, plus one or two of Yasir's brothers. Husayn, his younger brother, was there all the time. And, I believe, Nasr. Then others from the school came, most of them older boys. Once or twice the older boys tried to take over the leadership from Yasir, but he grew stronger and more persuasive and was able to resist them. So they ended up following him, although some remained jealous of his leadership. He did not look like a leader. He had none of the physical attraction of Abdelqadir, or of Majid Halaby. But he could talk. And he knew so much more than the rest of us."

Nasr al-Qudwa, Yasir's older brother, says he was only a sporadic member of the group. "At this time my other brothers and myself were in the middle between Yasir and our father. Our father kept his word to Abdelqadir and did not attempt to interfere with what Yasir was doing. But he did not like Zaeed or me or Husayn to join with Yasir. Of course, Yasir tried always to get us on his side. So I would go to meetings once in a while. But only to please him, really. At that time in my life I was not very interested. I had heard so much of it, so much arguing and fighting. Husayn, though—he became a follower.

"Yasir was very serious about it, it was all he cared about. And it changed him immensely. He received a sense of power and authority from his activities, and he became more outgoing and gregarious. He would go into coffeehouses and get into discussions with older people about what should be done. These men were usually members of some underground resistance group themselves. Or else they were local politicians. Yasir would argue with them. At first they would be amused, some even resenting his impertinence. That was at the time when the al-Husayni movement was suffering a decline in prestige because of the Mufti. The men were disillusioned with the Haj Aminists. But Yasir would defend them with great force and loquaciousness."

Hassam al-Fahum, another Gaza youth who drifted into Yasir's group, remembers him thus: "Yasir became another person in the period of a year. When I first knew him, he was still withdrawn and suspicious. He had a great love of secrecy and mystery. But as he saw the society expand, he became outgoing. He was all the time very serious and dedicated, but he began to make a joke here and there, to smile once in a while. Also he became very conscious of himself as an al-Husayni. He talked and acted as though his al-Husayni blood automatically conferred respect upon him. It was a bit ridiculous at first. In the beginning he was copying Majid Halaby. Then he added a bit of Abdelqadir to his mannerisms. It was ridiculous because he was so unlike either of them. But we became used to it, and after a while it seemed natural.

"Yasir had some struggles with other boys, though, who didn't take to the idea of him leading us. There was a boy who was related to the Nashashibi family, who kept belittling the al-Husaynis and Yasir. He tried to form a rival group. I remember that Yasir organized five or six of us to attack the boy one day. We gave him a wicked beating and he was not heard from again. Yasir did not take part, however. He simply stood and watched.

Taysir al-Aref was a nephew of Aref al-Aref, the Palestinian who collaborated with Haj Amin in the early anti-Zionist Arab riots. His immediate family had moved from Jerusalem to Gaza in the late 1930s, and he eventually became a member of Yasir's society. Today he lives in Cairo and earns his living as a dealer in cotton. "The Martyr Abu Khalid Society was just one of many youth groups that formed in Gaza toward the end of the war," he recalls. "I believe Badir al-Qudwa even had a group of his own that was a rival of Yasir's. I know that I began in another group in 1943, before Yasir started his. Our group broke up, though, and some of us ended up joining with Yasir.

"Yasir became more fanatical as he gained more confidence in himself as leader. And as he became more fanatical, he grew more ruthless. When the news came that Haj Amin had arrived here, it was a great moment of prestige for Yasir. He had kept faith in Haj Amin and Abdelqadir while almost everyone else had lost it. When the news came, he was vindicated. But then he did a strange thing. By that time we had twenty, twenty-five members. Yasir organized us into squads of five or six each. We were to seek out other groups and make them join us. If they refused, we were to beat them into submission. We would have clubs and knives, and would make surprise raids. With the Mufti back on the scene, Yasir was out to win over all the other groups to his side. He said at the time that he was acting under orders from Abdelqadir, but I doubt it. I seriously don't believe he had any contacts with Abdelqadir during these months. I believe he was doing it on his own initiative. He wanted to dominate all the youth groups. But he found that persuasion took too long. So he tried to do it through violence and intimidation. To a certain extent he succeeded, for by the end of 1946 we had about three hundred boys involved with us."

According to Hafez Ayubi, then a marginal member of the Abu Khalid Society and today a Palestinian communist, despite the group's expanding size it accrued little to its credit in the way of accomplishment. "We were really playing games, that is all," he complains. "No one in the higher echelons of the resistance leadership took us seriously, thus we had nothing serious or worthwhile to do. Jews were pouring into Palestine by the boatloads despite the

British immigration restrictions, and there was great confusion in the movement about how to deal with this. The British were preparing to abandon Palestine, but in the meantime they did everything to favor the Zionists and everything to hinder us.

"I must say, though, Yasir kept us together. He was a good organizer. Our group became the largest in Gaza. We got so big we had to have our meetings in sections. He kept us together mostly by rhetoric. The entire point of the society was that we were awaiting the call to arms from Jerusalem, from Abdelqadir. We were to be the storm troops of Arab liberation. When rhetoric failed, he would use violence. He had an inner circle of eight or ten boys, and he would send them out to beat the ones who showed signs of drifting away.

"But for all of that, we ended up doing nothing, accomplishing nothing. Yasir and his inner circle had no idea of politics in those days. Their thoughts and notions were all centered on fighting for the al-Husayni liberation. They were totally focused on Haj Aminism and the Jewish settlement, and had no awareness of anything else going on in the world. They knew nothing of government, nothing of political ideology, nothing of public opinion. There were some of us who were older who tried to introduce political ideas into the meetings, to weigh one political approach against another. After all, what was the so-called liberation going to mean if it had no political foundation? But Yasir saw this as some kind of deviation from the true purpose of the society. We were to be soldiers, not politicians. We were preparing ourselves to be martyrs for the cause of liberation, et cetera, et cetera. He was very big on the martyr business. Once, one of the boys in the group was killed in a perfectly ordinary accident. He was riding a horse, the horse fell, he broke his neck and died. I forget his name, but let's say it was Kamal Sabri. Yasir immediately pronounced Kamal Sabri a martyr, and created the Martyr Kamal Sabri Brigade as the name of one of our so-called guerrilla groups."

14

The Approach of Partition

The Martyr Abu Khalid Society finally got its call to arms in the spring of 1947.

During the previous year a joint Anglo-American Commission of Inquiry was sent to postwar Palestine to explore yet another solution to the Arab-Zionist problem. The commission concluded that "Palestine cannot be regarded as either a purely Arab or purely Jewish land. . . . It is therefore neither just nor practicable that Palestine should become either an Arab state or a Jewish state."

The commission's report proposed a nebulous form of binational administrative government for Palestine, then recommended that the 1939 British restrictions on Jewish immigration and land purchase be lifted and that 100,000 Jewish refugees in Europe, concentration camp survivors, be immediately permitted to immigrate.

The United States, then in the process of taking over many of Britain's interests in the Middle East, reacted enthusiastically to the commission's recommendations on immigration. Britain, at the same time endeavoring to revitalize its imperial interests and restore Arab favor, did not. Consequently, British Prime Minister Aneurin Bevan refused to lift the immigration restrictions.

In Palestine, the Jews launched a systematic wave of reprisals. Now wholeheartedly committed to the necessity of a Jewish state in Palestine as a result of the Nazi experience, they were preparing for all-out war to achieve it. In June of 1946 the Haganah blew up eleven major bridges linking Palestine with neighboring Arab countries. In response, the British imposed curfews and searched for hidden arms caches. A few days later the Haganah kidnaped six British officers. The British responded by arresting several leaders of the Jewish Agency and placing them in a detention camp.

In July the Irgun blew up a wing of the King David Hotel in

Jerusalem. The blast killed nearly a hundred British and Arabs, and even a few Jews. Thereafter, in response to each British countermeasure, the Jews escalated their violence, the Haganah hitting mostly military targets, the Irgun and Stern Gang striking everywhere. It was a Jewish repeat, on a much more militarily sophisticated scale, of the 1936–39 Arab revolt—except that this time the British had had enough. Despairing of ever being able to solve the Palestine problem, they announced their intention of giving up their mandate and, in February of 1947, turned the problem over to the United Nations.

The Arab nationalists, having just undergone a measure of reunification following Haj Amin's return in the spring of 1946, were immediately torn apart again as a result of the Jewish war against the British. The war inevitably spilled over onto the Arab population, and during the rest of the year the Arabs grew increasingly helpless and neglected. Nor did they fail to notice the abundance of modern arms possessed by the Jews, and the techniques used in their employ. Nor, either, did they fail to take note of the continuous stream of Zionist declarations concerning the imminence of a sovereign Jewish state in the land—the Anglo-American Commission to the contrary notwithstanding—they considered exclusively theirs.

Nationalist frustration was compounded by the fact that while the British-Jewish war intensified and Arab demands and aspirations were becoming obscured, neighboring Arab countries had begun to win their long-awaited independence with a great deal less bloodshed and destruction. Many had had to struggle, certainly, but in no other Arab state was there anything to compare to the violence in Palestine. Except for British control of Suez, Egypt had already obtained independence. In 1946 Syria and Lebanon became the next two Arab nations to be completely freed of foreign rule. In the same year the British Mandate over Transjordan came to an end, Transjordan assuming independence under the Hashemite king Abdallah.

After Britain put the problem of Palestine in the hands of the UN, a special committee was formed within the world organization to seek a solution. Known as the United Nations Special Committee on Palestine (UNSCOP), its members arrived in the beleaguered land in early May of 1947. Like so many commissions before them, they almost immediately took up the cause of partition. In August of 1946 the Jewish Agency had advanced a partition plan that would have given the Jews approximately 70 percent of Palestine and the Arabs 30 percent, despite the fact that there were half as many Jews as Arabs in the country. UNSCOP came up with a plan that modified the Jewish Agency plan but still gave the Jews more than 50 percent of the land—again despite the much larger Arab population.

Understandably, even moderate Arabs resigned to partition resented the plan because of its generosity to the Zionists in the face of the realities of population. Militant Arabs led by Haj Amin rejected it with unremitting outrage. They immediately mobilized all those groups throughout Palestine which had been forming and waiting during the years of World War II to mount the supreme effort to win exclusive Arab rule over the country. During the war the various Haj Aminist groups Abdelqadir al-Husayni developed had coalesced into a single large guerrilla force which came to be known as Futuwwah. The time had come for Futuwwah to do its work.

In May of 1947, intent upon demonstrating to the UN that the Arabs would accept no form of partition, Futuwwah, under the leadership of Abdelqadir, launched its first concerted attack. The enemy was no longer the British, but the Jews alone. Consequently, the attack was directed at a Jewish convoy on the Jerusalem-Hebron road. Half a dozen Jews were killed, and scores were wounded by Arab automatic rifle fire.

The Haganah and Irgun, while still intent on harassing the British, turned their attention to the Arabs. The Haganah retaliated by raiding a suspected Futuwwah office in Jerusalem, killing an Arab janitor. The Irgun responded by assaulting an Arab village near Hebron, killing sixteen Arabs and dynamiting their homes. The battle was joined.

Although, as usual, strong on rhetoric, Futuwwah was lightly armed in comparison with the Zionist military and guerrilla groups. Since what arms the Arabs did possess were controlled by Abdelqadir, he tended to keep them concentrated in Jerusalem. Thus, elements of Futuwwah scattered in the hinterlands were forced to make do with whatever weapons they could scrounge locally.

Futuwwah's first attack brought a general call to action by Abdelqadir to all the self-styled Arab guerrilla groups of Palestine. In

Gaza, Yasir al-Qudwa and his Abu Khalid Society responded with high enthusiasm. But so did a dozen other organizations, including one led by his oldest brother, Badir. The only trouble was that with the exception of two long-established groups—one Haj Aminist, the other Nashashibist—none of them possessed any weapons to speak of. In order to take part in any meaningful action, the groups lacking arms were forced to join themselves to the two armed groups, which were made up mostly of men in their forties and fifties.

"Yasir was visited one day by representatives of the Haj Aminist brigade," says Taysir al-Aref. "They told him they had orders from Abdelqadir to incorporate the Abu Khalid boys into the over-all Gaza Futuwwah. At first Yasir resisted, for he wanted us to remain independent. But we still had no arms, so many of us left and joined Futuwwah of our own accord. Finally, Yasir came over, but they relegated him and his closest friends to the back row. He was allowed no say in the tactics of the Gaza Futuwwah, and was not even permitted in the secret meetings where decisions were made. They thought he was too young. Occasionally they would say to him, 'Take a dozen of your boys and go to such and such a place and do this or that.' It was never anything important, and we never even got so much as a pistol."

As it became clear during the summer of 1947 that the UN favored partition, Futuwwah escalated its anti-Jewish terrorism. But Gaza remained relatively quiet, most of the action having deteriorated into a struggle for authority between the Haj Aminists and those who spoke for the more moderate Nashashibists. The Nashashibi faction now had a guerrilla force of its own, called Najjadah. Its arms supplies were more plentiful than those of the Haj Aminists because the Nashashibists had been more cooperative during the previous years with the British and thus had better contacts with British soldiers who sold black-market weapons out of British army arsenals. Consequently, the main war the Gaza Futuwwah fought during the summer of 1947 was against the Najjadah in an attempt to confiscate their arms.

Yasir chafed at the inactivity imposed upon him and his Abu Khalid Society by the more senior Haj Aminists of Gaza. Finally, in late November of 1947, along with his devoted fifteen-year-old brother, Husayn, and a couple of cohorts from the inner circle of the

Abu Khalid Society, he made his way to Jerusalem to offer their services as fighters to Abdelqadir himself.

Yasir's arrival in Jerusalem coincided with the vote by the United Nations to partition Palestine in accordance with the plan developed by UNSCOP. Jerusalem was in chaos. The Arabs, through Haj Amin in Cairo, announced their absolute rejection of the UN resolution and insisted that there was no possible way the world organization could impose partition. The Mufti was supported by the Arab League, which warned: "Any attempt to impose UNSCOP's recommendations or any similar scheme will be implacably resisted by all Arab countries. Let there be no doubt that the Arabs, if compelled, will fight for Palestine."

In the immediate wake of the UN vote the bickering factions within the Arab nationalist movement put aside their differences and united to wage war against the Zionists and against any British forces that interfered. December 2 saw Arab attacks against Jews break out all over Palestine. In Jerusalem Yasir and his companions, just arrived, joined a mob of more than two hundred Futuwwahists, armed with clubs and knives, who descended on the Jewish quarter of the city and wreaked havoc and injury. The next day they found one of Abdelqadir's lieutenants working out of a house in the Old City on plans for a wholesale war against Jerusalem's Jewish population. Yasir volunteered their services, and the boys were quickly conscripted as message runners between the various Futuwwah outposts in and around Jerusalem.

Salah Haddad was a young man of twenty at the time. His father was one of Abdelqadir's closest aides, and he himself was an avid member of Abdelqadir's forces. Today a follower of Georges Habash, the communist Palestinian revolutionary, he was assisting Sulemayn Ridha, Abdelqadir's lieutenant, when Yasir, his brother Husayn, and their companions showed up.

"Yasir did all the talking," Haddad recalls. "He was looking for Abdelqadir, who was conducting operations from a house on the Jericho road. Sulemayn gave Yasir and his friends assignments as messengers, but wouldn't tell him where Abdelqadir was. Yasir argued and argued. He claimed Abdelqadir knew him well, that he was an al-Husayni. Sulemayn had not heard of him before, and he did not want to be responsible for revealing Abdelqadir's whereabouts to someone he did not know.

"Yasir ran messages for a few days. He even came with me on a raid about a week later in which we killed a few Jews near the Hurva Synagogue. Still Sulemayn would not tell him where Abdelqadir was. Finally he went and got his grandfather, Mahmoud. His grandfather vouched for him to Sulemayn, so Sulemayn promised to get a message to Abdelqadir that he was looking for him and wanted to join him."

In reaction to the increasing Arab terrorism, Jewish forces stepped up their own attacks on the Arab population. On December 12, as Abdelqadir was making his way into the city through the Damascus Gate, an Irgun bomb exploded in a nearby bus station. Five Arabs died and close to fifty were injured, including Abdelqadir, whose face and arms were shredded by flying glass splinters. He was taken to a safe house nearby, where his wounds were cleansed.

"Word of Abdelqadir spread like lightning," says Haddad. "Everyone in the organization knew about it in minutes, and almost everyone knew where he'd been taken. Yasir found out, and an hour later he was presenting himself to Abdelqadir. At that time Abdelqadir was cut up and bleeding so badly no one was sure he would live. His wounds appeared much worse than they actually were. Abdelqadir smiled weakly at Yasir. Then he removed a pistol he had concealed in his shirt and gave it to Yasir. He told Yasir to become his surrogate, to kill as many Jews as he could with it. Yasir immediately rushed out with his brother to find a Jew to revenge the bomb in the bus station. But the city was shut up tight by the British, there were no Jews on the street. I ran into them later, still marching around looking for a Jew. I got him to come back to our hideout. We had a raid planned for the next day, and Sulemayn said that Yasir could join it, now that he had a pistol. So the next day we went out on the raid, down near the Dung Gate. We attacked some Jewish shops. There was some shooting from British police. Yasir pulled out his gun to shoot back, but pulled the trigger too soon. He shot himself in his thigh.

"We had to drag him out of there. He was yelping with fright and his brother was hysterical. We took him to his grandfather's house, but no one was there. So we had to take him all the way back to the house were Abdelqadir was. It turned out to be only a flesh wound. Abdelqadir laughed when he learned what Yasir had done. He took the pistol away from him, patted him on the head, and said, 'No more fighting for you, young man. From now on you will stay in the headquarters and make the coffee.'

"To say the least, it was a great embarrassment to Yasir, but he did what Abdelqadir ordered. He remained for the next few weeks at headquarters near Beit Safafa and did odd jobs. The others, his friends, his brother, were sent back to Gaza with his grandfather."

In January news came from Gaza of an outbreak of Arab-Jewish guerrilla warfare there. A Futuwwah group had ambushed a Jewish convoy trucking supplies from Gaza port to Beersheba and killed two Jews. A while later British soldiers escorting another convoy killed four Arabs. In February, Futuwwah raiders retaliated by killing several Jewish illegal immigrants sneaking ashore near Gaza. Reports of several other successful Arab raids reached Abdelqadir's headquarters.

"Yasir began to plead with Abdelqadir to return to Gaza to join in the fighting," says Salah Haddad. "Abdelqadir was by then so preoccupied with the resistance that he had no time for Yasir. He simply told him to keep quiet and remain in the background, his time to fight would come. Yasir was beginning to be a joke among the rest of us. He was doing a great deal of boasting about his exploits in Gaza, but from what we had seen of him he was quite inept. And of course Abdelqadir treated him in a condescending way.

"He could talk, though, and he did a strange thing. After the news of the Futuwwah raids started coming in, he began to take credit for them. He claimed that one of the raids was conducted by his own Abu Khalid warriors. We wondered what this Abu Khalid Society he kept talking about was. So he told us. He told us of the so-called Martyr Abu Khalid and of how Abdelqadir had assigned Yasir to start a guerrilla group named after Abu Khalid, and of how he had led and trained the group and now they were distinguishing themselves in guerrilla warfare against the Jews while he was trapped in Jerusalem.

"I knew nothing of this Abu Khalid at the time, but a couple of the men at the headquarters did. Well, Yasir kept going on about the famous Abu Khalid and how all of Gaza must be rallying round his Abu Khalid guerrillas as they went out on their raids. He was becoming a great annoyance to all of us, especially since we were beginning to lose a great number of fighters in Jerusalem. Here was this obnoxious fellow, who couldn't even shoot a pistol without hitting himself, telling us how his guerrilla fighters in Gaza would be much more successful in Jerusalem than we were.

"Finally one of the men in headquarters who knew the truth about Abu Khalid told Yasir he didn't know what he was talking about. Yasir argued back, as usual, so the man shouted that Abu Khalid was no martyr, that he was some idiot Abdelqadir had killed as a favor to Yasir's father. This was something new to Yasir, and of course he tried to laugh off the man's story. But then someone else confirmed it. He related the whole story—of how Abdelqadir had enticed Abu Khalid into thinking he was going to meet with him, and then had him taken as a prisoner and killed.

"Yasir still wouldn't believe it. He argued and argued. He showed us all the note he said Abu Khalid had written to him, told us of the final message Abu Khalid was supposed to have sent to him before being killed by the Jews. Everything he said the other two denied. They said Abu Khalid had been tortured into writing the note, that he had not been killed by the Jews while trying to smuggle arms to Gaza but had been killed by order of Abdelqadir months before. They said Abdelqadir had made up the story just to keep Yasir loyal and quiet."

Yasir was hurt and confused, unwilling to believe the story shouted at him in the heat of the argument, but unable to discount it either. He sat morosely about the Futuwwah headquarters for several days, his bluster and boasting silenced. His companions, seeing the weak spot they had uncovered in him, continued to play on the story, using the truth to taunt Yasir about the delusions he had let himself live under; just as his belief in the heroics of Abu Khalid was a delusion, they teased, so were his boastings of the Abu Khalid Society achievements in Gaza.

Yasir at first fought back, vehemently insisting that his claims about Abu Khalid were the truth. But with each passing day his companions chipped away at his certainty and he rapidly became immersed in an agony of doubt and uncertainty.

"Abdelqadir had been away from Beit Safafa for several days," Haddad recounts. "During this time Yasir sulked and would not talk to anyone. The men who had let the truth out were now afraid that if Abdelqadir found out he would punish them. They pleaded with Yasir not to mention it to him. Yasir would not even listen to them. He was planning to confront Abdelqadir with the story the moment he returned. The two men grew so anxious about this that they even plotted between themselves to get rid of Yasir before Abdelqadir returned, to kill him and bury him without a trace and make it appear that he had simply disappeared.

"Someone overheard the two and warned Yasir. Suddenly he was gone. I discovered later that he made his way back to Jerusalem and took refuge in his grandfather's house. A few days afterward Abdelqadir returned. Yasir must have heard he was back, for the next day he reappeared, demanding to see Abdelqadir. Abdelqadir was very busy in a meeting. Yasir burst right in on him and in front of everyone demanded to know the truth. Abdelqadir was caught by surprise. Whether it was because he was preoccupied by other things and could not collect his wits or because he decided that the time had come for Yasir to realize the truth I don't know. But he confirmed the story the two men had told Yasir. He did it very casually, almost as though it didn't matter that Yasir had discovered the lies he had told him. He certainly had no anticipation of the effect it would have on Yasir.

"Yasir became hysterical and tried to attack Abdelqadir. The others had to drag him off. Then Abdelqadir slapped him in the face several times until he became quiet, while the others held him. Abdelqadir lectured Yasir that it was time to grow up and be a man, to forget the foolish Abu Khalid. Yasir stared at Abdelqadir with pure hate in his eyes. Then he was pushed out the door so the meeting could continue. That was the last we ever saw or heard of Yasir until a few years later, when he reappeared in Cairo as Yasir Arafat."

PART II

AFTER ISRAEL

15

The Birth of Israel

We now come to that time in his life Yasir Arafat does not hesitate to talk about. It is a time that coincided with the creation of the nation of Israel in the spring of 1948. It is a time that he describes as his baptism of fire.

"I was in Jerusalem when the Zionists tried to take over the city and make it theirs," he is fond of saying, contrary to the testimony of other members of his family. "I fought with my father and brothers in the streets against the Jewish oppressors, but we were outmanned and had no weapons comparable to what the Jews had. We were finally forced to flee, leaving all our possessions behind. The Jews were killing Arabs indiscriminately during those days. Women, children—it didn't matter to them. They were blowing up entire blocks of houses. We learned that our house was to be blown up. My father gathered us—my mother, my brothers and sisters, our grandparents—and we fled. We walked for days across the desert with nothing but a few canteens of water. It was June. We passed through the village of Deir Yassin and saw what the Jews had done there—a horrible massacre. Finally we reached Gaza, where my father's family had some land. We were exhausted and destitute. It was upon our arrival that I vowed to dedicate my life to the recovery of my homeland."

As it happened, the eighteen-year-old Yasir was already in Gaza when the Zionists declared themselves an independent Jewish nation on May 14, 1948. According to both Taher Khalidi and Wajih Halef, young men who were involved with Yasir's brother Badir in a group carrying out acts of anti-partition civil disobedience against the British, Yasir reappeared in Gaza in early March. Word of his having shot himself in the leg had come back several months earlier with the return of his brother Husayn and the other boys who had originally gone to Jerusalem with him. The story had traveled the grapevine of Gaza's militant youth, probably embellished and exaggerated along the way, so that upon his arrival Yasir found himself the laughingstock of his fellows.

"The reason I know he was in Gaza in March," says Taher Khalidi, who today lives as a cripple in a refugee camp near Beirut, "is because our group was to take part in a large raid on the Zionist settlement of Nizzanim, which was north of our city. The raid was on March 22, I believe, and Yasir had shown up at one of our meetings with his brother a week or two before, while the raid was being planned.

"Badir brought Yasir to this meeting because he was trying to persuade him to go along on the raid. He said that Yasir had just come back from Jerusalem, where he had fought at the side of Abdelqadir. Of course, we had heard the story of his shooting himself, and we all joked at him, telling him to show us his wound and so on. He was very subdued. We asked him questions about Abdelqadir and he wouldn't talk about him, or if he did he would curse him. We couldn't understand this. Before he went to Jerusalem, Yasir was the most avid champion of Abdelqadir, always talking these big guerrilla ideas. Now he downgraded Abdelqadir, and didn't seem to care at all about fighting. He told us we were wasting our time going on this raid to Nizzanim, that anything we did in the name of Abdelqadir was a betrayal of true Arab ideals.

"Yasir did not go on the raid, and his behavior all through these months of struggle against the Zionists was strange. He took part in nothing. He remained by himself in his father's house and would not move. Later on we learned from his brothers about what had happened in Jerusalem with Abdelqadir over Abu Khalid. I imagine that explained it. In any event, we saw very little of Yasir during those days."

The United Nations, in voting in November of 1947 for the partition of Palestine into separate Jewish and Arab states according to the UNSCOP plan, had recommended that Britain maintain its civil and military administration there until August, 1948. The British, increasingly beleaguered by both Arabs and Jews after the UN vote, rejected the recommendation and announced their intention of removing all their forces and institutions as soon as possible. During the late winter and early spring of 1948, as the British began to withdraw troops and administrative personnel, fighting between Arabs and Jews escalated. During February and March troops from Syria and Iraq crossed into Palestine to join with the Futuwwah and other Arab resistance organizations in trying to prevent the implementation of partition. Throughout March and into April all roads leading out of Jerusalem were besieged by Arab forces. The Jewish community of the Holy City was cut off from Tel Aviv, and other areas of heavy Jewish settlement were separated from each other. The Arab League loudly reiterated the intention of all the neighboring Arab countries to wage a full-scale war against the Zionists unless partition was abandoned, and soon troops from Egypt and Lebanon joined those of Syria and Iraq.

At the beginning of April the Haganah launched a concerted counteroffensive against the Arabs along the Tel Aviv–Jerusalem road and elsewhere. As the British continued their withdrawal from the areas of Jewish population, Arabs and Jews engaged in bloody battles to win control of them. As April ground on, the Jews began to gain the edge. In the last two weeks of April they won control of Tiberias, Haifa, and Acre. In early May they conquered Jaffa and Safed, and reconcentrated their efforts to reach Jerusalem.

In the course of the battle for the Tel Aviv–Jerusalem road in April, Abdelqadir al-Husayni, the Arabs' most celebrated resistance warrior, was killed by Jewish forces.

The British completed their withdrawal from Palestine on May 14. On the same day the Zionists declared the land partitioned to them the independent state of Israel. The following day six Arab armies —those of Egypt, Syria, Transjordan, Lebanon, Saudi Arabia, and Iraq—invaded the freshly minted state. They advanced rapidly, clearly threatening to demolish the Jewish nation almost as quickly as it had come into being.

By June 1 large portions of territory allocated to Israel by the UN were occupied by the Arabs. But then the Jews, their backs to the sea, struck back. Throughout the rest of 1948 and into January, 1949, fighting what they called their war of independence, the Jews managed to reopen the road to Jerusalem, win control of the coastal plain, secure Upper Galilee, and drive the Egyptians from the Negev desert.

The central hill region, which had been part of the proposed Arab state under the UN plan, remained in the hands of the Arab army of King Abdallah of Transjordan. When it became clear, despite a cease-fire arranged by the UN, that the Arabs of Palestine would never accept this truncated Arab state, King Abdallah annexed it for himself, joining it to Transjordan and declaring the two sides of the Jordan River the new Kingdom of Jordan. The annexed land, at whose core stood Jerusalem, would eventually come to be known as the West Bank.

The Gaza region, extending southward into the western Negev desert, had also been earmarked by the UN as part of the Arab state. Although driven out of the Negev, the Egyptians managed to retain control over the coastal portion of Gaza. Egypt did not annex this narrow strip of land that pressed like a finger into the underbelly of Israel, however. Instead, once the Arab-Israeli truce was executed, it established administrative control over it.

By the time of the 1949 truce Israel had not only managed to retain all the land allocated to it by the UN but had conquered approximately half the territory assigned to the Arabs—the Arab portion of the Negev bordering on Egyptian Sinai; an irregular crescent of the central hill region, including part of Jerusalem but not the traditionally holy Jewish quarter of the Old City; and a chunk of northern Galilee fronting Lebanon. The new frontiers established in 1949 would become Israel's de facto borders until 1967.

Another consequence of the first Arab-Israeli war was the flight of Arab refugees from the territories either assigned to Israel by the UN or won by the new state during the war. Refugees from northern Palestine for the most part fled into Lebanon and Syria, where they were gathered by the respective governments into isolated camps in the expectation that they would soon be able to return to their homeland. Refugees from central Palestine made their way to both West and East Bank Jordan. Arabs from the coastal region moved into the Egypt-administered Gaza Strip, where eight camps were established to accommodate them.

It soon became clear that the refugees—more than 700,000 in number—would not be able to return to their homes. For various reasons the host governments rejected proposals that they incorporate the homeless Arabs into their populations. To do so would, from the Arab point of view, constitute Arab recognition of the legitimacy of the existence of Israel. Such recognition, according to every Arab and Islamic tradition, was impossible; it was impossible according to the precedents of international law, as well. In short, the Arabs maintained that the creation of Israel in Arab Palestine in 1948 was as illegal as the creation of Palestine itself out of Syria in 1919. Certainly, in the context of international law, they had a case. Unfortunately for them, they did not know how to prosecute it before the bar of world opinion. Yet they would continue to cling to their position of nonrecognition for the next three decades, and the chief pawns in their argument would be the disfranchised refugees of the miserable camps of Gaza, Jordan, Syria, and Lebanon.

Wajih Halef was a friend and cohort of Taher Khalidi and Badir al-Qudwa in the spring of 1948 in Gaza. He recalls Yasir al-Qudwa in much the same way that Khalidi does. Nearing sixty years of age and still a resident of Gaza, he says of that time, "Yasir came back from Jerusalem like a boy in mourning. He didn't even get upset at our jokes about his famous leg wound. He just moped about doing nothing. I remember when the Egyptian army came through in May on its way toward Tel Aviv, we all gathered along the road to cheer the soldiers on. Some of us even joined the columns marching northward. But not Yasir. He refused to come out.

"But then he changed. It was a few weeks later, and the news was bad. The Egyptians were retreating back into Gaza, and on other fronts the war was going badly. There was tremendous gloom all through Gaza, and the town was filling up with refugees. I encountered Yasir on the street and he was like his old self. He was talking of joining up with the Egyptians. I said, 'What has happened to make you so cheerful?' He didn't answer, but his brother Husayn was with him, so I asked him. And Husayn said, 'Didn't you hear? Abdelqadir is dead.'

"Yasir spent many weeks rejoicing over the death of Abdelqadir. We all knew by then about his experiences with Abdelqadir, and I suppose in retrospect you would have to sympathize with his feelings. But at the time no one sympathized. He became very unpopular. So did Husayn, for Husayn parroted everything Yasir said. They were even set upon by refugee boys who heard them talking so blasphemously about Abdelqadir. They received a terrible beating. After that we did not see much of Yasir for a while. He stayed close to home. Then he went to Cairo."

If Yasir Arafat was a refugee of any kind, it was as an escapee from Gaza to Cairo. In July, 1948, as the Arab-Israeli war continued to rage and as Gaza spilled over with genuine refugees, Abdul al-Qudwa grew afraid of an eventual Israeli conquest of Gaza. Accordingly, he packed up everyone in his family except Badir and moved them back to Cairo.

Nasr al-Qudwa says it was a journey his brother Yasir made without any objection. "My father still had the house in Cairo, which he was renting to a cousin of ours. When the Egyptian army came back out of the desert and took up positions around Gaza, he began to worry about an Israeli invasion. His attitudes about the Jews were well known, and he feared that if the Zionists invaded he would be among the first to be arrested. In addition to that, gangs of refugees were breaking into our shops and looting them. There was no way to stop it because Gaza was without any law enforcement. So my father announced one day that we were leaving that night to return to Cairo. It took us five or six days to get there. We all went in a lorry he hired from one of his friends. We were stopped in El Arish for two days by the Egyptians until my father convinced them we were not refugees but residents of Cairo. Then we ran out of petrol near Ismailia, and it took another two days to bribe some soldiers for some.

"On the journey my father talked a great deal to us about renewing his ties with the Ikhwan. He said Hassan Banna had become very powerful in Cairo and that the Ikhwan was to be the wave of the future. He regretted having gone along with Abdelqadir, and this pleased Yasir very much. Yasir and my father talked a great amount on that trip. At first Yasir had been angry with my father because of his part in the business with Abdelqadir and Abu Khalid. But now my father was apologizing to Yasir, saying that he too had been duped by Abdelqadir. Yasir was pleased to hear this, and he began to talk to my father again. By the time we reached Cairo, even though it was a difficult trip, they were friendly. Yasir wanted to join the Egyptian army, but my father said, 'No, let us wait. In the meantime you must go and finish your education.' He did not want

Yasir to go into the army because he felt the army was corrupt and weak. It was the tool of King Farouk, and would be used by him to try to put down the coming Ikhwan revolution that my father was predicting. Surprisingly, for once Yasir agreed with my father."

16

Return to Cairo

Arriving in Cairo in the summer of 1948, the al-Qudwa family found the Egyptian capital in the throes of mounting civil and political turmoil, sparked mostly by Hassan Banna's increasingly powerful Muslim Brotherhood.

World War II had broken the back of the two institutions within Egypt that had come to mean the most to the Egyptian masses: the Wafd party and the monarchy. In 1942, at the time the Axis armies were preparing to march across Egypt, the youthful King Farouk engaged in secret talks with the Germans for the purpose of entering into an alliance. In view of Britain's sixty years of de facto control of Egypt, it should not have been surprising that Egypt's leaders had little sympathy for the British cause in World War II. With the exception of a British military presence in the Suez Canal Zone and a naval base at Alexandria, Britain's military occupation of Egypt had been terminated by the Anglo-Egyptian Treaty of 1936. But when the British learned of Farouk's negotiations with the Germans in 1942, they sent a force of troops and tanks into Cairo to surround the royal palace. By so doing, they compelled Farouk to publicly disclaim his Axis sympathies and proved that they still had the last word in Egypt's foreign affairs.

Britain's intervention was seen as a violation of the independence granted to Egypt under the 1936 treaty, and Farouk's capitulation was a severe humiliation to those avid nationalists who had been living under the myth of Egyptian self-determination. During the war, moreover, Farouk's scandalous personal behavior—public drinking, gambling, wenching—deeply offended Egypt's pious Muslims. The enthusiastic acclaim he had received when he succeeded the British-appointed King Fuad was replaced by contemptuous unpopularity. His conduct was particularly repulsive to the Muslim

Brotherhood, and the Ikhwan used it to expand its own influence and win converts.

The esteem in which the Wafd party had been held before World War II was shattered when one of its leaders, disgusted with the secret corruption and graft that permeated its upper ranks, published at the end of the war a documented exposé of Wafdist financial wrongdoing. This was another scandal that played into the hands of the Ikhwan.

The war had shut down most of Egypt's foreign trade, and by 1946 the Egyptian economy was on the verge of collapse. Whatever economic gains and social reforms had been achieved in the 1930s were dissipated; the country had regressed to the point at which it had been decades earlier under the Ottomans, with the small, avaricious upper class running things and the large peasant *(fellahin)* and petit bourgeois classes enduring deprivation and seething with bitterness.

Also contributing to the discontent was the postwar reaction to Zionism and the imminent partition of Palestine. Zionism was no direct threat to Egypt politically, but there already existed an inbuilt abhorrence of it by virtue of native Muslim empathy, of age-old Arab tribal traditions concerning territorial imperatives, and of increasing Egyptian xenophobia. The Egyptian political establishment found it an easy matter to inflame mass emotions against the Zionists. Such methods tended to unite public opinion and to mask the establishment's own failings.

The strategy backfired, however, when the well-equipped Egyptian armies were repelled by the comparatively ill-equipped Israelis in 1948. By the commitment of its forces to the battle, by the heat of its anti-Zionist rhetoric, and by its stirring prophecies of Israeli annihilation, Egypt had thrust itself to the forefront of all the member states of the Arab League as the chief defender and liberator of Palestine. All the more profound, then, was the sense of national shame that flowed from the Egyptian defeat. As a result of the defeat, which was directly attributable to the inherent corruption of the military establishment—where class privilege, as in the old days, went before personal merit—and to the ineptitude and uncertainty of the political leadership, the last vestiges of public faith in Egypt's governmental institutions was shattered. By the time the al-Qudwas arrived in Cairo in July of 1948, Egypt had deteriorated into a political vacuum, with civil discontent reaching into every corner of the country.

Into this vacuum stepped the Muslim Brotherhood of Hassan Banna. The Brotherhood had managed to expand greatly during World War II and had gained even more adherents in the wake of the Egyptian rout in Palestine. It had developed a well-armed clandestine paramilitary organization which it began to use to assassinate establishment political leaders, terrorize the ruling class, and whip up mass sympathy for its goals. It had succeeded in winning over many young army officers to its cause of reforming Egypt from top to bottom, and also had a strong following among the *fellahin* populace. In addition, it received the wholehearted support of Egypt's rapidly increasing Palestinian Arab population following the debacle in Palestine.

Indeed, Haj Amin, recently returned to Cairo and now the sole Arab League–sponsored spokesman for Palestinian nationalism and anti-Israelism, began to publicly support the Brotherhood. Soon he and the Ikhwanites entered into an informal alliance under which, in exchange for further Haj Aminist support, the Brotherhood, once it seized power in Cairo, would devote much of reformed and zealous Egypt's energies and resources to the annihilation of Israel and the installation of a Haj Amin–led Arab state in all of Palestine.

Haj Amin's attraction to the Ikhwan was understandable. In addition to its fundamentalist religious orientation, it appeared at the time quite capable of making good on its promise to seize power in Egypt. Although Haj Amin was not as fanatically orthodox as Hassan Banna and his close associates, between them they had a strong identity of interests—to restore to their respective countries the primacy of religious rule.

Abdul al-Qudwa settled his family in their old house in Cairo. Delighted to find the popularity of the Ikhwan almost universal throughout the Palestinian community and quickly filled with a sense of the imminent rise of the Brotherhood to power, he set out to re-establish himself in the organization, which was now operating freely aboveground. On this visit to Cairo he was also pleased to be able to show to his contemporaries that he had all his sons on his side. Although Badir had remained in Gaza temporarily, Zaeed,

Nasr, Yasir, and Husayn were with him. All acted as loyal and devoted Arab sons should, and Yasir—yes, even Yasir—was no trouble.

Yasir, just turned nineteen, enrolled with Nasr in an Egyptian technological high school in order to complete his pre-university education. The faculty of the school was dominated by Ikhwanites, and, according to Nasr, much of the students' time was devoted to the surreptitious manufacture of crude bombs and rifles under the direction of faculty members in the school's shops.

"Yasir fell into this with great enthusiasm," recalls Nasr. "He showed a talent for machinery, and he even invented new ways to package explosives. He did not get terribly involved with Ikhwan politics at the school, but he received great enjoyment from making explosive devices. The other students and the teachers looked up to him for his ingenuity, and he reveled in their praise."

Muhammad Adwan, a classmate who claims to have know Yasir better than most, said, "One of the teachers organized a shooting club, and we would go to the outskirts of the city once or twice a week to practice firing our rifles at targets. Yasir was not a good shot. Nor was I. So we ended up always shooting last. In this way we became friends. We all knew he was related to Haj Amin, and he used to tell me stories of his experiences in Gaza and Jerusalem. Over a period of time he became very enthusiastic about the Ikhwan. He used to say that someday he would become the leader of the Ikhwan in Palestine."

By late 1948 the Ikhwan had reached the height of its influence in Egypt. In September, Haj Amin's reconstituted Arab Higher Committee, with Ikhwan support, formed a "government of all Palestine" and established it, with a governing assembly, in Gaza. Haj Amin moved to Gaza, still under the administration of Egypt, as president of the assembly. His idea was to use the hundreds of thousands of refugees swelling Gaza as his primary constituency and to organize most of them into a militia to be armed and trained by the Ikhwan.

Abdul al-Qudwa made contact again with both Hassan Banna and Haj Amin after his arrival in Cairo and, although he was not thought highly of by either, was given a minor position in the exile government. Thus in January of 1949 he returned to Gaza with his family.

There he and his sons became functionaries of Haj Amin.

At the same time, the Ikhwanites made their bid for power in Egypt, pursuing a year-long campaign of terror and insurrection against the Wafdist government. Hassan Banna, however, had become more cosmopolitan in his outlook, more politically oriented in the modern sense, perhaps because of his exposure to Haj Amin, while many of his closest lieutenants remained rooted in the original religious fundamentalism of the Ikhwan. Because of the differences that developed between Banna and some of his followers, the Brotherhood had begun to splinter into competing factions. In the end, then, the Ikhwan revolt against the Wafdists failed. Thereafter the Brotherhood's influence would wane, but the revolt exacerbated tensions within Egypt and left it in a mood of even more intense revolutionary discontent than before.

Once the Brotherhood's struggle for power was turned back, Egypt slipped into a state of near anarchy. Unable to take the rage of their 1948 humiliation out on Israel, vying Egyptian revolutionary factions turned it on the British forces that still remained in Egypt under the terms of the 1936 treaty. Armed bands of Ikhwanites clashed with the British and with other nationalist groups along the Suez Canal, and the fighting soon escalated into steady guerrilla warfare. Demonstrations and violence in Cairo and Alexandria continued sporadically into 1951 as a coalition of Ikhwanites, communists, socialists, and others agitated against the continuing British presence on Egyptian soil.

Finally, in October of 1951, in order to placate the dissidents, the Wafdist government proclaimed the termination of the Anglo-Egyptian Treaty and ordered all British military forces out of Egypt. It was a desperate and daring move, for Britain might well have been expected to respond by sending in more troops to enforce the treaty, which had five years to run. But after their unhappy experience in Palestine, the British were utterly tired of the Middle East. They went quietly, leaving only a small force to police the Suez Canal.

The Egyptian government expected its triumph in expelling the British to put an end to internal dissidence and violence. But this expectation was mistaken. Still Wafdist in its majority, and still suffering from the deep stain of corruption, the government's ouster of Britain unleashed an orgy of violent celebration that was quickly turned upon the Wafdists by the revolutionary coalition again seeking their overthrow. In riots in Cairo in January of 1952 over seventy-five people were killed and much property destroyed. The following months witnessed further violence as the Wafdists attempted to rule under martial law. Finally, on the night of July 23, 1952, a group of dissident army officers who had come under combined Ikhwan and socialist influence and who had been quietly plotting since the 1948 humiliation to restore Egyptian dignity and balance staged a coup d'état. Among them was a chauvinistically impassioned colonel who, as a junior officer four years before, had been witness to the Israeli rout of the Egyptian army. His name was Gamal Abdel Nasser.

17

First Guerrilla Training

It was during these events that Yasir al-Qudwa al-Husayni went through the final stages of his transformation into Yasir Arafat.

On his arrival back in Gaza in January of 1949 with his father, Yasir, along with his brothers, fell into a daily routine of combined Haj Aminist–Ikhwan activities. Cairo's Ikhwanite revolutionary mood had spread throughout Egypt and spilled over into Gaza. With its indigenous population, plus its refugees, plus the thousands of Egyptian administrative personnel recently arrived to oversee the Gaza Strip, plus the hundreds of people and dozens of organizations and committees involved in Haj Amin's new Government of All Palestine, Gaza had become a maelstrom of intrigue. It was not long before Yasir was sucked into it.

During February and March he was kept busy by his father doing odd jobs for the purely Ikhwan branch of the Government of All Palestine, which Abdul was trying to organize out of his old Ikhwan cell. Yasir worked faithfully for his father—distributing leaflets, harassing reluctant joiners, running errands, and the like. With pro-Ikhwan sentiment now strong in Gaza, and with Ikhwan ideals carrying the endorsement of Haj Amin, Abdul had little difficulty putting together a society of a couple of hundred members.

According to Anwar Sayigh, a young Gazan whose father had joined, it was largely an ineffective organization. Sayigh, until recently an economist and financial planner for one of the Arab oil-producing nations, says, "Abdul al-Qudwa had this air of braggadocio about him, he was always making himself more important than he really was. This attracted men like my father, who was basically weak and without any initiative of his own. My father was poor, as were most of the men who followed al-Qudwa. They joined his new Ikhwan group not out of any strong convictions but because they knew they might obtain a job in one of the al-Qudwa family businesses or might be able to borrow money from Abdul.

"Abdul would lend money to people as an inducement to join. Once he lent money to someone, he would never let them forget that they owed him, and if they did not constantly toady to him he would read them out in front of the others. Everybody knew that Abdul had access to the Mufti, that he had some sort of blessing from the Mufti, and Abdul used that to build up his Ikhwan organization. But it was never effective in any sense—just a bunch of old men—sycophants, really—who were looking to live off Abdul.

"Of course, Abdul tried to make his group seem very important, very military. His son Badir was his chief of staff, sort of, and he was even more overbearing and self-important than Abdul. Badir's 'army' consisted of two or three of his brothers, Rahman—or Yasir, as everyone called him—among them. Just about the only thing they did was go out and terrorize the families of men who wandered in their obedience to Abdul. I didn't know Yasir very well, but I used to see him roaming the streets with his brothers, all looking very severe and dedicated, searching out members of Abdul's group who had missed a meeting.

"My father was basically a peaceful, contemplative man, very apathetic about politics and all these other things that were going on in Gaza. He was content just to sit around and read newspapers. He was strongly religious, however, and I suppose that is one of the reasons he joined the Ikhwan. After he joined he got kind of a part-time job with the al-Qudwas. Then he lost it, and because he was bored with the rantings and ravings of Abdul al-Qudwa, he stopped attending the Ikhwan meetings. Then, one day, Yasir and his brothers came round to our house looking for him. He was not there, so they started cursing me and my two brothers. We were younger than they, and we were appropriately intimidated. But then they began to manhandle our two sisters. My brothers and I became enraged and went after them.

"To tell you the truth, they gave us a severe beating. But they used clubs, these old English billy clubs they had got from somewhere. Yasir was particularly brutal. The others wanted to stop after they'd drawn some blood, but not Yasir. He continued to beat and beat on us. He grew crazed by the sight of our blood."

As events unfolded in 1949, King Abdallah of Transjordan made known his intention of annexing the central hill region of Palestine which his British-trained army had occupied and held in the 1948 war. This region, bordering the West Bank of the Jordan River and including the Old City of Jerusalem, had been included as part of the Palestinian Arab state in the UN partition scheme. King Abdallah's decision to annex it, incorporate it as part of his new and larger Kingdom of Jordan, and transform all its permanent residents into citizens of Jordan created a furore within Haj Amin's Government of All Palestine.

King Abdallah's move brought nearly one-third of prewar Palestine's Arab population under his control and thus removed it from Haj Amin's influence. Abdallah—son of the Hashemite Husayn ibn Ali and brother of Feisal, the two who many Palestinian nationalists believed were primarily responsible for the failure of Arab self-determination at the end of World War I—was excoriated and vilified by the various Haj Aminists headquartered in Gaza. And when Abdallah appointed Raghib Nashashibi, the leader of the traditionally more moderate Palestinian nationalist view and therefore Haj Amin's chief rival, as military governor of the West Bank, Haj Aminist emotions became murderous.

In his first few months in Gaza, Haj Amin and his agents tried hard to organize a new Futuwwah or guerrilla force out of the large refugee population to operate against Israel. The majority of the refugees, however, were uneducated and unsophisticated. Moreover, they were badly confused and dispirited; on the one hand the Government of All Palestine was promising them an immediate return to their homes, on the other it was predicting many years of struggle and sacrifice to liberate their homeland.

As a result, the Haj Aminists had little success in drawing upon the refugees. They thereupon turned to the indigenous Arabs of Gaza, and to the Egyptians. "I recall that one day my father announced he had been summoned to meet with the Mufti," says Nasr al-Qudwa. "This was just after King Abdallah's declaration. He returned from his audience and immediately called a meeting of the Ikhwan. He said the Mufti had told him that we now had two enemies, the Jews and the Jordanians. We were to immediately form ourselves into a guerrilla group, along with other groups in Gaza.

This time there was to be no mucking around—the Haj Aminists had much money and we would immediately receive training and arms from the Ikhwanites in Egypt.

"The following month many of us were taken to a place near Suez City and underwent three or four weeks of guerrilla training. It was there that my younger brother Husayn had his name changed. It was Yasir who suggested it. As usual, Yasir knew more about things than the rest of us. We were living in tents, having Ikhwan lectures, training with rifles and grenades, practicing infiltration techniques. The Egyptian instructors were very tough. Yasir was not very good at the physical things we were made to do, and the instructors used to get very angry with him. But he would get back on their good side by knowing so much about tactics and strategy.

"Anyway, one day he came into our tent raving about the evil of the Hashemites. He said he learned that King Abdallah had a grandson who was named Husayn, after Abdallah's father. He said it would not do for a Haj Aminist guerrilla fighter to have such a name. He insisted that Husayn, our brother, replace that name with another."

Fth is an Arabic root for words meaning "conqueror" and "conquest." According to Nasr al-Qudwa, the Ikhwan instructors at the camp were fond of calling their charges *fathi,* an Arabic slang expression for "little conquerors." Thus, in seeking a change of name for his brother Husayn, Yasir took to calling him Fathi. Soon he was Fathi to everyone.

Yasir then circulated throughout the camp attempting to persuade all boys who bore the name Husayn to change it to "Fathi." He did the same with youths who had such names as Feisal, Abdallah, Ali, and others identified with the Hashemite dynasty, but met with only mixed success.

"He got a movement going about the business of names," says Ali Douad, an Egyptian whose father was an Ikhwan leader and who took the training at the same time as Yasir. "He had a small gang of boys from Gaza, and they would go around trying to force us to accept new names if we had names the same as the Hashemites. They got most of us to do it, but as soon as we left the camp we started using our regular names again.

"Yasir," Douad adds, "was disliked by the instructors. When they heard about this name changing, they confronted him with his own name and his relation to Haj Amin. They were Egyptians and tough men, and they didn't have the kind of slavish adoration for the Mufti that the people from Gaza had. They said to Yasir, 'Eh, you are an al-Husayni. Before you go around changing Ikhwanites' names, change your own. Or better yet, get the Mufti to change his from al-Husayni to something else.'

"Yasir tried to claim that family names didn't count, but I'm sure it irked him. Despite the fact that the instructors didn't like him, had a certain contempt for him—you see, he complained a lot about the physical hardships of the training—despite that, he admired all of them for their manliness and fearlessness. So when they put that notion of his al-Husayni name in his head, even though he said family names were not important, it stuck there. I think the fact that he carried the al-Husayni name made him feel less in the instructors' eyes than he would have liked to feel."

Yasir returned to Gaza in August of 1949—the month of his twentieth birthday—more or less proficient in the basic use of arms. He could now, according to Nasr, fire a pistol without hitting himself, shoot a World War II–vintage German rifle fairly accurately, toss a hand grenade a safe distance of ground, and light a Molotov cocktail without having it blow up in his face. His newly acquired skills were put to immediate use by the Haj Aminists, but not, as he had hoped, against Israel.

During the war of 1948 many members of Palestine's Nashashibi clan had taken refuge in Gaza. When King Abdallah declared his intention in 1949 to annex the West Bank and name Raghib Nashashibi as its military governor, his declaration gave Nashashibi prestige a considerable boost throughout the Arab areas of Palestine. At the same time, it diluted al-Husayni authority, particularly when, despite Haj Amin's efforts to get the Arab League to prevent Abdallah's move, the annexation was completed in 1950.

Aside from the Ikhwan group which the al-Qudwa brothers trained with, Haj Amin had financed the organization and training of several other guerrilla groups since his arrival in Gaza as head of the Government of All Palestine. When he failed to stop Abdallah's annexation, he unleashed these groups on the Nashashibis.

"Yasir and his brother Fathi were in the same group that I was in," recalls Amin Hegoub, the son of one of Haj Amin's advisers who today sells mutual funds in Europe. "We thought we were being trained to fight Zionists, but all through 1949 and 1950 we did nothing but terrorize the Nashashibis and their followers in Gaza. At first Yasir was a very avid fighter. He started on the lowest rung in our squad, because of his ungainliness in the field, but he rapidly became the leader of the squad. Not because of any special exploits, but simply because he was the sharpest thinker and tactician.

"The Mufti's purpose was to use us to intimidate the Nashashibis in Jerusalem into giving up their alliance with Abdallah and resisting annexation. Of course, it had the opposite effect. The more damage we did to the Nashashibis in Gaza, the more convinced the Jerusalem branch became about the idea of having the protection and citizenship of Jordan.

"One mission I remember was when our squad—just our squad alone, about twenty of us—was sent to the outskirts of Gaza to burn some orchards owned by Nashashibi interests. Yasir was our leader by then, and he planned the entire operation. There was one member of our squad no one quite trusted—I don't know why, but he just had the look and manner of someone you didn't trust. His name was Rork Hamid, and he was known to have been friendly with some Nashashibis before the partition, even though his father was very active in the Ikhwan.

"Well, we went on our mission, but as we entered the orchard we were ambushed by a gang of Nashashibi laborers. They had clubs and knives, and every one of us except this Hamid took a wound or an injury before we could get away. We regrouped back in the city, in a shed behind the cemetery. It was just dawn. We were all bruised and bloody, all but Hamid. He looked very sheepish. We had several pistols stored in the shed. Yasir kept looking accusingly at Hamid, I guess we all did. We were all thinking to ourselves that he was the one who had forewarned the Nashashibis of our mission. Finally, in a very soft voice, Yasir spoke what we were all thinking. Hamid vehemently denied it. Yasir stood up and we all noticed he had a pistol behind his back. He walked over to Hamid, who was by now in tears over our accusations, and shot him in the head.

"We were astounded. Yasir turned to us with a weird smile on his face and said something like 'Let that be a warning to any and all of you who would betray the holy Ikhwan.' He then swore us all to secrecy about the killing, and ordered us to take Hamid's body to Falastin Square and hang it in Ikhwan style.

"We discovered later that it hadn't been Rork Hamid who betrayed us. It was one of Haj Amin's own men, and it was done deliberately in the hope that we would be killed and the killings would turn the whole of Gaza against the Nashashibis. When Yasir learned this, it did not bother him in the least that he had killed Hamid. I remember him saying that Hamid had been the first person he had ever personally killed, and for that reason Hamid had served a valuable Ikhwan purpose."

Muhammad Mujaya, another member of the squad, corroborates the story and describes the twenty-year-old Yasir. "He was almost what you call a dual personality, very diffident at times, very hyperactive at others. He was short and squat, as he is today, and wore a thick moustache in the Turkish style. He had two ways of looking at you with his large eyes—very softly, like a man looking at a woman he desires, or blankly, as though his eyes were going right through you. This was really his hallmark, the way he looked at you. Once you were looked at by Yasir, you never forgot him.

"He was very vain about his hair. He began to lose his hair at this time, and this was a great source of irritation to him. There was a girl he fancied—the daughter of Magib al-Hourani, who was in Haj Amin's assembly. Her name was Derona, and she had been educated in London. She was a few years older than Yasir, and very European in her ways. She really wouldn't look at Yasir twice, but he imagined that she would have him if it wasn't for his hair.

"One day several of us saw him in the street wearing a Western jacket and trousers, and, lo and behold, he had a full head of hair. We said, What has happened to Yasir? We found out he had got someone to steal a wig. He was walking around hoping to cross the path of Derona al-Hourani. He wore the wig for about two weeks. Then, suddenly, he was not wearing it any more. We heard from his brother that he had finally encountered Derona and approached her with some romantic prattle. She giggled at him, and he became so furious he slapped her. That was the end of Derona. And the end of the wig.

"Yasir definitely had a buffoon's quality in many of the things he did, but that was counterbalanced by his glib tongue and sharp mind in intellectual matters. There was always a temptation to laugh at him, but it was almost as if he could read the laugh forming in your brain, and he would cut it off with that look of his.

"The shooting of the Hamid boy put an end to any temptations we might have had not to take him seriously. It was like an initiation rite for him, and at the same time a symbol of his authority over us. He was the first of us to have actually killed anyone, and after that our guerrilla activities became a deadly serious business. Especially because of the repercussions of the shooting.

"When Rork Hamid's father learned of his son's death, he became enraged. He went to Yasir's father and demanded to have the killer delivered over to him. He knew the killer was an Ikhwanite because of the way Rork's body was hung in the square. Yasir's father knew it was him—I'm sure he beat the information out of Fathi. He refused to do what Rork's father demanded. So Rork's father hired a gang of thugs to terrorize us until one of us told who the killer was. When Yasir found this out, he again swore us to silence and said he would kill anyone who betrayed him.

"Well, one of us eventually did betray him. I don't know who, but Rork's father learned it was Yasir who had killed his son. He sent his thugs after Yasir, and Yasir went into hiding. Finally, Yasir's father hired his own thugs to kill Rork's father before he could get to Yasir. We had the beginnings of a real family war in Gaza between the two leading Ikhwanites.

"But then the Mufti heard about it. He summoned the two fathers before him. When he heard their stories, he demanded to see Yasir. He asked Yasir if he had killed Hamid. Yasir said he had, and that he did so because Rork had been a spy for the Nashashibis. It was the first time Yasir had met the Mufti, but he was not at all fazed. He spoke straight out to Haj Amin and showed no special deference, the way most people did.

"That was when Yasir learned the true story of our betrayal to the Nashashibis. Being an al-Husayni, he got off the hook. The Mufti officially pardoned him for the killing, explained the circumstances to Rork's father, and ordered him to give up his vendetta against Yasir.

"But Yasir was not impressed by the Mufti. I remember him afterwards complaining over and over about how it was the second time he had been betrayed by an al-Husayni. From then on Yasir always spoke badly of Haj Amin."

The Arab world's bellicosity toward Israel began to lose its steam as the feud between the al-Husaynis and the Nashashibis in Palestine intensified and spilled over into 1951 and the shaky governments of neighboring countries struggled to resist revolutionary overthrow. The nationalist liberation movement led by Haj Amin became thoroughly turned in upon itself as a result of the Mufti's obsession with Jordan's King Abdallah. As far as Haj Amin was concerned, Abdallah was the symbol of all those collaborationist tendencies that had infected the Arab soul for decades and prevented true Arab national self-determination. Until these tendencies were obliterated, the fight to recover Palestine would have to take a back seat.

Yasir continued his activities with his ersatz guerrilla band into the fall of 1950, but as time passed he grew more vocal in his criticisms of the Mufti. His attitude again brought a rift with his father. Abdul was now fully committed to his combined Ikhwanism and Haj Aminism, despite the fact that the Egyptian Ikhwan had lost its struggle for power in Cairo and that Haj Amin's Government of All Palestine in Gaza was proving ineffectual. With the exception of Yasir and Fathi, Abdul's entire family followed his lead, continuing to revere the Mufti while at least paying token respect to Ikhwan philosophy.

In October of 1950 an order came out of Haj Amin's headquarters calling for the integration of all separate Palestinian militia and guerrilla groups under the Mufti's authority into a single armed entity. The new "liberation army" was to consist of two brigades, one to be named after the 1930s guerrilla leader Izzaddin al-Qassam, the other after Abdelqadir al-Husayni. According to the order, Yasir al-Qudwa's small band was to be incorporated into the "Abdelqadir Brigade."

The order brought a vigorous protest from Yasir. He refused to allow his band to join. Word of his refusal soon got around. His father and family were hectored by loyal Haj Aminists. Abdul confronted Yasir and demanded that he follow orders. Yasir refused. Abdul then pleaded on the basis that Yasir's intractability was causing the entire family to lose their status in the Haj Aminist hierarchy. Yasir still refused.

The standoff continued into the summer. Abdul finally came to Yasir with a proposition. If Yasir would agree to leave Gaza and go to Cairo, his father would pay all the expenses of a university education.

Yasir, most of his band having joined the Abdelqadir Brigade over his protestations, realized that there was little point in remaining in Gaza. He knew also that he would never be able to be a part of the Haj Aminists. So he accepted his father's offer.

18

Becoming Yasir Arafat

Arab families of any means in Palestine traditionally sent as many of their male offspring as possible to schools of higher education, priority flowing from the oldest sons down to the youngest. Palestinians had, and still have, as powerful a compulsion to educate their children as Jews are said to have. This probably derives from Palestine's location at the heart of the Middle East and its religious importance for the rest of the world; Palestinians have for centuries been exposed, more than any other Arabs, to sophisticated influences from other parts of the world. Moreover, the education of children has always stood as a symbol of a family's success and ranking in class-conscious Palestinian society. The more children a father could say he had in some university, the more self-esteem he and his family could assume.

Abdul al-Qudwa was not different from most Palestinians in his concern that his sons be educated. However, the vagaries of events in the 1930s and 1940s and his own involvement in them had played havoc with the normal order of things. By 1950 his oldest son, Badir, had long since forsaken the educational opportunities his father had offered in order to devote his energies to the Ikhwan. His next eldest, Zaeed, had decided to marry and enter his father-in-law's machinery-repair business instead of continuing at school. Nasr had had a year at King Fuad University in Cairo but had recently dropped out and, bored with the turmoil in Gaza, was working there as a taxi driver.

Thus, when Yasir consented to go to Cairo and enroll at King Fuad, Abdul was both pleased and relieved, although he held no high hopes for his son's resolve to remain there. Nevertheless, he settled a generous amount of money on Yasir, enough to allow him to live comfortably for a year, and sent him on his way.

Yasir arrived in Cairo in December and presented himself at the university. There he learned he lacked certain credits in Arab literature and composition; before he could be accepted as a student at King Fuad he would have to make up for his deficiency. Arrangements were made for him to be tutored by teachers at the university during the spring and summer of 1951.

For the first two months Yasir lived with the family of his uncle —one of his father's brothers—in Abdul's house in the Palestinian quarter in which he had grown up. Within weeks he was embroiled in a controversy.

The neighborhood was dominated by a gang of young men in their twenties, several of whom remembered Yasir as the strange boy Rahman al-Qudwa. They were by now fierce Haj Aminists, although not one of them had been to Gaza. Knowing that Yasir was freshly arrived from Gaza, they asked him to bring them up to date on the Mufti's achievements there. It displeased them mightily to hear Yasir denigrate Haj Amin; his anti-Mufti perorations confirmed for them that Yasir was still the unbalanced Rahman of fifteen years before.

One day in the spring of 1951 the gang lured Yasir to a meeting place in the neighborhood with the intention of taking its wrath out on him. Yasir did not go unprepared. Strapped around his leg was the pistol he had brought from Gaza. When it became clear to him that the members of the gang were going to beat him, but before they could do so, he drew the pistol and trained it on them.

"It caught us completely by surprise," recalls Jabal Yazid, who was a member of the gang. "He held us at bay in that room for four or five hours, lecturing us on the evils of the Mufti and painting a picture of himself as having been a great guerrilla fighter in Gaza. He told us this story of how Haj Amin had caused his squad of freedom fighters to walk into a trap in some battle near Ashqelon with the Zionists. He said the Haj Aminists betrayed him because they feared the popularity he was winning for his heroic exploits. He told us his whole squad had been wiped out, and that he had personally killed those responsible for the betrayal with the very pistol he was holding in his hands. The reason he had come to Cairo, he said, was to start a new liberation organization out of the Palestinians here. He claimed that the liberation of the homeland would never come to anything as long as the Mufti was alive. His first task, he told us, was to form an assassination squad to go back to Gaza to kill the Mufti.

"He was talking at a great rate, and by the time he was finished he had most of us believing him. Then he put down his pistol on a table and sat down on the other side of the room. 'There,' he said, 'there is my pistol. Now, who in this room is going to pick it up and shoot me?' We were mesmerized. No one made a move for the pistol. Then one of us said, 'Okay, okay, you can go if you wish, we do not want to harm you.'

"But Yasir did not go. He smiled at us, and then he said, 'Who of you wants to join with me?' And someone said, 'What, to kill the Mufti? No, we cannot do that.' And he said, 'Oh, no, I was only joking about that. I cannot kill the Mufti, we are of the same family. But who of you wants to join with me to work toward the liberation of Palestine?' "

Yasir had no takers, but Yazid says that news of his talk about assassinating the Mufti got around to some of the older citizens of the neighborhood. One night a delegation of angry men showed up at the al-Qudwa family's house and demanded that Yasir's uncle expel him from the house and from the neighborhood for his heresy. Although the house was owned by Yasir's father, he went without protest after his uncle voiced fears for his own children's safety.

He located his brother Nasr, who was living in a single room near Cairo's main *souk,* and moved in with him. "He stayed a few months," says Nasr. "He had learned from one of his tutors about a group of students, younger boys, from Palestine who attended King Fuad University. He told me that they had started an organization called the Union of Palestinian Students. He became very eager to get into the university when he heard that, so he spent most of his time while living with me studying for the tests he had to take. Yasir was very bad in writing and grammar, although he was brilliant with numbers. I had been at the university the year before, and I had some friends who were still there. One day one of my friends came to visit, and when he heard that Yasir was studying to take the qualifying tests, he said he could get a copy of the writing and grammar test. He was just talking idly, but Yasir took him seriously, and for the next few months he hounded this fellow. My friend finally stole a copy of the test, but he was discovered by the authorities and was expelled from the university because he refused to confess who it was he stole it for. Yasir memorized the test, and when it came time for him to take it he passed it almost perfectly."

Admission to King Fuad University entitled Yasir to lodgings in a university-owned residence. He reported for registration during the latter part of August, 1951.

A few weeks earlier agents of Haj Amin had shocked the Middle East by assassinating King Abdallah of Jordan in retaliation for the king's annexation of the West Bank and for his moderate stand toward Israel (Abdallah had actually conducted negotiations with Israeli leaders, behavior that was in profound violation of Haj Amin's long-standing insistence that no Arab leader acknowledge the existence of the Jewish state). What particularly repulsed the Arab world was the fact that the assassination was carried out at the revered al-Aqsa mosque in Jerusalem. To a majority of devout Arab Muslims this was an outrage. To the Muslim Brotherhood it was an unholy desecration.

Haj Amin was denounced from many quarters, and a general anti–Haj Aminist mood quickly sprang up in all the Arab countries. The mood was especially virulent in Egypt, despite the fact that the Ikhwan itself was pursuing a policy of widespread assassination and terrorism in its struggle to overthrow the regime of King Farouk. Although the Ikhwan espoused assassination as a political device, it interpreted Haj Amin's assassination of Abdallah as an anti-Islamic act.

The leaders of the Brotherhood had had enough of Haj Amin. Their enemies—Farouk and the Wafdists—had caused Egypt grave humiliation ten years earlier by flirting with the Nazis and then bowing before the British pressure. In many of his recent declarations about the Israelis Haj Amin had been invoking memories of his wartime alliance with the Nazis.

The Egyptian Ikhwan, appreciating the fact that identification with an Arab leader who was still sympathetic to the universally discredited Nazi cause would harm its own attempts to gain the sympathy of world public opinion, set out to separate itself from the Mufti and destroy what was left of his prestige. With frequent references to his desecration of the holy mosque and to his Nazi past, it mounted an anti-Mufti propaganda campaign in both Egypt and Gaza that soon turned public feeling strongly against the Haj Aminists. One leading Ikhwan newspaper headlined an analysis of Abdallah's assassination with the assertion: "The Time Has Come to Remove the al-Husaynis." Another, distributed throughout Gaza, read: "The al-Husaynis Have Outlived Their Usefulness to Arab Self-Determination."

Anti-Mufti tirades reached their height at the time Yasir was registering at King Fuad University. Sensing that his future was with the Ikhwan and not the Haj Aminists, when he came to the place on the registration form that called for him to insert his full and true name, he wrote "Yasir Muhammad Arafat." He dropped "al-Qudwa" because he had heard that his father and brother in Gaza, having had to make a choice of allegiance between Haj Amin and the Ikhwan, had chosen Haj Amin. If he were to remain an Ikhwanite, it would not help him to be known as either an al-Husayni or an al-Qudwa.

Yasir Arafat enrolled in the civil engineering course at the university; although he had no specific career in mind, he believed that his previous experience with explosives and his facility in mathematics proved that his aptitudes lay in this direction. Besides, he has told me, "I often saw advertisements in the Cairo newspapers for engineers in the oil countries. I knew that was where the money would be made, so it was in the back of my mind when I elected to go into engineering. As a homeless Palestinian, I knew I would someday have to make a living in some other part of the world than my own homeland."

The Ikhwan was extremely active at King Fuad, as were various Egyptian socialist parties, communist organizations, and a small core of Syria's Baathist party. All were competing against one another in the general atmosphere of rising dissidence in Egypt to enlist students to their respective causes and gain dominant political power. Although the Ikhwan's influence had waned somewhat since 1949 and the organization had broken into several factions, with its essentially religious rationale and its militant political activism it was still the most attractive to the majority of students.

Arafat wasted no time in using his Ikhwanite background to make his presence felt at the university. Older than most of his fellow entering students by two or three years, skilled in arguing the ins and outs of Ikhwan philosophy, by the end of 1951 he was an important organizer and recruiter for the Ikhwan branch still loyal to the changing ideals of Hassan Banna.

Banna no longer hewed to the original purely Islamic line of the Ikhwan. In the years immediately following World War II, as a result of his exposure to nationalist movements throughout the Arab world and of his participation in the general Egyptian wave of curiosity about Soviet communism, he had modified his Islamic fundamentalism to fit it more comfortably into the increasingly popular non-sectarian nationalist ideologies of socialism and pan-Arabism.

Communism itself had little appeal for an Arab world that had been, for so long, so deeply imbued with the idea of an all-powerful God. But much of its political and economic machinery was well suited to this same world which, again for so long, had developed nothing in the way of indigenous political institutions and was unaccustomed to distinguishing between religious and political authority. Thus Hassan Banna grafted socialist theory onto his religious fundamentalism to produce a nationalist ideology that was more palatable to the new generation of youth in Egypt than it would otherwise have been under the original precepts of the Ikhwan.

Yasir Arafat, in retrospect, says that he was drawn to the new Ikhwanism principally because it was involved in militant action of the sort he had longed for in Gaza but had seldom seen. "The difference was," he recalls, "that in Palestine the liberation movement had ground to a halt, that as time went on after 1948 there was less and less chance to participate in guerrilla war. In Egypt, on the other hand, the chances were increasing all the time. We had weapons, we had organization, and we actually went out and waged liberation war."

That the war was against the British and against the Egyptian regime rather than against the Zionists mattered little. "The point was," Arafat says, "that we young Palestinians got a chance to do some actual fighting. In fighting the British we were fighting those responsible for the tragedy of Palestine. We could at least take out our frustrations on them, which made it better than not fighting anyone at all."

Another reason Arafat became such a strong partisan of the Egyptian Ikhwanites was the promise he saw in their struggle to promote a revolution in Egypt. Says Mustapha Kamel, who was close to Arafat at the university and who is today the manager of a cotton-processing factory near Cairo, "Much of the recruiting literature aimed at the Palestinian students of the university declared the Ikhwan's solidarity with the liberation of Palestine and stated in no uncertain terms that, once Egypt was liberated from its own corrupt regime and from continuing British influence, she would unite the entire Arab world in a holy war on the Zionists. The Ikhwan convinced the Palestinians that the first order of business was to gain power in Egypt. The Palestinians became so intent on this that many eventually forgot about the liberation of Palestine and became intent on the struggle for Egypt for its own sake. If you travel around Cairo, you will meet many Palestinians who were students in those days and who fought with the Ikhwan but who never joined the struggle for Palestine later on. When I knew Yasir Arafat, he was the same way. He lost interest in Palestine and became totally and solely devoted to the Egyptian cause—that is, until President Nasser outlawed the Ikhwan. Then he began to remember Palestine again."

One of the Palestinian students mentioned by Kamel is Marwan Sharif, and he still lives in Cairo. "It is true," he agrees. "Life was infinitely better in Cairo in those days than in Gaza. At least we were fighting, and for many of us the cause in Egypt became the only one. It was the same with Yasir. He used to talk of rising to some important post in what we thought would be an Ikhwan government of Egypt presided over by Hassan Banna. We all thought, Well, there is no future for us in Palestine, the Jews have the land, the Hashemites have the rest of it, so what is the use of dreaming? Perhaps someday the Ikhwan will run the Jews out, but don't count on it, we said. Our future is here, in Cairo. Many of us even became Egyptian citizens, despite the fact that we were members of the Palestine Student Federation. The federation was largely an Ikhwan-sponsored organization in the beginning, and for many of us our loyalties became more toward Egypt than toward Palestine. Even Yasir—he tried to become an Egyptian citizen."

Arafat denies ever having considered becoming a citizen of Egypt. He is equally vehement in his denial of having had any ambitions for himself in an Ikhwanite government of Egypt or of having ever lost sight of what he has always said was his true mission. But the testimony of two others who knew him at the time, if accurate, points to a different conclusion.

Ismael Riad, another engineering student at King Fuad University in the early 1950s, says he shared a desk with Arafat for two years and that they became quite friendly—so much so that he even took Arafat to his family's home in Alexandria on several occasions. "My father was a successful businessman in Alexandria and we lived rather well," says Riad, who today is the submanager of a shipyard in Alexandria. "Yasir, when I met him, was quite commanding, a few years older than me. He was a lonely sort, but a rabid Ikhwanite, which I was for a while, and a spellbinding speaker, although his Arabic was never very good. But he did not speak with his voice so much as with his body—his hands, his eyes, his dramatic pauses, his up-and-down inflections.

"Anyway, we became friends. Yasir had become enamored of a girl he met at the university who was also from Alexandria and whom I knew. Her name was Jinan al-Oraby. She was a fat, dumpy girl, not much to look at, but for some reason he took a fancy to her. She was very timid and made no effort to respond to Yasir's advances, but he pursued her anyway. He would come to Alexandria on holidays just so he could be near her.

"Finally he got a reaction out of her—I don't know what it was, she smiled at him, or touched him, or something. Well, he went mad with joy and said he was going to marry her. He came to Alexandria once and asked her, and evidently she said yes. So he came back to my house and said he must become a citizen. My father had connections in the Interior Ministry, and he begged my father to expedite matters for him. He told us that Jinan's father had given them permission to marry provided that Yasir became a citizen—he did not want to lose his daughter to Gaza, or wherever Yasir might go.

"My father put in a word, and soon it was all arranged for Yasir to become a citizen. But then, at the last moment, there was a change of mind—either by Jinan or her father. They decided she would not marry Yasir, and as far as I know he dropped the citizenship idea."

Riad suggests a third likely reason for Arafat's loyalty to the Egyptian Ikhwan. "He usually never mentioned his personal life, you know, his family background and so on. I did not even know until much later that he was an al-Husayni, and he got very annoyed at people who probed into his past. But he did talk about his father a great deal. He used him as an example of an Ikhwanite who couldn't adapt to the changing times as Hassan Banna did, and he would often describe his father, in the most uncomplimentary ways, sitting and festering in Gaza while the real work of Arab liberation was going on in Cairo. I received the impression that he hated or resented his father, and was a bit ashamed of him. I believe his dedication to the Ikhwan in Cairo, and his desire to stay in Egypt, stemmed from a desire to show his father up in some way."

Jinan al-Oraby, now in her forties, is the mother of six children and a resident of Cairo, where her husband works as a printer. With much reluctance she recounted to me her experiences with Yasir Arafat in the fall of 1951. "He was a strange young man. He had a certain charm which he could use to great advantage. But he also had a dark streak, a sort of permanent irrational anger that was always simmering below the surface.

"I don't know why he took a liking to me, except that perhaps we were very much alike. I was rather a bit on the shy, withdrawn side, and so was he. I had never been with a man, and he said he had never been with a woman. I believed that, because he was always very awkward around me. He was not like most young men who were always so sure of themselves.

"He pursued me for about six months and was always telling me he wanted me to be his wife. Finally he asked my father. My father was in the construction business, building houses in Alexandria. I believe my father saw in Yasir someone he could take into his business because of his interest in engineering, so he said yes, that we could get married.

"But all the time he was pursuing me, Yasir never made any approaches to me. He would simply talk, telling me of political things, of Egypt and the future and how he hoped to someday be an important person in the government. He never mentioned Palestine or the Jews, and I never even knew he was from there or that he had another name. Then a terrible thing happened.

"We had neighbors in Alexandria who were Jews. They were not very popular, for they had for some time been trying to emigrate to Palestine. But I was friendly with their two daughters, Rachel and

Miriam. One day Yasir came to my house to visit and found them there. Thinking back on it, I realize he was playing very innocent, leading them on. When he discovered they were Jewesses, I could see his mood change, he became very tense. He started asking them leading questions, and they revealed that they would soon be going to Israel to live. He became even more tense, yet continued to play the innocent, asking more questions, personal questions about their father, where he worked, that sort of thing. They thought he was just making idle conversation, as did I. I had no idea he had any particular feelings about Jews or Israel.

"Well, two days later Rachel and Miriam's father was murdered. It was a terrible shock to our neighborhood. Because they were Jews they were not popular, but still, no one I knew would have liked to see them harmed. It was also a shock because Mr. Harkabi—that was his name—was found hung upside down from a tree on the street where we lived.

"At first I made no connection between Yasir and Mr. Harkabi. But a few days later I was with Yasir. We were alone in my house. I told Yasir about Mr. Harkabi, and I began to weep for my friends Rachel and Miriam. Yasir went into a rage. He struck me and shouted at me never to weep for a Jew. I argued that these were my friends. That just got him more enraged. He proceeded to beat me, tearing my clothes off and cursing and pummeling me. I was frightened to death, helpless and ashamed at my nakedness. Then he stopped beating me and threw himself on me. He removed his trousers and tried to penetrate me, but he could not do so. This made him even more irrational. He began to beat me again, then forced me to do horrible things to him. Finally he threw me aside. That is when he told me he had been responsible for the murder of Mr. Harkabi.

"He acted as though nothing had happened between us, that all would go on as before. He said that he had arranged for the death of Mr. Harkabi to save Palestine from receiving another Jew. And he threatened to have Rachel and Miriam killed if I ever talked to them again. He acted as though we were already married.

"He continued to come around for the next few weeks, but I was unable to say anything to him. I was so terrified of him. At the same time I was terrified of saying anything about what had happened to my father or anyone else. Yasir became his old self again, as though nothing had happened, and when I didn't talk to him he began to concentrate on my father, trying to get closer to him.

"As the date for our marriage grew closer, I became more terrified. I did not want to marry Yasir, but it had been arranged and there was no way for me to get out of it short of telling my father of his behavior, which I couldn't do. But then fate intervened. Part of the agreement that we would be married was that Yasir would become an Egyptian citizen. My father had agreed to be one of his sponsors, and had sent off the necessary letters and forms to Cairo. There came back in the mail one day an official letter to my father saying that there was no record of a Yasir Arafat, but that there was a record of so-and-so and such-and-such. What it came to was that the letter revealed who Yasir really was, not who he had said he was to my father. This accidental finding out disturbed my father very much, for he had always been favorable toward the British and had never liked the Mufti or anything to do with the al-Husaynis of Palestine.

"He confronted Yasir with this information. At first Yasir said it must be all a mistake. But then he was forced to admit the truth. He begged my father, saying how much he hated Haj Amin too, but my father would not forgive his attempt to deceive him. He ordered Yasir out of the house and declared the marriage agreement ended. I was so relieved I can't tell you, although I made sure to make it appear to my father that I was heartbroken by his action.

"I only saw Yasir once after that. He didn't even look at me."

Yasir Arafat, when asked, claims never to have known a girl named Jinan al-Oraby.

19

"The Scimitar"

It was the winter of 1951–52. A few months earlier, in order to placate its increasingly dissident populace, the Wafd government of Egypt had unilaterally terminated the Anglo-Egyptian Treaty of 1936, which still had five years to run. The mood of national celebration that followed was quickly seized upon by the Ikhwan and other aspirants to power in Cairo and transformed into an escalating round of anti-government demonstrations throughout Egypt.

During the months Yasir Arafat was traveling to Alexandria to court Jinan al-Oraby, he was also busy at the university in Cairo securing himself a place of importance in the Ikhwan-sponsored Palestine Student Federation. When, in November, his impending marriage to Jinan fell through, he returned to the university and began to work full time on PSF projects, which consisted mostly of organizing banner-filled Ikhwanite student marches on the various institutions of government in Cairo. The primary purpose of the marches was to elicit violent police responses, which could then be escalated into general rioting. One such riot broke out in January of 1952, and his contribution to it cemented Yasir Arafat's star in the PSF firmament.

It began as a general student march on the Abdin Palace of King Farouk and his mother, Queen Nazli, who was the real power behind the Egyptian throne. Student groups from most of the schools in Cairo had been secretly organizing for weeks for the march, some representing the Ikhwan, others representing competing nationalist organizations. Yasir, almost single-handed, rallied the PSF, which theretofore had been relatively dormant in the rising tide of dissidence, so that by the day of the demonstration PSF students and their supporters were among the largest groups assembled.

The march began peacefully enough from Cairo's largest square, a mass of chanting students filling the boulevard as it made its way toward the palace. As its self-appointed leader Yasir marched at the head of the PSF contingent, three or four groups behind the lead organization. Strapped to his leg was his trusty pistol. As the lead group neared the palace, policemen with loudspeakers warned it to proceed no farther. The group hesitated, but the press of humanity from behind pushed it forward again. Suddenly the march gathered speed and, like a giant phalanx, bore down on the palace gates. From behind the gates stepped a dozen members of the palace guard, automatic weapons blazing.

Dozens of students in the first rows were hit. Panic seized the tightly compacted mob and it exploded into a frenzy of flight, everyone seeking an escape route. Portions of the mob spilled down side streets, while the main body, retracing its steps in a stampede, found its way blocked by a wall of water suddenly built by half a dozen fire hoses.

Arafat managed to avoid being trampled and found an escape route through a side street. With his pistol now in his hand, he led a group of his PSF cohorts through a series of alleys that led to the rear of the palace. At the high wall surrounding the grounds, he concocted a plan. He issued rapid-fire orders to his dozen or so companions, waving his pistol about as he pointed out directions. The plan was for them to vault the unguarded wall and, with Yasir's pistol as their only weapon, to mount an assault on the palace itself.

"With him waving and pointing the pistol, none of us was going to argue with him," says Rashid Bulami, one of those who had followed Arafat. "Yasir suddenly became like a man possessed. He thought up this idea on the spur of the moment and gave each of us specific assignments, threatening to kill anyone who disobeyed. His idea was to charge the palace and assassinate the king in retribution for the palace guard's shooting at the students. He said that since we were all from Palestine, we were all *fedayeen* and must always be prepared to die. He claimed that by assassinating the king we would open the way to the Ikhwan revolution, which would bring about the liberation of Palestine, and that we would all become heroes of a free Palestine, that monuments would be built to us. I must say, in the heat and panic of those moments, when our hearts were beating so furiously with fear, he electrified us into wanting to go over the wall.

"Fortunately—or unfortunately, depending on how you wish to interpret it—Yasir spent too much time on his propaganda. Before we had a chance to go over the wall, an army lorry filled with soldiers raced into the street and the soldiers surrounded us. Someone must have seen and reported us. The soldiers took Yasir's gun, then marched us around the palace to the front. The rest of us were too frightened to speak, but Yasir kept hurling insults at the soldiers. He even spat in the face of one. He received a rifle butt on the side of the head as a reward, and we had to drag him the rest of the way.

"At the front of the palace there were dead and wounded students lying all over. We were loaded onto a bus with others who had been captured and taken to a barracks across the river. We were held there for three days with nothing to eat but bread and water. We were questioned, but none of us told of our allegiance to the Ikhwan or said we were members of the PSF. We simply said we were taking refuge behind the palace when we were arrested. Yasir had more difficulty explaining his gun, but he finally got them to believe it was only for self-protection. They even gave it back to him when they released us."

When he was released, Yasir returned to Cairo to find the city in a state of martial law. The rioting that had been touched off by the student march had spread throughout Cairo; when it ended, there were close to a hundred people dead, thousands nursing injuries, and hundreds of burned and battered buildings.

King Fuad University remained closed for several more days. When classes resumed a week later, Yasir discovered that he had become a hero among the members of the PSF. His companions in the aborted assault on the royal palace had spread the word of his derring-do—although, as Rashid Bulami says, the story grew in exaggeration each time it was related. "We were all still so excited by what we *almost* did that by the time the story made the rounds we had actually done it. That is, we had actually scaled the wall and begun an assault on the palace itself, only to be stopped by the king's troops." Nevertheless, recalls Bulami, Yasir returned to classes to find himself almost universally admired by his fellow Palestinian students.

The rioting in January of 1952 and subsequent civil turmoil set the stage for the coup d'état, six months later, that eventually brought Gamal Abdel Nasser to power in Egypt. During these six months

Yasir Arafat exploited his increased prestige among the Palestinian students at the university and spent most of his time seeking to mold the PSF into a more active and effective instrument of what he thought, still, would be the eventual Ikhwan revolt and seizure of power.

The surprise July coup of the Nasserites, who called themselves the Free Officers Movement, momentarily took the wind out of the sails of Arafat's—indeed, of all of Egypt's Ikhwan followers'—ambition. In view of the Free Officers' former Ikhwan associations, the Brotherhood leadership took a wait-and-see attitude toward the new regime as the Nasserites installed the popular General Naguib as the country's figurehead leader and imposed a system of rule by military fiat.

Arafat, however, along with a small circle of newly made friends, continued to restructure the Palestine Student Federation at the university—renamed the University of Cairo by the new government. At this time, too, he redirected the PSF's attention to the question of Israel. Immediately upon their accession to power, the Nasserites had expressed their intention of recommitting Egypt to the annihilation of Israel and the recovery of Palestine. The declaration was part of Nasser's general vision of uniting the entire Arab world into a distinct power that would, with its vast petroleum resources and large population base, have a say in the affairs of the globe. Such a united Arabdom would be led, of course, by Egypt.

Arabs of many political stripes were impressed by the Nasserite vision, not the least of whom were the politically conscious but still confused Palestinian students of Cairo University. The new regime's inflammatory pronouncements about Israel rekindled the pride and chauvinism of these students, most of whom had been too young to be involved in the Palestinian nationalism of the 1940s. In Yasir Arafat they had a young man, slightly older, who had been involved, but who had rejected the fruitless ways of the Haj Aminists and was receptive to a potentially more productive alternative. The Ikhwan had long promised such a commitment to the liberation of Palestine but had lacked the power to fulfill their promise. No matter that the Free Officers were not avowed Ikhwanites; they now had committed Egypt to Palestine and possessed the power to follow through.

Arafat used the Nasserite declarations to further expand his influence within the PSF and to enlarge its membership. He began to extol the Free Officers regime and explained away his initial Ikhwan-inspired reservations about it by predicting the development of an eventual Nasserite-Ikhwanite coalition that would rule Egypt. As a result of the wide popularity of General Naguib, the apparent leader of the Nasserites (Nasser himself was still keeping himself in the background, although it was becoming increasingly clear as time went on that he was the brains and power behind the government), Arafat had little trouble in overriding Ikhwan objections to his hasty espousal of the new regime. In December of 1952 he called for an election among the students to officially establish a PSF leadership. Not surprisingly, he was elected president of the federation, with his closest friends being chosen for the chief suboffices.

One of these friends was a young man from Haifa named Walid Jiryis. Today an Egyptian petroleum engineer, he says, "I became friendly with Arafat just after the Nasser coup. Up to then I had done little at the university in the way of political acts. I had joined the PSF, but I had been concentrating more on my studies than anything else. Then Yasir began to come around. He found out that I was distantly related to al-Birah, the old guerrilla fighter, and he told me stories of his friend Abu Khalid, who was a protégé of al-Birah. He was very enthusiastic, very intense, and very insistent that I do more. I was impressed with him, I suppose, for he was older than me and had gained a good deal of prestige among the students. He befriended me, and got me very involved. When they elected him president of the PSF, he got me elected as one of the vice-presidents.

"The unity did not last long, though. In the beginning the offices were held by students from various parts of Palestine. But once everyone found out that Yasir was from Gaza, it was the students who came from Gaza that became the most full-time workers. As time progressed, Yasir lost interest in the idea that the offices of the federation should be filled by representatives of every region of Palestine. His Gaza friends wanted the organization to be led strictly by Gazans. It was not long before Yasir began to ignore meetings of the elected officers and make decisions and take initiatives on his own, supported by his Gaza supporters.

"There was soon a rebellion by some of the others, but it did not last long. We called for another election in 1953, and this time most of the offices were filled by students from Gaza. In fact, the PSF eventually became an almost exclusively Gaza organization. Yasir and I fell out, and I finally quit the federation in 1954.

"In my opinion, winning the presidency of the PSF turned Yasir into a power maniac. Just the way he behaved after his election—he suddenly began to thrive on his position. He learned what it is to be president of something, to be able to issue orders, form committees, handle money, push people around who disagreed with him. He became arrogant. He became pretentious. He used to say that he could no longer have close friends because there might be times when he had to discipline or dismiss or even punish someone, and if he was a friend . . .

"There was an occasion when he did this. There was a student whose parents had sent him out of Palestine in the '48 war to live with relatives in Cairo but who themselves remained behind. When the war ended, his parents found themselves living in what had become Israel. They were suddenly Israeli Arabs. They adapted to this existence, but the Israelis would not allow the boy to return to his parents. He was very unhappy about this, but he never spoke of it. We all simply thought he was from Cairo. He was a very malleable boy. He had no sense of himself, but would follow the lead of anyone who showed any friendliness toward him. Yasir had recruited him—this was the time when Yasir was building the PSF and trying to get as many boys on his side as he could so that he could take it over. The boy had been among those who attacked Farouk's palace during the 1952 demonstrations. He worshiped Yasir.

"Then—oh, a year later—Yasir discovered the story of the boy, that his parents were living in Israel. What is worse, they were apparently satisfied there. Yasir tried to get the boy to publicly denounce his parents. The boy would have done just about anything for Yasir. But this! This he could not do. He was torn by the conflict—loyalty to his parents, loyalty to Yasir.

"So, Yasir began to hold him up to ridicule. Still the boy would not agree to condemn his parents. Yasir, I would say, really loved the boy. He was delicate, sensitive, like a flower. He was very much a part of Yasir's inner circle—four or five boys who lived in the same place and, well, you can imagine what I mean. And what did Yasir do?

"There was another boy—we used to call him The Scimitar—who came from Bedouin people. He was totally ruthless. Yasir held a kind of formal hearing for the boy whose parents lived in Israel, who wouldn't denounce them. He gave this speech about us all being *fedayeen.* He cried as he pointed to the boy. He said, 'My heart aches for Ahmed (or whatever his name was), my *feday* soul bleeds for dear Ahmed. We are as brothers,' he said, 'we are as creatures whose veins are joined, whose blood runs from one to the other. . . .' It was very dramatic. And then he said, 'But my Arab brother Ahmed cannot bring himself to be a true *feday,* so he must be taught.' Thereupon the boy we called The Scimitar appeared with a knife. Yasir sobbed and sobbed as The Scimitar proceeded to castrate the boy. The next day the boy was dead. He had killed himself. After that, Yasir used to say he could have no friends."

Other eyewitnesses to this extraordinary event confirm the account given by Walid Jiryis.

20

The Algerian Cause

Naguib's popularity did not endure. It became clear during 1953 that the nominal head of the military junta did not have the ambition to bring the reform to Egypt that had been hoped for by extremist elements like the Ikhwan. As a result, a concerted anti-junta propaganda campaign was mounted by the Ikhwanites, and a new round of civil disturbance began as the Ikhwan dispatched trained assassins and terrorists in another attempt to gain power.

These events forced Yasir Arafat onto the horns of a dilemma within the Palestinian student community at the university. As president of the PSF he had been extolling the junta for its rabid denunciations of Israel. Now he was forced to reverse himself in order to adhere to the Ikhwanite party line. According to one observer, he did not move quickly enough. That, and the fact that he had packed the PSF executive with students from Gaza, provoked an anti-Arafat rebellion on the part of the more strict Ikhwanites among the federation's membership.

The struggle for leadership intensified into the fall of 1953. To demonstrate his Ikhwanite resolve and to compensate for his tardiness in joining the general anti-Naguib movement, Arafat took a number of his Gazan cohorts to the Suez Canal Zone in October of 1953 to link up with Ikhwanite terrorists harassing the canal administration. Arafat's group managed to achieve little at the canal; they had hoped to receive arms and join in terrorist operations, but they were not accepted by the Suez Ikhwanites and were soon told to leave. When they returned to Cairo, they discovered that they themselves had been victims of a coup; in their absence they had been voted out of office in the PSF.

Arafat and the ousted Gazans immediately started a new organization, calling it the Palestine Student Union. Arafat assumed the presidency of the PSU, and his first act was to declare a propaganda war on the PSF.

"Along with the students from Gaza," recalls Ismael Nabbani, an early member of the PSU and now a teacher at an Arab school in Kuwait, "several Egyptian boys came into Yasir's group. One of them had a father who owned a printing plant, so we had access to a press, which is something the PSF didn't have. This is when Yasir learned how to write his manifestoes. He started writing these long tracts against the PSF. The Egyptian student would have them printed in great numbers for free, and then Yasir would send us out to distribute them to all the students at the university. They would be filled with hundreds of errors, both in grammar and in typography, and often it was almost impossible to make any sense of them. But although they were crude, they had great effect. Earlier, only the Palestinians among the student population knew who Yasir was. Soon the entire student body had heard of him through these pamphlets."

Among those who heard of him was a group of students from Algeria who were busy trying to enlist student support for the nascent Algerian struggle for independence from France. At the time, France was occupied in an unsuccessful war in Indochina, trying to retain its colony of Vietnam in the face of Vietnamese strivings for independence. The French experience in Vietnam had fueled similar strivings in Algeria, another French colony; consequently, an Algerian revolutionary movement had evolved to give voice to and do battle for Arab Algerian aspirations of self-determination. The dominant organization in the movement was called the Algerian National Liberation Front, or FLN.

The leaders of the FLN student group sought out Yasir Arafat after seeing several of his broadsides against the PSF, ineptly written mixes of Ikhwan fervency and conventional anti-Zionist propaganda that seemed to have no political focus whatsoever. The Algerians' intent, according to Ismael Nabbani, was not to explore Arafat's philosophy, but simply to discover the source of his free printing facilities.

"The FLNists were having trouble getting money for printing pamphlets. At the end of each of Yasir's, there was a credit line that said something like 'Printed Free by a Friend of Arab Palestine.' The

Algerians thought they might get the friend of Palestine to be a friend of Algeria too.

"But then it became more than that. The Algerians were amused by Yasir. They were more sophisticated than he was, and they were able to speak very glibly about political ideologies, economic systems, colonialism, imperialism, and so on. Yasir had heard of all these, of course, but he had never discussed them, analyzed them, or even thought much about them.

"He was extremely impressed by the Algerians, and I am certain that it was from them that he first learned how to get across his point more effectively. He cultivated them, attended their meetings, began to support them in his pamphlets. He arranged for them to obtain some free printing, so they tolerated him. After a while, there began to appear in his pamphlets words and phrases he picked up from them, phrases like 'colonial oppressor,' 'imperialist exploiter,' that sort of thing. And he began to use the word 'liberation' a great deal in relation to Palestine. He had never used that word before, and he was surprised at the favorable effect it had."

The effect was that, as soon as Arafat began to couple references to Palestine in his pamphlets with the concept of national liberation, his Palestine Student Union experienced an influx of new students. Many of them came over from the rival PSF, while others were new Palestinian students at the university who had not yet made any commitments. By spring of 1954 the PSU had more than two hundred members. The idea of approaching the problem of Palestine in terms of its "liberation" proved to be a potent magnet.

Ikhwan-sponsored agitation against the junta escalated throughout the spring of 1954 as Naguib began to admit back into government circles Wafdist politicians who had been ousted in the 1952 Free Officers coup. Nasser, having remained largely behind the scenes, grew impatient with the figurehead ruler, then angry when Naguib started to ignore the dictates of the Free Officers' brain trust and act on his own authority with regard to political appointments. Hence, in the summer of 1954, the Nasserites ousted Naguib and installed a new leadership, with none other than Nasser himself at its fore.

The change did nothing to mollify the Ikhwan. Shortly after Nasser assumed full dictatorial power, an Ikhwan assassination attempt was made on his life as he was delivering a speech in Alexandria. According to Muhammad Heikal, for many years editor of Cairo's largest newspaper and a confidant of Nasser, the new Egyptian leader did not flinch as six bullets whizzed past his head. "He just stood there, braving the assassin as the bullets whistled past him. He spoke to the people as the shots rang out: 'My fellow countrymen, stay where you are. I am not dead, I am alive, and even if I die all of you is [sic] Gamal Abdel Nasser. The banner would not fall.' "*

The incident catapulted Nasser into universal popularity in Egypt and sounded the death knell for the Ikhwan. Partly to cool Ikhwan disgruntlement, partly to reinvigorate the regime's 1952 commitment to lead the Arab world toward the solution of the Israel problem (and wholly, according to many experts, to divert attention from Egypt's internal problems), Nasser almost immediately ordered the establishment of an Egyptian-organized and trained guerrilla force in Gaza. Made up mostly of Arab Palestinians recruited from Gaza's refugee camps and, to a lesser extent, from the indigenous populace, the force, to be led by Egyptian army officers trained in commando tactics, would be the spearhead of an eventual war of liberation that would not only return all of Palestine to the Arabs but also serve as the template for Nasser's vision of a unified federation of Arab states which, led by Egypt, would become an important third power bloc in the world.

To sharpen the focus of his vision for the rest of Arabdom, Nasser repeatedly declared: "I am an Arab, we are all Arabs," meaning that one Arab's struggle was the struggle of all Arabs, and that the fight of one Arab nation was the fight of all. To a people imbued with the ancient tribal tradition of "The friend of my enemy is my enemy, the enemy of my friend is my enemy," Nasser's declarations had wide appeal throughout the Arab world. Not the least of those inspired were the several million Arabs who made up the Palestinian diaspora.

Nasser's rise to power and the commencement of guerrilla operations from Gaza and northern Sinai early in 1955 caught Yasir Arafat by surprise. Still caught in his Ikhwan-Nasserite dilemma, he

*Muhammad Heikal, *Nasser: The Cairo Documents* (London: New English Library Ltd., 1972).

was puzzled to discover from one of his brothers in January that Egyptian military cadres had been in Gaza for the previous three months recruiting and training guerrilla squads to operate out of the refugee camps. For several months Yasir could not decide on how to react to the news. On the one hand it was still instinctive Ikhwanite policy to resist the Free Officers regime; Nasser himself, after all, had once been an Ikhwanite but had renounced his allegiance to the Brotherhood. On the other hand Nasser, in his establishment of an Egyptian-sponsored Palestine liberation guerrilla army, was accomplishing what the Ikhwan had long promised but never fulfilled. Yasir had been taking a strong Ikhwanite line in his most recent pamphlets in an endeavor to re-establish his influence in the Palestine Student Federation and wed it to his PSU. To reverse himself again and come out in praise of the Nasser regime would jeopardize that effort and, he recognized, seriously erode his credibility as a spokesman for Palestinian students in Cairo.

His dilemma was solved in part by the sudden appearance in Cairo of two young men from the Al Bureij refugee camp in Gaza. Named Khalil al-Wazir and Salah Khalef, each was a member of a family from the vicinity of Jerusalem that had fled during the 1948 war. Younger by a year or so than Yasir, they had spent their adolescent years in the teeming squalor of Al Bureij and had been members of various terrorist groups that had formed, only to quickly dissolve again from lack of leadership, arms, and training, in the late 1940s and early 1950s. Toward the end of 1954 they received secret recruiting posters distributed throughout the eight camps for young Palestinian men to form a "*fedayeen* army" to be trained by Egypt. They enlisted. Upon going through some basic training, they were found by their Egyptian instructors to have leadership potential and were selected, along with several other recruits, to be sent to Cairo for more specialized advanced training at a military base nearby.

Al-Wazir and Khalef arrived in Cairo in April of 1955. It was their first visit to the Egyptian capital and, with a few days on their own before they were to report to the military base, they wandered the streets like sightseers. In the course of their wanderings they stopped at a coffeehouse near the university frequented by Palestinian students. Immediately pegged as refugees by the more affluent students, they were snubbed by all but one, a homosexual who promised them sleeping accommodations for the night. They accepted.

The student was a member of Yasir Arafat's PSU. During the night he learned the purpose of al-Wazir's and Khalef's presence in Cairo and the next day mentioned it to Yasir. Yasir was interested in hearing more about what the Egyptians were doing in Gaza, so he asked the student to bring the two refugees to see him. Al-Wazir and Khalef came. After several hours of talk, Yasir and the two struck up a friendship. A day or two later the Gazans left for the military base with the promise to return at the end of their stay to fill Yasir in on the details of their training.

Return they did, a month or so later, with tales of their training in infiltration techniques and explosives work. They told of a new miracle explosive—plastique—which could be hand-molded into any size and form desired. It had tremendous concussive effect and, when stuffed with nails and metal shards, could kill and wound great numbers of people. Yasir was fascinated by his friends' descriptions; somewhat of an explosives expert himself, he had heard stories about plastique from several of the Algerians he knew and was anxious to experiment with it himself. But what was of even more interest to him was the fact that al-Wazir and Khalef had returned with commissions as lieutenants in a special Gazan brigade of the Egyptian army. They were now being paid a regular salary to fight against the Jews.

21

Suez

Al-Wazir and Khalef returned to Gaza in June of 1955, leaving Yasir in Cairo to chew on his indecision. Soon tales began to filter back to Cairo of the successes of the Egyptian-sponsored guerrilla groups operating out of Gaza and striking into the heart of Israel. Israeli vehicles were ambushed, farms and settlements were attacked, fields were booby-trapped, roads were mined.

Fedayeen cadres from Gaza, funded by Egypt, had also begun to infiltrate into Jordan, Syria, and Lebanon and to organize guerrilla cells there. By August Israeli casualties were running at a rate twice that of previous years' guerrilla actions.

But so were guerrilla casualties. The Israelis, infinitely better armed, trained, and equipped, responded to serious *fedayeen* raids with reprisal raids of their own, swarming into Arab villages and camps in Gaza and Jordan, destroying homes, and taking suspected guerrillas—they preferred to call them terrorists—into custody or killing them on the spot. One such raid late in August was directed at Khan Yunis, at the southern end of the Gaza Strip. Khan Yunis was the site of a guerrilla training center run by the Egyptians, and not only were scores of Gazan trainees killed but also forty Egyptian military personnel.

Among those killed in the raid was Yasir Arafat's brother Badir. News of Badir's death put an end to Yasir's indecision over his loyalties toward the Ikhwan and the Nasser regime. Nasserite propagandists used the raid to call for the launching of a holy war against Israel, summoning Palestinians of all ages to join what they promised would be an enlarged and better equipped guerrilla army.

Yasir responded to the call by presenting himself, in the company of several of his PSU cohorts, at a recruiting center in Cairo. He could not boast of his previous experience in the manufacture of bombs on behalf of the Ikhwan, because the Ikhwan, after trying to kill Nasser, was growing increasingly out of favor. He did, however, impress the Egyptian recruiting officer with his knowledge of explosives, particularly plastique, and asked to be sent for training at the same military base that Khalil al-Wazir and Salah Khalef had attended. His request was approved, and in October Yasir left Cairo for the base, which was near El Mansura in the Nile Delta.

Before his departure he had sent word back to al-Wazir and Khalef in Gaza that he had been accepted for training at El Mansura. They responded by advising him to seek out one Anwar Ghalib, a Jerusalem-born Egyptian army captain who had been their chief instructor the previous spring. Yasir did so. According to Ali Badnan, another trainee at the time and now an Egyptian agricultural official, the acquaintance the two struck up was responsible for getting Yasir his first attention from the Nasser regime.

"Anwar Ghalib was a demon of an instructor," says Badnan. "He had received military training in England in the 1930s, and he was an expert on commando warfare. What is interesting is that he was also a member of the Ikhwan. A secret member, because Nasser, once he came to power, tried to discourage any further Ikhwan activity in the army. What is even more interesting is that he was very involved at El Mansura with Egyptian intelligence. In addition to training guerrillas, he was also recruiting spies for the intelligence service, which was headed by a colonel who was once his commanding officer and also English-trained.

"Yasir and I were sent to El Mansura at the same time. Yasir immediately impressed everyone with his stories of the fighting in Jerusalem in 1948. He made himself known to Anwar Ghalib, and Ghalib immediately took a liking to him—much to the dismay of the rest of us in the training brigade, for we were all vying for Ghalib's approval.

"Yasir's specialty was explosives. He knew more than any of us about the properties of the various explosives we were trained to use, and it was not long before Ghalib had him teaching the classes. He had no fear handling explosives, and he was always carrying about small handfuls of plastique and shaping them like clay into likenesses of notorious Zionists such as Ben-Gurion. He would then entertain us by setting them off.

"Out of every training group of a hundred or so men there would be four or five who would be selected for officer's reserve commissions—second lieutenancies. Yasir was really not very capable in field exercises—he tired easily and was on the clumsy side. But since he was a whiz with explosives, Ghalib selected him for a commission.

"He selected him for something else, too. He recruited Yasir for the intelligence service. One day a man came down from Cairo to interview Ghalib's three or four selections for intelligence. He interviewed Yasir, and a few days later we learned that he had been taken on. His job was to return to the university after his training was over and organize a new unified Palestinian student organization out of all the different Palestinian groups there. This was supposed to be a secret job, but Yasir was too proud to keep it quiet. He told us that the new organization he was to form had top priority, that he would have all the money and other means he needed to put the organization together, and that it would be used by the Nasser regime for political purposes. He even said that as soon as he returned to Cairo he would have a meeting with Nasser himself."

Yasir returned to Cairo with his lieutenant's commission in December of 1955. He did not have a meeting with Nasser, but was soon contacted by a man named Mohar Takieddin, an Egyptian intelligence functionary. Takieddin restated Yasir's mission, gave him several hundred Egyptian pounds to establish an office near the university, and promised him any other resources he needed to get the new organization started—including enforcers.

Within days the university was inundated by a flood of anonymously written pamphlets demanding that the various Palestinian student groups cease squabbling among themselves and unite into a new entity that would support and contribute to the Nasser regime's war against Israel. Proposed to head the new organization, which would be called the General Union of Palestinian Students, was Yasir Arafat. A few days later a rally was announced at which Yasir would speak to all Palestinian and other interested students. Implicit in the language of the announcement was the threat that those Palestinian students who failed to attend would regret their failure.

The leaders of Yasir's by then arch-rival PSF took exception to what they perceived to be his mysteriously financed grab for power.

They responded with a pamphlet of their own which disclaimed Yasir's authority to speak for all Palestinian students. The day after the pamphlet appeared, several top officers of the PSF were found dead.

Yasir denied any knowledge of the murders. He was probably telling the truth. Although he had to assume that the killings were engineered by his new benefactors in the Egyptian intelligence service, he had no foreknowledge of them and had no idea who actually committed them.

After a further blitz of pamphlets the rally took place late in January, 1956, and was well attended. Yasir read a speech, secretly written for him by Mohar Takieddin, in which he formally proposed the establishment of the General Union of Palestinian Students. The union, he rhapsodized, would become the matrix of the future government of liberated Palestine. The liberation of Palestine would be accomplished chiefly by "our beloved surrogate, Gamal Abdel Nasser," and the new Arab nation would then join and support the "United Arab Republic" envisioned by Nasser to bring about a renaissance of Arabdom's and Islam's world glory.

Even those closest to Yasir looked at each other perplexedly. On the orders of Takieddin he had told them nothing of his mission; any resistance, he had been promised, would be taken care of. His sudden glorification of Nasser caught them by surprise, and the next day several of his cohorts in the PSU began plotting to remove him as head of the group.

Hassan Salim, although not a part of Arafat's inner circle in those days, was a member of the PSU. "Three or four of Yasir's closest friends disagreed with his praise of Nasser and his offer to put all Palestinian students at Nasser's service. What happened thereafter was rather startling. They confronted Yasir at a meeting of the PSU the next day and denounced him. They demanded he resign, and there was a good deal of agreement on the part of most of the others.

"Yasir simply smiled sadly in that way he had when he knew that he knew more about something than you did. One of the students against him had become his real enemy—they disliked each other immensely. Yasir said very little, he just said that any attempts to oppose him would be regretted by those who engaged in them. He reminded us all of what had happened to the PSF leaders.

"The following day this one student—Yasir's enemy—persisted. Along with several of his friends he began to circulate a petition calling for the removal of Yasir. The following morning he was dead."

During February momentum gathered toward the formal creation of the General Union of Palestinian Students (GUPS). According to Salim, who today occupies his time as a press agent for the Palestine Liberation Organization in Beirut, Yasir disclosed to his inner circle the fact that GUPS was being backed by Egyptian intelligence and promised that those who remained loyal to him would be rewarded in the years to come.

"It was first two, then three, then four people who learned of Yasir's connections, but with the tendency we all had to gossip it soon became common knowledge in the PSU that he was working for the Egyptians. In fact, he finally told us all at a meeting that March, just before the elections were to be held for the General Union. He said, yes, he was a part of Egyptian intelligence, and that the new organization would be generously financed and supported. But he warned us not to confuse his public approval of Nasser with his private feelings. As people without a country, he said, we must take our friends where we find them. The Egyptians would use the General Union for their own purposes, but we would use the Egyptians for *our* purposes."

Elections were held at another rally in March, and Yasir, with the help of emissaries of Mohar Takieddin circulating through the crowd, was chosen chairman of the newly constituted GUPS.

The election was held in an atmosphere of increasing tension in Egypt. Nasser had refused to join in the Baghdad Pact, a military alliance proposed by Britain between herself and various large Middle Eastern nations. Nasser's objections were rooted in his contempt for the British and their decades of colonial exploitation of Egypt. He was not able to prevent Iraq—another former Arab colony of Britain—from joining, however. Moreover, he was in the midst of a dispute with the United States over a 1952 American promise to sell $500 million worth of arms to Egypt. The Eisenhower administration had held up the sale under British pressure for fear the arms would be used against British troops still occupying the Canal Zone.

The British had agreed to evacuate the Zone by 1956, but after they had persuaded Iraq to join the Baghdad Pact in 1955, thus marring Nasser's vision of a united Arab world, he felt compelled to get the British out of Suez immediately. For this he would need a much better equipped army than he had. When the United States continued to withhold the arms it had pledged, and when Nasser learned that France had secretly agreed to supply Israel with arms, he turned angrily to the Russians and through them found a willing supplier.

Egypt and Czechoslovakia signed a large-scale arms agreement in September of 1955 over the vocal objections of the United States, which saw the deal as a Soviet attempt to impose its influence on the Middle East. Britain too was dismayed, and from then on its prime minister, Anthony Eden, became obsessed in his denunciations of Nasser.

At the time of the founding of GUPS and the election of the twenty-six-year-old Arafat to its chairmanship, Nasser had just given diplomatic recognition to Communist China. The United States responded by withdrawing its promise to help finance the building of the Aswan High Dam. Britain followed suit. With Czech arms now flowing into Egypt and pledges of financial support and friendship emanating from Moscow, Nasser replied in this escalating battle of nerves by nationalizing the Suez Canal on July 26, 1956, and summarily ordering the British out.

The British left. But Nasser, according to Muhammad Heikal, knew they would be back in force—possibly accompanied by the French, with whom they had shared the operations of the Suez Canal Company—to try to recover the canal. It was only a question of when. In the meantime Egypt exulted at Nasser's daring, and tens of thousands flocked to join the army when he warned of a probable Anglo-French invasion. The invasion came in October of 1956. With it came an unexpected twist that would profoundly change the geopolitical face of the Middle East. The twist was Israel.

After Nasser's nationalization of the canal, Britain and France secretly invited Israel to join them in a war against Egypt. All three parties would benefit from such an alliance. The strategy was for an Anglo-French force to parachute into the Canal Zone while an Israeli armored force invaded the Sinai Peninsula, thus distracting the Egyptian army. Britain and France would justify their part in the invasion on the grounds of Egypt's "illegal" seizure of the canal. Israel would justify its participation on the fact that Egypt, by financing and mounting Palestinian Arab commando raids from Gaza, was in effect waging war against Israel. Also, more recently, Egypt had set up a blockade of the Gulf of Aqaba, thus cutting off Israel's southern port of Eilat. In exchange for its participation Israel would receive increased arms support from Britain and France.

When the war broke out in October, the world was astonished by Israel's success. England and France were universally condemned for their actions, even by the United States. Israel was chastised as well, but the ease with which its forces knifed across Sinai, chasing the Egyptians before them and destroying everything in their path, tempered the world's disapproval with admiration. In only eight years Israel had transformed its army from a ragtag civilian militia into a highly disciplined, mobile, advanced, and audacious force.

Although the English, French, and Israelis were soon pressured into withdrawing by the United Nations, thus giving Nasser a "moral victory" and a considerable propaganda triumph, the Israeli performance served notice on Egypt and the rest of the Arab world that their dream of recovering Israeli Palestine would be difficult if not impossible to realize. As a result of the war, Nasser's popularity soared throughout much of Arabdom, reinforcing his vision of becoming the supreme leader of a unified Arab world. But the war also dulled the intensity of Nasser-inflamed Arab passions concerning Palestine. The big-power politics involved in the conflict drew the world's attention away from the question of Palestine, and the performance of Israel took the wind out of the bombast of the Arab "liberation" movement.

No one was more demoralized than Yasir Arafat. Just before the war broke out, he was called into the service. He was assigned as a sub-lieutenant to a demolitions detachment in Suez City, at the southern end of the canal. The group's mission was to blow up former British security stations along the southern reaches of the canal should it appear that the British would be successful in their attempt to regain control of the waterway. A secondary assignment was to destroy the British-developed oil-producing facilities at Abu Rudeis, farther south along the Gulf of Suez.

Arafat saw no action, but when the news arrived in Suez that Israel had joined the British and French, he was as stunned as everyone else in Egypt. On the third day of the war he learned that the Israelis had captured Gaza and were driving across Sinai toward the canal. By then the morale and discipline of the Egyptian army had disintegrated. On the fourth day it became known that the Israelis had captured the Mitla Pass, thirty miles due east of Suez, and were driving on the city itself. Exhausted Egyptian soldiers fleeing the Israeli advance poured through Suez with terrifying tales of Israeli firepower and mobility. Thereupon the commanding officer of Yasir Arafat's detachment, and then the second in command, disappeared, followed by most of the enlisted men.

Yasir was left with three men out of an original detachment of forty. The tiny group blew up an Egyptian ammunition depot on the outskirts of Suez. As it turned out, the Israeli intention was not to capture Suez City, which was on the western bank of the canal, but merely to secure the eastern shore as part of its plan to control all of Sinai. Arafat's destruction of the depot, then, ironically served only to cost Egypt several million dollars' worth of ammunition.

He could not be faulted, though. He had remained while those about him were fleeing. As he says, "It was when my faith in Egypt's ability to help the Palestinian evaporated. It was sickening to watch thousands of Egyptian soldiers running toward Cairo. Nasser had experienced the same thing in 1948, and he kept telling us how it would never happen again while he was president of Egypt. Yet he had been in power for four years, and here it was happening again."

Arafat says that he remained in Suez with his three faithful enlisted men, waiting for the Israelis to invade and preparing to make a final stand. "We were praying for the Zionists to come," he insists. "We were ready to die. But before we did we wanted at least one Zionist soldier each. We set up an ambush on the second story of a store. We had a bazooka—an American bazooka—and only half a dozen shells. We were not sure how to operate it, but we were determined to make it work. We knew that the first Zionists to come into the city would come in tanks, and we had the bazooka zeroed in on a corner where we thought they would first enter. By then the city was almost empty. We stayed there for five, six days, waiting. But the Zionists never came."

For all practical purposes the war was over within a week. Israel possessed all of Sinai, while British and French troops occupied Port Said and Port Fuad, respectively, at the Mediterranean end of the canal. At the beginning of November, prodded by the United States and Russia—each acting out of its own international interests—the United Nations organized a cease-fire. The cease-fire remained more or less in effect, with the combatants remaining in place, until March of 1957, when the British and French agreed to withdraw from the occupied ports and the Israelis agreed, under particularly severe pressure from the United States, to return Sinai to Egypt.

During the early stages of the cease-fire Yasir Arafat made his way back to Cairo and, with the help of his friends in the Egyptian intelligence service, was immediately mustered out of the army. The reason for the haste with which he was discharged was that the communist-bloc countries were organizing an international student convention in Prague, Czechoslovakia. In an attempt to further ingratiate themselves in the Arab world, the communists had invited several Arab countries to send delegations of students. Egypt suggested that a delegation of Palestinian students be invited as well. When approval of the suggestion came back, the Egyptian government placed the details of the trip in the hands of its intelligence operatives, who, through Arafat, controlled GUPS.

Arafat was ordered to call a meeting of GUPS to inform the union of the invitation. Meanwhile, Arafat's intelligence contacts manufactured thousands of posters picturing Arafat being greeted by Nasser and describing Arafat's heroic exploits in the recent fighting. In actuality, according to several Palestinians who were involved in the student administration of GUPS, the photo was manufactured as well. Arafat had still not met Nasser. Indeed, Nasser had no idea at the time of the connection between Egypt's intelligence service and GUPS. The picture was a standard one of Nasser greeting some Arab dignitary, except that the dignitary had been airbrushed out and Arafat superimposed in his place.

The posters were distributed to the GUPS membership before the general meeting on the Prague conference, thereby increasing Yasir's prestige. They also found their way into other corners of Cairo's

Palestinian population. Among those who saw them were Khalil al-Wazir and Salah Khalef, the two young Gazans Yasir had befriended and who were indirectly responsible for his initial Egyptian intelligence contacts. They immediately sought Yasir out.

They found him two days before the meeting. According to Zaeed al-Qudwa, who was visiting Yasir at the time, they fell into an animated all-night discussion (Arafat himself will not discuss the beginnings of his relationship with the two). Al-Wazir and Khalef told Yasir of having escaped from Gaza after their Palestinian guerrilla unit, attached to the Egyptian army, had fled in disarray before the surprise Israeli thrust across Sinai. They had ended up in Cairo, but were afraid to report their presence lest they be reconscripted into the army. They were bitterly enraged at the Egyptian performance and vowed to carry on the fight against Israel on their own.

Their sentiments were shared by Yasir, Zaeed recalls. "Yasir ranted for hours about the shame of the Egyptians and about how that shame also stained the soul of every Palestinian. He had this pile of posters within reach, and he picked one up and tore it to pieces, condemning Nasser and shouting of how he was ashamed to be seen shaking his hand."

It was an emotional night. The three commiserated with one another, each fueling the others' rage. Zaeed says that several students close to Yasir wandered in during the night and joined the discussion, raising the level of anger and the decibel count. By the time dawn arrived, there were fifteen or sixteen GUPS members on the scene, in addition to Yasir, al-Wazir, and Khalef. It was during this all-night session that the seeds for what eventually grew into the organization known as al-Fatah were sown.

22

The Generation of Revenge

Much of the talk during that night late in 1956 was of the generation that had lost Palestine, first to the British, then to the Jews. It was the generation of Haj Amin al-Husayni, of Abdul al-Qudwa, of Sulaymain al-Wazir and Wabdi Khalef, the fathers of Khalil and Salah. "It is the generation of disaster!" said Khalil. "Then we," replied Yasir, "must become the generation of revenge!"

"Generation of revenge." The phrase echoed more than once through the room that night. The next day Yasir, Khalil, and Salah made a covenant among themselves, vowing to become the generation of revenge in more than words alone. Meanwhile, there remained the problem of what Khalil and Salah were to do.

Yasir, according to his brother Zaeed, came up with the solution. They were, at least nominally, still Egyptian army officers. They had taken the training at El Mansura. They had been personally trained by Anwar Ghalib, who also recruited intelligence people for Mohar Takieddin, Yasir's own contact with the intelligence service. Yasir would talk to Takieddin about Khalil and Salah.

That afternoon he did, and when the GUPS meeting was convened the next evening to choose who would be selected to go to Prague, Khalil and Salah were on the list of candidates. Yasir was the first elected. He immediately gave a speech demanding that his two friends, Palestinians who had fought bravely for Egypt, be appointed to accompany the delegation as "security specialists." The demand was approved. Several other students were chosen, and the meeting came to an end.

Takieddin handled the travel and passport arrangements. Yasir had so far remained in the dark about the connection between his visit to the student convention and Egyptian intelligence needs. But the night before the delegation was to leave, Takieddin at least partially enlightened him. The operative informed Yasir that there was a plot afoot among secret Ikhwan elements within the government, and particularly within the intelligence community, to depose Nasser. The plot was being financed and masterminded by agents representing the Soviet Union, which believed that Nasser's accession to power in Egypt had been secretly engineered by the American CIA. Since Nasser's accession Ikhwan fortunes had waned, and several secret Ikhwanites had learned that Nasser intended to outlaw the Brotherhood. The American installation of Nasser as head of the Egyptian government called for a Soviet countermove, explained Takieddin, as the CIA and the KGB were bitter enemies. The secret CIA sponsorship of Nasser also meant that the United States was an enemy of the Ikhwan.* Operating according to the old Arab axiom that "the enemy of my enemy is my friend," the Russians had approached the Egyptian Ikhwan with their scheme to oust Nasser, replace his regime with an Ikhwanite one, and build Egypt into a modern military power. Very important secret Ikhwanites in the government had agreed to the scheme, Takieddin assured Yasir, even men who were trusted aides of Nasser. It was of vital importance that the plan be implemented before Nasser had a chance to crow over his "triumph" in getting the United Nations, and the United States, to force Israel, Britain, and France to withdraw from Egyptian territory, and before he had an opportunity to outlaw the Ikhwan. Yasir's mission in Prague, therefore, was to make contact with Soviet agents and transport back to Cairo certain forged documents that would "prove" Nasser to be a pawn of the CIA.

Yasir listened to Takieddin's tale with increasing wonderment. With all his old Ikhwanite instincts reawakened and his disillusionment with Nasser heightened by his discussions with al-Wazir and Khalef, he could only approve of the plot. The fact that he would be dealing with Russians doubly impressed him. Moreover, as Takieddin promised, he would be well rewarded for his work once the coup was completed. The Ikhwan government would immediately establish a Palestinian government-in-exile and he, Yasir, would certainly be appointed to a prestigious post. What's more, intimated

*Recent revelations by Miles Copeland, author of *The Game of Nations,* and others lend credence to suspicions that the CIA had a hand in the operations of the Egyptian government.

Takieddin, the government would have the full backing of the Soviet Union, which would bring its power to bear in the United Nations to help it achieve its objectives.

As it turned out, of course, none of this came to pass. Yasir left for Prague with his delegation of GUPS students—including al-Wazir and Khalef, the two outsiders—and a generous packet of various European currencies provided by Takieddin. He had been warned by Takieddin to tell no one about his assignment. But he was too excited about the Ikhwan plot, and his role in it, to keep it quiet. On the plane to Prague he shared the details with al-Wazir and Khalef, swearing them to secrecy.

In Prague the three attended a succession of meetings devoted to discussions of the virtues of socialism and its application to "emerging" or "third-world" nations. Yasir and his fellow Palestinian delegates lobbied vigorously to get a resolution passed that would "deny" the legality of the creation and existence of Israel. They were unsuccessful. One delegate, Rahim Jibril, recalls that they were not only unsuccessful but that, because of Yasir and his two new friends, the Palestinian delegation quickly became riddled with dissension.

"Yasir let al-Wazir and Khalef take over the delegation—these two refugees who were not even students," says Jibril, today a rich businessman in Beirut. "They acted as though they were the leaders, not Yasir, and their favorite discussion tactic was to threaten and intimidate. Yasir seemed to approve of this, and after a while none of the rest of us could even say a word. It was always the other two, screaming about the conditions in the camps, shouting of Zionist atrocities in Gaza. Every panel discussion we attended they would take over. Yasir would just sit there—he never spoke much himself—and nod his approval.

"At one meeting the chairman—I believe he was a Yugoslav—berated al-Wazir for his hysterical language. Yasir immediately stood up and protested. The chairman ordered him to sit down and be quiet. He refused. He turned to the rest of us and ordered us all to follow him in a walkout. He, al-Wazir, and Khalef marched out of the auditorium. A few others followed, but the rest of us did not. We were fed up with Yasir and his two henchmen. Later he was so furious he dismissed us from the delegation. But it didn't matter.

There was no effective delegation left anyway. It was just Yasir and his two friends, who knew nothing about debating procedures and cared less."

Yasir, al-Wazir, and Khalef waited expectantly throughout their first week in Prague to be contacted by Soviet agents. No attempts were made to contact them. Then came worrisome news. The students Yasir had dismissed from the delegation earlier in the week, including Jibril, had left to return to Cairo. On their arrival at Cairo airport they were arrested. Word of the arrests reached Yasir a few days later. It was then announced in Cairo that the Nasser regime had uncovered the Ikhwan plot. Many prominent Egyptians were arrested, including several close to Nasser himself and a number of functionaries in the intelligence service. Other collaborators, the news reports went on to say, were still being sought.

"When we were arrested," Jibril remembers, "we were accused of being part of the plot, and we were soon able to disprove that to the satisfaction of the police. It became clear to us during the interrogations we were subjected to that the police had information connecting the General Union of Palestinian Students to the plot, however. We were asked many questions about Yasir. The police did not know about al-Wazir and Khalef being with him in Prague, but we were forced into telling them. When the police let us go, it was obvious they intended to arrest them when they returned. We only learned later that the General Union had been set up by the Ikhwan plotters in the intelligence service, and that Yasir had been acting as a front man for them."

Jibril says that someone in GUPS sent a cable to Yasir in Prague warning him not to return to Cairo. He received the message the same day newspapers in Prague carried the Egyptian government's announcement of the discovery of the plot. The next afternoon he, al-Wazir, and Khalef were intercepted on their way into a convention meeting by two emissaries from the Egyptian embassy, who handed them an order instructing them to accompany them to the legation. Knowing what the order meant, al-Wazir punched one of the emissaries and the three fled back to their hotel room.

There they mulled over their options, which at first seemed to be only two. They could either return to Egypt or seek political asylum in Prague. Neither prospect appealed to them, yet because they were traveling on restricted passports they could go nowhere else. But then Khalef had an idea.

During the late 1940s and early 1950s many Arab Palestinians had left the Middle East and emigrated to West Germany to take advantage of the plentiful work opportunities created by Germany's postwar economic recovery. Among these were many members of the Khalef family who had settled in and around Stuttgart, where a large Palestinian community had developed. Khalef had several cousins at the University of Stuttgart, which similarly had a large Palestinian student population.

Khalef's idea was for the three of them to somehow get to Stuttgart. The question was—how? It was answered almost immediately.

One of the members of Yasir's inner circle when he founded the PSU was a young student from Gaza named Zuhayr al-Alami, a nephew of Musa al-Alami, the man who had been the Palestinian representative to the Arab League before Haj Amin's return to the Middle East after World War II. Zuhayr had initially been impressed by Yasir's denunciations of Haj Amin, with whom his uncle had vied for leadership of the nationalist movement. When GUPS was formed and Yasir installed as its chairman, Zuhayr went along with him. He was present the night of the impassioned discussion between Yasir, al-Wazir, and Khalef, and had voiced his approval of their condemnation of the "generation of disaster," which included his uncle, and their self-appointment as leaders of the "generation of revenge." He had sought and received election as a member of the Prague delegation and was one of the few who had remained loyal to Yasir when he split with the delegates who were displeased with al-Wazir's and Khalef's domination of the proceedings. He was still in Prague but was growing unhappy over the fact that Yasir, al-Wazir, and Khalef were excluding him from their discussions.

However, he had a passport that enabled him to travel freely. When Yasir mentioned this, Khalef saw it as the solution to their problem. Yasir still had the money given to him by Takieddin. They would use some of that to send Zuhayr al-Alami to Stuttgart with a letter for one of Khalef's cousins. The letter would instruct the cousin to send Zuhayr back to Prague with three valid Palestinian passports borrowed from students at the university. Using the passports, with their own photos pasted in, Yasir, al-Wazir, and Khalef would be able to travel to Stuttgart and find refuge from the Egyptian authorities.

They summoned al-Alami and put the plan to him. They told him of his probable arrest if he returned to Cairo at the end of the student convention. They also explained that Nasser had just outlawed the Ikhwan in Egypt and that the regime had obtained lists of all Ikhwan members and was making wholesale arrests, so that they all stood in jeopardy if they returned.

Eager to please Yasir and flattered that he had been taken once again into his confidence, Zuhayr agreed to the scheme. The next day he left for Stuttgart. Four days later he was back in Prague with three passports and tales of the existence of an active Palestinian nationalist organization in the German city. A day later Yasir and his three friends departed for Stuttgart.

23

From Germany to Kuwait

Yasir arrived in Stuttgart to find, as al-Alami had said, a strongly entrenched Palestinian movement. But it was one that was foreign to his sensibilities. Based on European socialist political ideals, its leaders scoffed at his Ikhwanite perceptions. Thus, rather than try to marry his own ideas to those of the local Palestinians, he and his three friends feverishly endeavored to discredit the local leadership and form a new group based on converts from the old.

"He and his friends made a few attempts to intimidate people," says Sabri Hadawi, then a student at Stuttgart University and today a banker in Frankfurt. "But it was a time when the movement was losing steam. The Suez war had demoralized everyone. The war was not even fought over Palestine, and afterwards the Palestinian cause was lost in all the other things that were going on. Most of us in Stuttgart were tired of it all, bored. Not even this fellow Yasir Arafat with his strong-arm henchmen and his secret ways could impress us."

Yasir lasted three months in Stuttgart. With the money from Takieddin running out, he and his three companions tried to raise funds among the local Palestinians in conjunction with their efforts to set up an independent liberation group, but had little success. Although there were many jobs to be had in Stuttgart's industry, they were afraid to apply for any lest their illegal presence in Germany be discovered. There was, moreover, the problem of the language barrier. The four spoke only Arabic; they understood a little English, having heard it spoken often in Cairo, but German confounded them. Rebuffed by most of the Palestinian community, then, but unable to communicate with anyone else but the Palestinians, low on funds, and generally uncomfortable in Germany's harsh late-winter climate, they began to fish about for a new opportunity.

One day in April of 1957 they found it. Yasir noticed an advertisement in the local Arab newspaper. Inserted by the government of Kuwait, the ad announced that Kuwait was seeking skilled construction workers to emigrate to the tiny Persian Gulf sheikhdom to help in the building boom that was going on there as a result of the country's petroleum riches. The ad promised all sorts of worker benefits previously unheard of in the Arab world, appealed particularly for displaced Palestinians with engineering degrees, offered free transportation and housing facilities, and, to sweeten the offer, promised that no questions would be asked about the applicants' personal backgrounds other than their academic qualifications.

When Yasir and his companions showed up the next day at the address given in the ad, they found a swarm of Palestinians there—recent graduates of Stuttgart University and those about to graduate—all eager for a free trip to warmer climes. In his years at the University of Cairo, Yasir had spent comparatively little time in its classrooms, and when the time came for his class to graduate he was woefully behind in his studies in the engineering program. Indeed, he would not have graduated. His arrangement with Takieddin had taken care of that, however. As chairman of GUPS and leader of the student delegation to Prague, it was imperative that Yasir be able to prove himself a bona fide student and graduate of Cairo. So, despite the paucity of his scholastic credits, at the behest of Takieddin he was issued an official degree in civil engineering. He had taken it with him to Prague, and was able to produce it at the Kuwaiti hiring hall in Stuttgart.

He was immediately hired and within a few days was issued the necessary travel documents, plane ticket, and expense money. With the special Kuwaiti passport he was told he would receive, he decided he could safely risk a visit to his family in Gaza on the way to Kuwait. He persuaded the Kuwaiti representative to authorize the detour, and his air ticket was routed via Cairo.

Khalil al-Wazir and Salah Khalef were not so lucky. Lacking any academic credentials, they were not hired. But Zuhayr al-Alami was. The four discussed the problem just before Yasir's departure. They agreed that once Yasir arrived in Kuwait he would scout opportunities and as soon as possible arrange for Khalil and Salah to join him and Zuhayr. In the meantime, they would communicate by letter; Khalil and Salah would remain in Stuttgart and continue to try to organize a Stuttgart student liberation group based on Ikhwan principles.

Yasir and Zuhayr left Stuttgart the morning of May 16, 1957, on a flight to Cairo. By now Zuhayr was a full-fledged member of the four-man "generation of revenge." He had been told of the other three's involvement in the Egyptian intelligence plot and was wholeheartedly committed to a future of radical activism on behalf of the Arafat-conceived new-style liberationism. Zuhayr had also managed to persuade the Kuwaiti recruiters to give him a side trip to Gaza, and when he and Yasir arrived at Cairo airport, they were passed through the immigration stalls without more than a perfunctory glance at their Kuwaiti passports.

They did not linger in Cairo, but headed straight for Gaza. The Israelis had only recently evacuated Sinai, and Egypt had not yet been able to restore full transport service to the Gaza Strip. Yasir and Zuhayr had to wait for three days in Port Said before they could arrange to get on a bus to Gaza. Along the route they saw graphic evidence of the Israeli military achievement of six months before—hundreds of charred and wrecked Egyptian tanks and other armored vehicles. The sight enraged them, and Yasir spent much of the trip muttering Arabic obscenities at both the Egyptians and the Israelis.

The scene in Gaza was even more depressing. Not only was the city scarred and battered, the population was depressed and demoralized. Yasir visited his father, expecting to find a man consumed with vengeance. What he found was a man defeated, his voice a steady lament of resignation. What was even more embittering to Yasir was the fact that Abdul even spoke kindly, almost wondrously, of the Israelis who had occupied Gaza for five months.

With the exception of Fathi, his younger brother, all the other members of the family were similarly resigned. Zaeed and Nasr had had enough of the conflict, and when Yasir tried to arouse them they refused to listen, wishing only to help their father resurrect his ruined business and lead peaceful lives under the restored Egyptian administration. Zaeed urged Yasir to give up his liberationist dream; the time had come, he said, to recognize reality and get on with life and forget the idea of annihilating the Jews. "We have seen them," Zaeed declared, "we have lived among them. They are too powerful, we will never overcome them." Yasir spat on his brother.

After a week in Gaza, Yasir and Zuhayr made their way back to Cairo. Before leaving for Kuwait they made an ill-advised secret visit to the GUPS office near the university and were surprised to find it still functioning. They encountered several of their student acquaintances, and Yasir was angered to learn that one of his former enemies from the Prague trip had been named to the chairmanship of the organization. "The fellow," says Rahim Jibril, "had purged the union of all its Arafat followers and had put it directly at the service of the Egyptians. He also, in line with Egyptian policy, made any further Ikhwan activity illegal. He brought the union back to the policies of the Mufti, and when Yasir came by and found out about it he was outraged. He went looking for the new chairman, whose name was Nissim Qarnaubi, and I'm sure he had it in his mind to kill him. But he never got a chance. One of Qarnaubi's followers reported to the police that Yasir was back. The police came round looking for him. Now, I had no great love for Yasir, but I didn't want to see him arrested. So the next time he came to the office I intercepted him and warned him that the police were waiting inside. He said, 'Is Qarnaubi in there?' I told him yes. 'Then I will go in and kill him,' he said. 'That is something worth being arrested for.' And he would have gone in, except this fellow he had with him, Zuhayr al-Alami, would not let him. Zuhayr demanded they leave, and finally Yasir agreed. But before they left, Yasir pulled out a wad of money and waved it in my face. He said it was mine if I would kill Nissim Qarnaubi before the night was over. He said he would meet me the next day at a certain place, and that if I brought Qarnaubi's severed hand with me, he would give me all the money. The hand would be proof that Qarnaubi was dead. It was very recognizable to all of us, for it had two missing fingers. But I said no, I could not do such a thing. So they left, and as far as I know the police never found him."

They didn't find Yasir because the next day he and Zuhayr left Cairo for Kuwait. The sheikhdom, situated at the top of the Persian Gulf and squeezed between Iraq and Saudi Arabia, was all desert except for the port town, also called Kuwait. It was here that they arrived after a plane ride to Baghdad, a truck journey to Basra in southern Iraq, and a two-day boat trip through the stifling midsummer heat of the Persian Gulf.

They found Kuwait city a dust-choked maze of building projects, all in their beginning stages, creeping from the edge of the original town into the desert itself. The city was crowded with Palestinians, and living conditions were crude. Yasir and Zuhayr reported to the Ministry of Public Works and were immediately assigned jobs and living quarters—a tent overlooking a beach south of the city. "We might as well be at Nuseirat," Yasir commented wryly, referring to a refugee camp near the beach in Gaza.

Yasir's job was in the Department of Water Supply, and his principal function was to interpret engineering diagrams submitted to the Public Works Ministry by private foreign companies making bids for construction contracts. He soon came to the realization that with all the private work being let out he could do better for himself by starting his own contracting company. Using the balance of the expense money he had been given in Germany to get to Kuwait, he purchased a third-hand American-made pickup truck, gave it a new coat of paint, lettered in Arabic on its side doors "The Free Palestine Construction Company, Y. Arafat, Proprietor," and announced himself in business. His first bid was on the plumbing for a new block of apartments to be built near the beach to house Palestinian workers. Since he still held on to his job in the Department of Water Supply, it was his task to study all the bids and recommend the awarding of the contract for the plumbing project. The contract went to the Free Palestine Construction Company.

In order to fulfill the contract, Yasir had to hire workers. He had received two or three letters from Khalil al-Wazir in Stuttgart telling of progress in organizing a group there, but expressing a desire still to join Yasir in Kuwait. Yasir went to his superiors in the Ministry of Public Works and put in applications for Khalil and Salah to be brought to Kuwait; jobs would be guaranteed them by the Free Palestine Construction Company. In the meantime, he searched the local Palestinian community for four or five workers to sign on with his fledgling company. But he could find no one. There were many more jobs in Kuwait than there were workers to fill them, and Yasir would have to pay a premium to draw workers away from other jobs. So he took to stalking new arrivals off the boats at the port, and in this way got his first complement of laborers.

One of them was a young Palestinian named Faruq al-Qadumi, a Nazarene who had been languishing in a refugee camp at Deraa,

Syria, since 1949. Al-Qadumi had been a member of a Syrian-sponsored commando unit that had made several raids into Israel the year before. He brimmed with liberationist fervor and was immediately drawn by Yasir's nationalist intensity.

Al-Qadumi began work for Yasir as a pipe fitter on the plumbing project. Over the next few months the Free Palestine Construction Company received several more assignments, and Zuhayr al-Alami left his job at the Ministry of Health to join Yasir and Faruq.

24

Fatah

It was now the beginning of 1958. The Arab world's concern for the Palestinian question had thoroughly dissolved in the wake of the Suez war. Except on those occasions when an Arab leader such as Nasser invoked the plight of the refugees to make propaganda capital, little was thought of, and less achieved, on behalf of Palestinian nationalism.

Jordan had much of what would have been an Arab Palestinian state under the 1947 partition resolution—the West Bank—within its control, and for the most part Jordanian Palestinians seemed content with their lot. Egypt had Gaza and, although the mood there was not as docile as in the West Bank, there was little initiative left among its Palestinian populace to attempt to bring about a change in the status quo.

After the 1956 war the major Arab countries became involved in a fresh round of power struggles among themselves. Nasser used the popularity he had won by nationalizing the Suez Canal and then forcing the withdrawal of French, British, and Israeli forces from Egyptian territory to try to advance his vision of a unified Arab world with himself at the helm. He achieved this in part with Syria in 1958, forming what the two countries called the United Arab Republic. Nasser had earlier proclaimed the political ideology of Egypt to be "Arab socialism" and had established the Arab Socialist Union as the country's only valid political party. In Syria the Baath party, representing a looser type of pan-Arab Marxist socialism, was on its way to power, as it was in Iraq. The Egypt-Syria union would turn out to be short-lived as the Baathists, finding the Egyptian brand of socialism too parochial and reactionary, would themselves attempt to take over from Nasser as the dominant power in the Arab world.

Nasser preached reform of the entire Arab world on the model of his version of Arab socialism. Implicit in his reformist philosophy was condemnation of the old-style Arab monarchies represented by such nations as Jordan, Yemen, and Saudi Arabia. Egypt therefore supported revolutionary movements in these countries, and eventually committed a large force in Yemen to fight against royalist troops supplied and reinforced by Saudi Arabia. Moreover, it sponsored attempts to depose the Hashemite monarchy of Jordan and endeavored to sow civil strife elsewhere.

The only country that remained relatively unaffected by the increasing turmoil was Kuwait. Ironically, it was here that the most violent expression of Arab—especially Arab Palestinian—frustration was born.

By mid-1958 Yasir Arafat was well ensconced in Kuwait, the master of a thriving business and an increasingly important bureaucrat as well. Educated Palestinians continued to flow into the country, and soon he was at the center of an expanding circle of friends sympathetic to his ideas and drawn to his deepening confidence in them. Included among these friends, aside from Zuhayr al-Alami and Faruq al-Qudami, were Muhammad Yusef an-Najjar and Kamal Adwan, both originally from Jerusalem. With the exception of al-Alami, all had at one time or another since 1948 been residents of refugee camps and members of embryonic guerrilla groups. Each was in his mid-twenties and each now worked, either full or part time, for Yasir's construction company.

Late in 1958 Yasir managed to pull the strings necessary to obtain entry permits for Khalil al-Wazir and Salah Khalef, still in Stuttgart. Al-Wazir arrived in Kuwait in February of 1959. Khalef was taken ill at the last moment and was unable to make the trip, so in his place al-Wazir brought a friend he had made in the German city, Khalid al-Hassan. Al-Hassan was a student at the University of Stuttgart, although he was already in his late thirties, and was the leader of a Palestinian student association that had been organized after Yasir left.

Arafat says that he was astonished at the change he noticed in the personality of his friend Khalil al-Wazir. Previously mercurial and hotheaded, he had become even-tempered and deliberate. It was obvious that Khalil had come under the strong influence of the newcomer, al-Hassan, who, Arafat recalls, was an intellectual, spoke German fluently, and was measured and remote in manner.

According to Salmon Yusef, who was briefly a member of the Arafat circle in Kuwait, Yasir greeted the unexpected arrival of al-Hassan with a great deal of resentment. "He was expecting Salah Khalef, and al-Hassan arrives instead. He sees the influence al-Hassan has on Khalil and he doesn't like it. Yasir is used to being the leader, the idea man, and here comes this stranger Khalil is always praising, and Yasir does not like it, he is jealous. Besides that, al-Hassan is not very impressed with Yasir. Khalil had obviously told al-Hassan a great deal about Yasir and—well, you know how expectations come about. He probably arrived expecting to find Yasir some sort of heroic figure. Instead, Yasir stays quiet, does not seem pleased that al-Hassan has come, sees him as a threat to his own influence.

"But Khalid al-Hassan ignores this, and soon he has us all excited by his ideas. He has become very important in Germany, you see. He is friendly with many Algerian revolutionaries there. He has even been to Algeria and circulated in the FLN underground. He has allied the Palestinian students in Stuttgart with the Algerian students, and he has become a friend of Muhammad Khaidar, one of the FLN leaders.

"Khalil al-Wazir confirms all this—in fact, Khalil knows Khaidar too. They both talk to us a lot about the FLN and the revolutionary struggle against the French in Algeria. They say the Algerians have not waited around for years and years like us Palestinians, waiting for other Arab countries to liberate Algeria. They are doing it themselves. They do it through well-thought-out political principles and highly disciplined guerrilla action. And they do it by winning over the people of Algeria to their cause. It is the first principle of any revolutionary liberation movement, they say, to win over the native people and then organize them into revolutionary cells.

"We have these meetings in the office of Yasir's company every night. Yasir disagrees with what Khalid al-Hassan says. He is still a believer in the Ikhwan principles—terrorism, sabotage, assassination. Yes, yes, Khalid says, but that is why the Ikhwan failed in Egypt. That is all they did. They did not organize the people, though. Instead, they made the people afraid. It was the same with the Haj Aminists in Palestine. They were very good at killing Arabs who disagreed with them, but they were no good at motivating Arabs into action.

"Khalid said many things that were hard for Yasir to swallow. Ah, they were hard for all of us. We had been raised on Ikhwanism, on Haj Aminism, and here he was telling us it was all useless. If Palestine is to be liberated, it will be done by Arabs who follow modern revolutionary principles. He pointed to China, to Vietnam, to Algeria. These are modern revolutions. And who are the people who keep us from being free? The Zionists, who occupy half our land. And the Jordanians and Egyptians, who occupy the other half. These are our French. And look what the Vietnamese did to the French! Look what the Algerians are doing to their French occupiers! Palestinians must do as the Vietnamese and Algerians."

Yusef, a Syrian who today is employed as a diplomatic representative of the Kuwaiti government, says that Yasir continued to resist al-Hassan's arguments until a split in loyalties developed between those in the circle who were swayed by the force of al-Hassan's personality and logic and those who remained devoted to Yasir—mainly because he was their source of employment.

"But the issue was resolved a month or so later when Salah Khalef arrived from Germany. He too had become very much a follower of al-Hassan and his Algerian theory. When Yasir saw this, he was at first dismayed and refused to talk to Salah. But Salah had brought with him many Algerian FLN pamphlets. Yasir started to read them, and soon he began not to argue with Khalid so much. Khalid was older, and he was more of an intellectual than a doer of deeds. Yasir was still one who would not hesitate to pick up a gun and use it against an enemy. We all admired him for that, and we admired Khalid for his mind. Khalil al-Wazir made it clear to Yasir that although he admired and followed Khalid, he did not wish to admire Yasir any less, or follow him any less. Then Salah told him the same thing. He said to Yasir, 'Give up Kuwait, come back to Germany, that is where the real action of Palestinian liberation is happening.' But Yasir did not have good memories of Germany. And that is how Fatah started.

"It was the middle of the summer. Khalid and Khalil's temporary visas were about to run out, and they had to return to Germany.

Khalid was saying how it would be good to do something now, to create a link between his followers in Stuttgart and Yasir's in Kuwait, to make a new Palestinian liberation front based on FLN principles. He said he had been promised the help of the FLN. Yasir agreed, and then everyone agreed. We all wanted to be a part of it. There were about twenty of us then, but it was Yasir, Khalid al-Hassan, Khalil al-Wazir, and Salah Khalef who were the most enthusiastic among us. Faruq al-Qadumi, Muhammad Yusef, and Zuhayr al-Alami were also eager. The rest of us—well, I would say we simply went along with it.

"We were all living in tents near the beach, and the night before Khalid and Khalil were to leave we had a farewell party at the beach. We made a sacred covenant between us. Yasir had been talking a long time about the generation of revenge, and he wanted to call our group by that name. But Khalid said no, it was childish, it was an Ikhwan childishness that would not be taken seriously. He wanted something more dignified, like 'Front for the Liberation of Palestine.' Then someone else said 'Front for the Conquest of Our Palestinian Homeland.' The word 'conquest' caught on, but Khalid thought it would be misleading, for what we wanted was revolution and liberation, not conquest. Conquest was what foreign powers engaged in.

"We went on and on, toying with names, but nothing sounded quite right. Still, the word 'conquest' kept coming back, '*fatah.*' It was a word that meant a great deal to every Arab, Yasir said, for it symbolized the golden age of Islam. Then someone—I believe it was Salah Khalef—figured out that by reversing the word we would have '*hataf.*' *Hataf* would be the Arabic shorthand for *Harakat at-Tahrir al-Falastin,* which meant 'Movement for the Liberation of Palestine.' So there it was. Our group would be Hataf, but we would reverse it to Fatah.

"I don't mean to make it sound as though it was as simple as that, however. We called ourselves by several names during the next few months. It was really Khalid al-Hassan who popularized the word when he went back to Germany. It caught on among the students at Stuttgart, and Stuttgart was the place the Fatah consciousness first developed in any organized way."

25

Our Palestine

The infant Fatah was in most ways no different than the dozens of new younger-generation liberation groups that sprang up after the Suez war throughout the Palestinian diaspora. Rhetoric was its only weapon at a time when post-Suez Palestinian apathy and demoralization made rhetoric powerless. Like other groups, Fatah would most likely have died aborning. However, under the ideological guidance of Khalid al-Hassan it sprinkled its initial rhetoric with a concept that was new and unfamiliar to Palestinians, who for years had labored under the expectation that their homeland would be regained through the efforts of a unified confederation of Arab nations. The core of the concept was that the liberation of Palestine was being delayed by the trust most Palestinians had been programmed to place in the promises of non-Palestinian Arab leaders such as Nasser. The hope that Palestine could be wrested away from the Jews by surrounding Arab nations had been proved false by the Suez fiasco. The time had come for all Palestinians to recognize that the recovery of their land was primarily a Palestinian affair and could no longer be entrusted to the Arab states.

In a time when dozens of countries the world over were engaged in internal revolutionary struggles and the words "liberation" and "self-determination" were becoming increasingly popular slogans uttered to defend the justice of those struggles, the idea that Palestinians themselves were in the end the ones responsible for their own destiny soon caught on among the younger generation. The notion gave the rhetoric of the early Fatah an appeal, particularly among students throughout the diaspora, that was lacking in that of other groups and provided it with the sustenance it would need to survive.

Yasir Arafat likes to credit himself for the inspiration behind the new concept, but most of those who have been involved with Fatah from its beginnings, and who are willing to talk about it, claim that the credit belongs primarily to Khalid al-Hassan and secondly to Khalil al-Wazir, both of whom returned to Stuttgart from Kuwait with the intention of allying their embryonic Fatah group to the veteran and much better organized Algerian liberation movement. Yasir remained basically a fund raiser for the group, using his official position in the Kuwaiti government to pry financial contributions from the country's immensely rich governing family.

At this task he was rather successful, recalls Omar al-Hatab, an early member of Fatah who was wounded in a guerrilla action in 1969 and now recruits for Fatah in the refugee camps of Lebanon. "Yasir was the financial genius in those first years," says al-Hatab. "He made it more or less an official practice to get contributions to the organization from those who came to him seeking construction contracts. It soon became known that to get approval for a contract a company would have to donate a certain percentage of the contract's worth to the Palestine Liberation Committee, which is what we were calling Fatah back there in the beginning. He had got many of the people who worked in the ministry to go along with him on the scheme, which wasn't difficult since most were Palestinians.

"I would say that in that first year, 1959, Yasir raised about twenty thousand English pounds. But that is not all he did. He also recruited more people to the committee, including myself. Our principal task was to raise money also, through our jobs in the government. A friend of mine who worked in the Finance Ministry was a friend of two of the sons of the emir of Kuwait. He joined us, and he got the sons to persuade their father to give money to the committee to finance a newspaper Yasir wanted to publish."

The newspaper—actually a four-page handbill called *Falastinuna* (Our Palestine)—began printing in the fall of 1959, with Yasir the main contributor. It featured "eyewitness" stories by Palestinians arriving in Kuwait about alleged atrocities committed against Arabs by the Israelis during the 1956 war and unsigned editorials written by Yasir which developed the idea of Palestinians effecting their own national liberation.

Al-Hatab says that the paper was originally meant only for the Palestinian community of Kuwait, but that it was such a success and brought such a large influx of new recruits into the organization that

Yasir soon devised a plan to distribute it through the refugee camps in the northern Arab countries.

"Yasir went to Beirut about six months after the paper was publishing. He toured the camps and set up a distribution system. While he was there, he met with Khalid al-Hassan and Salah Khalef, who had come down from Germany. They were very impressed with the paper and were pleased to see how Yasir had come around to preaching Khalid's ideas. They were also impressed with the money Yasir had raised. In those days Yasir was not the frugal man he is today. When he went to Beirut he stayed at the St. Georges Hotel, and when the others came in from Germany he paid for them to stay there too—all out of the money from Kuwait.

"They were there for about three weeks, exchanging news about what they were each achieving in Germany and Kuwait. It was a very important three weeks, for it was then that they really organized themselves more formally into Fatah. Khalil al-Wazir joined them, coming from Algeria, where he had been working underground with the FLN. He told of how Algerian freedom fighters had been going to China for training and said that the FLN was arranging to send him. Yasir and Salah were very enthusiastic about this, and they asked Khalil to try to arrange for them to go with him.

"It was in Beirut that summer—the summer of 1960—that we formally became Fatah. Yasir and the others agreed that we would use that name only from then on. We would have three divisions. One in Germany, with Khalid and Salah in charge. One in Algeria, with Khalil in charge. And one in Kuwait, with Yasir in charge. Yasir's main job was to continue raising money, publishing the paper, and organizing Fatah cells in the camps. Khalid was to work on organizing cells in Europe, and Khalil's responsibility was to do the same in Algeria, which had many Palestinians living there. He had said that the FLN leaders would help our cause once they won their revolution.

"Muhammad Yusef, Faruq al-Qadumi, Kamal Adwan, and Zuhayr al-Alami came to Beirut sometime during that period and joined Yasir and the others. They all looked at each other and said, 'Here we are, we are the leadership, it is now or never that we must decide what we are to do.' Khalil told of how the FLN operated, using the principle of collective leadership they had learned from the

Chinese. So the eight of them decided that they would be the collective leadership of Fatah."

Following the Beirut meeting, the founder-leaders of Fatah dispersed to their various territories. They did not anticipate the difficulties of exercising collective leadership when separated by distances of thousands of miles, however, and during the next two years Fatah came close to foundering as a result of its confused direction. According to most of those familiar with the situation, it was only the industry of Yasir that kept the nascent movement alive. After the first few issues of *Our Palestine* were published, its Fatah message began to wear thin. Yasir received reports of diminishing interest in the paper from the camps of the north. In Kuwait as well, after the first rush of interest, enthusiasm for the Fatah cause lessened. Nevertheless, Yasir, through his control of the paper, was gradually becoming known throughout the camp world. He decided that to revive interest in the new movement he should use his modest notoriety to bring the Fatah message home in a more direct way. Accordingly, he set off late in 1961 on a personal tour of the camps in an effort to drum up enthusiasm among those he felt would be the most likely prospects for recruitment to Fatah—the refugees.

With him, according to al-Hatab, went Zuhayr al-Alami, Kamal Adwan, and Faruq al-Qadumi. With a forged passport easily obtained from sympathizers in Kuwait's Foreign Ministry, Yasir traveled under the alias of Dr. Muhammad Fawzi, representing himself and his fellow travelers as a medical team on a grant from the Kuwaiti government to inspect health conditions in the camps.

Arafat insists today it was this tour that burned into his soul the obsession with winning back Palestine from the Israelis. "I have been accused of being a political dilettante before I went on that journey," he told me. "And it is true, I *was* such a dilettante. I had been in a few of the camps in Gaza, a few in Lebanon, but I had never spent time in any of them, had never really got to know the degradation and humiliation so many of my people were forced to endure because of the Zionists. It is true, I was committed to liberation, but my direction was not certain. It only became certain during that trip, when I myself experienced the atrocity of the camps. It made no difference to me what logic the Jews used to justify the presence of Israel. It made no difference to me what the Jews had suffered in

Europe. What I saw was the Jews doing to us what the Nazis had done to them. And I decided then that I must devote my life, every ounce of energy and initiative I possessed, to rectifying the situation. It is all that has mattered to me ever since."

From an organizational point of view, the tour was only moderately successful. Yasir did not succeed in putting together a single Fatah cell in any of the camps he visited, undoubtedly because he left no one in his wake to do the actual organizing. He did, however, manage to introduce what might be called a Fatah consciousness within the refugee community, so that when he returned to Kuwait and began writing for *Our Palestine* again, his exhortations were more readily received than before.

Early in 1962, with the help of further funds raised through his Public Works office, Yasir expanded *Our Palestine* into a forty-eight-page monthly. Because Beirut had better printing facilities than Kuwait, he decided to have the publication printed there, and throughout 1962 and into 1963 he commuted once a month to the Lebanese capital to deliver the magazine's copy.

With the transformation of *Our Palestine* into an enlarged, better distributed, and more professional-looking publication, Fatah began to gain an image—first in the Arab world and then among concentrations of Palestinians abroad—of responsible spokesmanship for the new Palestine nationalism. The magazine still contained the basic message of Palestinian responsibility for the liberation of Palestine, plus virulent articles against what their authors perceived as the evils of Zionism, but on Khalid al-Hassan's insistence it also opened its pages to more scholarly and reflective essays by Arab intellectuals on the fine points of colonialism and imperialism and the legality of Arab revolutionary impulses.

On one of his trips to Beirut in 1962, Yasir met again with all but one of his Fatah co-founders; Faruq al-Qadumi was the only one missing. Yasir, after his tour of the camps, had renounced any interest in the good life, so this time they convened not in the swank St. Georges Hotel but in a tin-roofed shanty in Beirut's teeming Dekwaneh refugee camp.

The meeting was dominated by the reports of Khalid al-Hassan and Khalil al-Wazir. Al-Hassan told of the progress he was making in converting Stuttgart's revived Palestine Student Association to

Fatah principles. The association had become affiliated with the General Union of Palestinian Students in Cairo—the same GUPS which Yasir had headed back in 1956. The Nasser regime had cleansed the union of its Ikhwan and other anti-Nasser elements and was now funding and otherwise controlling it for the purpose of creating a network of pro-Nasser Palestinian student organizations throughout the Arab world and Europe. Egyptian influence, al-Hassan reported, still held sway in the Stuttgart association. But he had organized a large Fatah cell within it, plus cells in similar student associations at other universities in Germany and Austria. The FLN struggle in Algeria was rapidly approaching a successful climax. He predicted that once the Algerian triumph was complete, many of the Palestinian students of Europe who supported the FLN would be instantly transformed into followers of Fatah, since he had modeled his Fatah cells on the FLN's example. He further declared that *Our Palestine* was now reaching Europe and urged Yasir to sharpen its pro-FLN orientation.

Khalil al-Wazir brought news of events within Algeria itself. He spoke glowingly of the achievements of FLN guerrilla tactics, in which he had become quite expert, and told of how the French were on the verge of collapsing and evacuating the country. He boasted that he had become friendly with Ahmed Ben Bella, the FLN's top man, and had elicited promises from Ben Bella and other leading FLNists to provide full-scale Algerian support for Fatah once a revolutionary government was installed in Algiers.

Present at the meeting was Hassan al-Sharif, the son of one of the camp's elder leaders and a typesetter at the plant that printed *Our Palestine*. "Yasir was very quiet throughout," he recalls. "Even though everyone had agreed on collective leadership, there was little doubt in my mind that Yasir was the leader among leaders. He said little while all the others made their grandiose predictions. Once in a while he would interject a disagreement—he was not as enthusiastic about tying Fatah to the FLN as the others were. You could sense that the others were always worried about what Yasir was thinking. As they talked, they were always looking at him out of the side of their eyes in a worried way. This, I later found out, was because Yasir controlled the purse strings. He had opened a bank account in Beirut, and I understood it contained about fifty thousand pounds. He had got all this money in Kuwait, and it was he and only he who could sign the checks. Khalil was talking about opening a Fatah recruiting office in Algiers, and he wanted something like ten or fifteen thousand pounds from Yasir to do it. Yasir said no, he said do as we do in Kuwait, raise the money from the Algerians. There were many arguments about money, and I think Yasir enjoyed the power he held over the others on money matters. Of all the leaders he was the most conservative. What I mean is, his conservative attitude toward money created a conservative attitude toward other things, like policy and strategy. He believed the most important thing at that time was establishing *Our Palestine* and disseminating it as widely as possible.

Yasir's cautious approach was overwhelmed by events, however. Shortly after the Beirut meeting France gave up Algeria and the FLN revolutionaries took over the government. Immediately, Khalil al-Wazir returned to Beirut with the news that Ben Bella and the other FLN leaders wanted to see all the founders of Fatah in Algiers.

The eight made the trip in December of 1962 and were received by Ben Bella on Christmas Eve. Yasir was deeply impressed by the Algerian, who had just decreed Arabic to be the official language of the country. He listened to Ben Bella tell of the decade-long struggle of the FLN. Ben Bella related stirring tales of the sacrifices that had been made by Algerian freedom fighters and warned the eight that the struggle to liberate Palestine would be a long and arduous one. "But you must do it yourselves," he cautioned. "Seek all the help you can get from other nations, both Arab and non-Arab, but make no alliances and, in the end, trust only yourselves. To achieve an independent Arab Palestine, you must yourselves be independent."

Ben Bella made good on his promises to Khalil al-Wazir. At Yasir's request he authorized the setting up of a Fatah office in Algiers through which all Palestinians in Algeria would have to register to receive work permits; the permits would be issued only to those who pledged to donate a percentage of their salary to the Palestine Liberation Movement. The monies received would go toward setting up guerrilla training camps, to which Khalid al-Hassan would send trainees from among his burgeoning student following in Germany and Austria. In the meantime, Ben Bella said, "It is imperative that those of you who are serious about your duty to liberate Palestine go to China. It is the Chinese who made our revolution possible. They will make yours possible as well. We will arrange it."

Yasir returned to Kuwait fully converted to the FLN approach that al-Hassan had been promoting for so long. He immediately filled the pages of *Our Palestine* with articles singing the praises of the Algerian revolution and excerpts from the writings of Frantz Fanon, the black psychologist whose political treatises—particularly his book *The Wretched of the Earth,* which promoted violence as a cleansing force for the oppressed and colonized people of the earth —provided much of the philosophical inspiration for the FLN cause. Indeed, the romantic adulation of violence, which in Fanon's words "frees the native from his inferiority complex, from his despair and inaction," soon became the chief feature of *Our Palestine.*

In April of 1963 word came to Yasir from Algiers that the Chinese would welcome a visit from two representatives of Fatah. A hurried meeting of the founders was called in Beirut. Khalid al-Hassan was unable to get there from Germany in time, but the other seven met, again at the Dekwaneh camp, to vote on who should go. There was no question that one member of the delegation should be Khalil al-Wazir; he, after all, had initiated Algerian interest in Fatah and was still the group's primary link to the FLN. Al-Hassan had indicated by mail that he would like to be the other member, since his interest in Chinese revolutionism preceded that of the other founders of Fatah. But Yasir, who continued to think of Khalid as an intellectual rather than a potential guerrilla fighter, lobbied against al-Hassan's selection and declared that he should go. He argued that as the moving force behind *Our Palestine,* he would be able to print his observations of China and that such observations would be more valuable to the cause than anything al-Hassan could contribute. Yasir got the vote.

He and Khalil immediately flew to Algiers. There they joined a delegation of second-string FLNists—mostly Algerian college teachers being sent to China on a cultural exchange program—and took off for Peking. According to Said Hammami, today a spokesman for the Palestine Liberation Organization, they were dismayed at the reception they received on their arrival. They were met by functionaries of the Chinese cultural program who mistook them for members of the FLN. Thereafter during their two-week stay they had little to do but attend lectures on the communist revolution in China and visit agricultural communes. None of their guides understood Arabic, and their scholarly Algerian traveling companions, who did, had scant interest in Palestinian matters. They finally managed to convince their guides that they were in China on business other than that having to do with Algerian-Chinese relations. They demanded interviews with Mao Tse-tung, Chou En-lai, and other leaders of the revolution, threatening to expose the Chinese affront to the Palestinian revolution on their return to the Middle East if such interviews were not granted. They got to see none of the leaders but were eventually ushered into the presence of a Chinese army officer who had gained some fame as a guerrilla fighter during the revolution. Through an interpreter he regaled them with tales of Chinese guerrilla exploits. They made little sense to the two Palestinians, and they left China bitterly disillusioned by the indifferent reception they had received.

They were determined not to let the nature of their stay in China become known, however. On returning to Beirut in May of 1963, Yasir began to publish articles in *Our Palestine* glorifying China and claiming that in secret interviews with Mao, Chou, and others China had given its official support and approval of the Fatah cause. Drawing more on conventional revolutionary literature than on anything he had learned in his nonexistent audiences with the Chinese leaders, he wrote that the Chinese had laid out for him and Khalil a vital revolutionary scenario for the liberation of Palestine. The scenario called first for the establishment of a consolidated leadership, which, Yasir claimed, the revolution already possessed in the form of the collectively operating founders of Fatah. The next step was for the leadership to win the Palestinian people's confidence in it, to enlighten the people about their oppression, and to inspire and incite them to "revenge." The third step was to gain control of all the organizations and institutions that served the people so as to create a national discipline and organization. The climactic step was to organize and arm the people, and to begin the military struggle against the oppressor—in this case Israel, primarily, but also against anyone else who might stand in the way.

The key to the implementation of the scenario, Yasir claimed he was told by Mao, would be the occurrence of an imperialist event that would enable the revolutionary leadership to invoke the national emotions necessary to commence the process of revolutionary revenge. He was unaware of it, but such an event was then in its germinating stages, and it would provide the motive power for Yasir's and Fatah's leap into prominence in the Arab world.

26

The Palestine Liberation Organization

The event was the unilateral diversion by Israel of the upper waters of the Jordan River. Arafat himself credits the Israeli venture as being the catalyst of his and Fatah's ascendancy in the Arab world.

"The timing could not have been more perfect," he says. "We had made some progress in our attempts to indoctrinate our people in the necessity of a military solution to the problem of our disfranchisement, but it continued to be difficult. The Zionists didn't know about us then, they had no conception of revolutionary policies, so they could have no anticipation of the consequences of their illegal action. They were worried about how their action would be interpreted in the United Nations, yes, but in their typical arrogance they went ahead anyway, on the theory that once the diversion was accomplished the world would accept it, despite its illegality, just as the world accepted the existence of the illegal Zionist state.

"But it was precisely that arrogance that blinded them to the true consequences of their action. It would be accurate to say that everything that has happened in the Middle East in the last twelve years stems from the Jordan diversion project. The Israeli action gave us in the liberation movement a specific focus around which to build our cause. It put flesh on the skeleton of our ideology. It gave us the power and influence we had been struggling to achieve. It gave us a specific strategy and tactical approach that we could shape to our needs. But most important, it settled the issue once and for all—that is, that there would never be peace in the Middle East until the Palestinian people were given their rights, as individuals and as a nation."

The Jordan River diversion project had been secretly planned by Israel for several years, ever since the neighboring Arab nations had refused to join in a joint water management plan with the Jewish state. It consisted of a scheme whereby water from the upper Jordan at the Sea of Galilee, which was in Israeli territory, would be dammed and fed by canal into the Negev desert for irrigation purposes. News of the plan leaked into the Arab world in 1963, provoking a storm of protest. The diversion, it was claimed, would dry up the lower Jordan, which flowed through the territory of the kingdom of Jordan and was the source of the Jordan Valley's fertility. The valley's rich and varied agricultural base, the lifeblood of the Jordanian kingdom's fragile economy, would be destroyed.

The leaders of the major Arab states saw in the diversion project a timely anti-Israel propaganda vehicle. Although it would be excessively cynical to suggest that they used the issue solely as a device in their own respective struggles to gain the leadership of the Arab world, that they used it at least partially for that purpose was readily apparent at the time. The 1958 union between Egypt and Syria had broken up in 1961 in the face of Nasser's tendency to dictate Syrian policy, and feelings between the two countries were in a rising spiral of distrust and resentment, sharpened only shortly before when a Syrian military coup had solidified Baathist power in Damascus and attempted to rid the country of all Nasserist elements left over from the Syro-Egyptian union. The new Baathist leaders made it clear that they were not content with Egypt's claim that it possessed the answer to Arab unity, and set out on a course to discredit Nasser and take the unity movement down a more radical road.

While the Arab states argued the illegality of the Israeli diversion project, Arafat used it, in the pages of *Our Palestine,* to incite the Arab world to war. "This is what he means when he says the diversion plan gave Fatah its strategy," remarked Tewfik Khuri, who helped Yasir get out *Our Palestine* and subsequently became its editor. "Yasir and the others had been sustaining the position that the liberation was primarily a Palestinian business. But they knew Palestinians could not do it alone—we were too scattered and we had no means. What we had to do was force the Arab states who kept claiming they were our surrogates but who did nothing but talk, we had to force them to go to war. That became the strategy from 1963 onward. And it worked brilliantly. By 1967 we had forced the Arab states into a war. Although the Arab states lost, Israel was not the winner. We were the real winners, for the war put our cause before the world. That was Yasir's genius, and that is why he became the foremost leader of the liberation movement. By creating this strategy, he created the movement."

In 1959 Nasser, seeking to consolidate his hold over the Arab world, had characterized the community of Palestinian refugees as "the Palestine entity." This was his way of acknowledging the legitimacy of Palestinian nationalism. By coining the phrase and having it identified with him, he became the de facto chief proponent of the Palestinian cause, which at that time was still stumbling aimlessly through the hangover of Haj Aminism and post-Suez helplessness. He had maintained his symbolic leadership of the Palestinian cause up to the time the Israeli water diversion project became known in 1963, constantly cautioning other Arab groups not to take any independent initiative on behalf of Palestine lest they disrupt his carefully developed plans.

Yasir continuously ridiculed Nasser's leadership in *Our Palestine* following the disclosure of the diversion project. His perorations came to the attention of the Egyptian leader, who ordered his intelligence service to see to Arafat's liquidation. An old acquaintance of Yasir's from their days at Cairo University, Mahmoud Rasad, had an uncle in the intelligence service, and through him got wind of the assassination order. Although he was neither an Ikhwanite nor a Fatahist, he had been working in the Egyptian administration in Gaza and had developed a romantic interest in Yasir's youngest sister. He mentioned the order to her and she passed it on to her brother Fathi, then making his living as a cigarette smuggler. Fathi traveled to Beirut, announced his identity at a newly opened Fatah recruiting office at the Dekwaneh camp, and passed the warning on to Faruq al-Qadumi, who had been sent by Yasir to Beirut to run the office.

Within days Yasir, in Kuwait, knew of Nasser's order. "I was unnerved, to say the least," he recalls. "Yes, I was writing anti-Nasser material, but I never expected such reprisals. I was forced to close up my business and go underground to avoid detection by Nasser's agents. That was when I first learned to live the fugitive's life. It was not pleasant, I can tell you, for there are few places to hide in Kuwait. But I was a *fedayeen,* so sacrifice meant nothing. What was important to me was that my words had made an impact.

If the Egyptians wanted to kill me, then I knew that Fatah was working. I vowed that they would not silence me. To die at the hands of the real enemy, that would make me proud. But the real enemy was not the Egyptians, it was the Jews."

Arab protests against the Jordan diversion scheme got nowhere. Arafat stepped up his attacks on Nasser, writing from his hiding place that the Egyptian leader had ordered his assassination and warning other Fatahists to beware. Nasser responded by publicly denying Yasir's claim, but condemning his editorials calling for war. "We will only go to war for the Palestine entity when we are assured of success," he said in an interview with an Arab journalist. "And we will only be assured of success when we have a unity of effort. These cries of the self-described liberators of Palestine can only be disruptive of Arab unity. Besides, they are dangerous. Who is this Yasir Arafat? What does he know about fighting a war? If he wants to join our struggle, we will find a place for him in our army. But if he does not want to join, let him keep quiet and entrust the war to those who understand war, and its consequences."

It was the first public notice anyone in the forefront of Arab leadership had taken of Yasir. He viewed it as a signal to escalate his war of words against Egypt and an opportunity to expand the influence of Fatah. He secretly left Kuwait under his phony Dr. Fawzi passport and took up hiding at the Dekwaneh camp in Beirut, where he resumed his vituperative essays against Nasser for *Our Palestine.* Soon he broadened the scope of his criticism to include all the Arab nations. "There is a well-known children's story about a group of mice persecuted by a cruel cat," he wrote late in 1963 in a piece that was later mistakenly credited to others. "The mice had a meeting and decided that the best way to defeat the cat was to hang a bell around its neck, a bell that would warn of its whereabouts at all times. The only problem was which of the mice would hang the bell, and on this subject they could not agree. Today the situation is reversed. There are thirteen cats in the Arab League and not one of them hangs the bell on the Zionist mouse."

Yasir's combination of outrage and irony, although in linguistic terms clumsily composed, began to have an effect on the "Palestine entity" that Nasser had characterized as his special province. Early in 1964 Nasser called an Arab summit meeting to "unite the Arab world in the measures that should be taken" to counter the Israeli diversion project. When it became clear that neither Nasser nor other outspoken Arab heads of state were prepared to go to war over the issue, a sharper torrent of abuse flowed from *Our Palestine* and other nationalist publications. Yasir called for a "revolt" on the part of all Palestinian communities within each Arab country, a revolt that would force the inactive Arab governments to defend their rights "in deed as well as word."

In reaction, Nasser put through a proposal calling for the instant formation of an Arab League–sponsored organization that would thereafter represent the "Palestine entity" and speak for all the nationalist groups, conservative and radical alike. As the leader of the Arab world, Nasser feared that the provocations of such groups as Fatah would eventually drag Egypt into another war with Israel —precisely the strategy Yasir and his Fatah co-founders had settled on. Another war at that time would prove disastrous for Egypt, and the inevitable defeat would reveal to the world the Nasser regime's inability to win back Palestine. Such a revelation would be a shattering blow to Nasser's prestige. The only way to prevent it was for Egypt to completely control, through its pre-eminence in the Arab League, the entire Palestinian movement.

The result of his proposal was the Palestine Liberation Organization (PLO), at whose head Nasser installed Ahmed Shukayri, a fiery Palestinian lawyer who had previously worked as a representative of Saudi Arabia at the United Nations. Nasser called Shukayri an "experienced diplomat and statesman who is best suited to the task of leading the organization because of his widespread contacts in the international community of nations."

Yasir, along with other proponents of the radical approach, was astonished at Nasser's move. In the first place, Shukayri was a member of the "generation of disaster," and he still clung to the old-fashioned principles of the aging Haj Amin, who was then living in Beirut after being forced out of Egypt and Gaza in 1959 because of his continuing flirtations with the outlawed Ikhwan. In the second place, Shukayri had earned a reputation as somewhat of a bombastic buffoon during his service at the United Nations and was held in amused contempt by most of his "widespread contacts in the international community of nations."

"The appointment of Shukayri to speak for the cause of liberation was a clear reflection of Nasser's contempt for our cause," says Arafat. "It was obvious from the very beginning that the PLO was to be nothing but a paper tiger, a tool of the Egyptians to keep us quiet."

Shukayri immediately fulfilled all of Arafat's expectations. While traveling the Arab world in the spring of 1964 and making ringing declarations about Palestinian liberation, he recruited to the newly hatched PLO only old-line nationalists who had been active in the 1920s and 1930s but who had largely faded from any positions of influence with the new generation of revolutionaries.

The PLO was officially born in Jerusalem on May 22, 1964, when Shukayri convened the First Palestinian National Congress and delivered a keynote speech that rang with such phrases as "the liquidation of Israel," "death to Zionism," "the inevitability of battle," and "our sacred homeland." Not to be outdone, Arafat retaliated in the pages of *Our Palestine* with his own and others' vitriolic thoughts about Nasser, Shukayri, and the PLO. Yasir, departing radically from his years of Ikhwan conditioning, asked: "How much longer must we labor under the delusion of Ikhwanite dreams as represented by this impostor Shukayri? Is it not a measure of Gamal Abdel Nasser's cynicism that he makes of this PLO what he will not permit in Egypt itself?"

But Shukayri had several advantages over Arafat and other lesser known rivals. With the exception of Syria, the Arab governments, at Nasser's insistence, had wholeheartedly committed themselves to support Shukayri, and almost all the elder notables of the Palestinian communities in the Gaza Strip, Lebanon, Kuwait, and Saudi Arabia had endorsed the PLO. Shukayri had almost unlimited funds placed at his disposal; moreover, he was authorized to organize a Palestine Liberation Army, units of which would be trained by the various Arab countries and attached to their armies.

It was the Syrian exception that provided Yasir and Fatah with the final rung of their ladder-climb to prominence.

27

Terrorism

The other countries of the Arab League had followed Nasser's dictates with regard to the formation and support of Shukayri's PLO for various reasons, all of which nevertheless had to do with Nasser's desire to keep the Palestinian movement under his control. Should guerrilla activity get out of hand, each of the countries recognized that it would suffer, in one degree or another, from the by then well-known Israeli penchant for reprisals. Indeed, Nasser, after the formation of the PLO—and maintaining that war against Israel would only be launched at the proper time, and then only under the auspices of his newly formed Unified Arab Command—had placed a ban on Palestinian guerrilla activity.

Aside from Syria, the only other exception taken was by the Jordanians. But theirs was only half an exception. King Husayn, successor of the despised King Abdallah, was happy to have the Palestinian movement under the control of the Arab League. He was simply reluctant to have the PLO operate in Jerusalem and other sites in the West Bank—this because he understood the movement's resentment against the Hashemites in general, going back to World War I days, and against himself in particular, going back to his grandfather Abdallah's annexation of the West Bank in 1950. The West Bank had become vital to Jordan's economy, and Husayn knew that implicit in the ideology of the Palestine revolution was the idea that the West Bank was part of the land to be liberated.

Syria's exception was almost total. It stemmed not from any lack of desire to see the movement under over-all Arab control, however, but from its intensifying argument with Egypt and its determination, in the wake of its self-radicalizing Baathist coup in 1963, to discredit Nasserism and assume for itself the mantle of leadership in the Arab world.

The Fatah call to military action, orchestrated by Yasir Arafat in *Our Palestine* and other publications in reaction to the Israeli water diversion project, had produced what at first appeared to be a favorable response among young Palestinians, particularly those i geria and Europe. In Germany and Austria, Khalid al-Hassa heeded Yasir's exhortations to infuse the previously Cairo trolled Palestinian Student Association with a thoroughgoing F orientation, the basis of which was, of course, that the liberatio the homeland could no longer be entrusted to the Arab countries b must be achieved by Palestinians themselves. The Fatah cells th al-Hassan had quietly implanted in the various European branche of the association, and which had been gestating since 1961, suddenly sprang to life. Under Fatah prodding hundreds of Palestinian students left their classes to be flown to Algeria, where they were inducted into guerrilla training camps supervised by Khalil al-Wazir and sponsored by the Algerian government. Al-Wazir got word back to Yasir in Beirut that soon he would be sending to the battleground (Palestine) a brigade of superbly trained freedom fighters who would become the vanguard of the future Fatah war of liberation.

The formation of the PLO in May of 1964 diverted much of the Fatah-inspired resolve, however, as Yasir and his fellow spokesmen became almost exclusively involved in elaborate condemnations of Nasser, Shukayri, and the Arab world in general. Moreover, most of the young Palestinians in Algeria, having experienced the rigors of training and now facing the actuality of engaging in real violence, had second thoughts. Soon the majority of them were on their way back to their universities. Only a handful made their way to Beirut, where they joined the profoundly disappointed Yasir Arafat.

Arafat called a meeting of the founders of Fatah to discuss their problems. In the wake of the defection of so many trainees, Algeria had informed Khalil al-Wazir that it was going to reduce its support for the organization, as Fatah did not seem a viable force, particularly in view of the strength of the PLO. The creation of the PLO had also caused Fatah funds from Kuwait to slow to a trickle; most money was now going to PLO organizers. And *Our Palestine* had only enough money to publish one or two more issues.

The founders, joined by a dozen or so additional members who had gained Yasir's trust, met at Dekwaneh throughout the third week of September, 1964. "It was our darkest hour," confesses Arafat. "All of us were in one way or another outcasts, fugitives, and we all feared for our lives at the hands of Nasser's agents. But that only stiffened my sense of purpose. Many of my colleagues were discouraged. Al-Hassan came from Stuttgart with bad news about his organization there—the students were giving up on Fatah. Al-Wazir came from Algiers with equally bad news—the Algerians had closed the training camps. Everyone was feeling defeated, but I knew that it was at moments such as these when bad fortune inevitably reverses itself."

Good fortune came in the guise of one Hazim al-Khalidi, a Jordanian who had fought with distinction in the British army during World War II. Al-Khalidi was an acquaintance of Khalid al-Hassan and had become sympathetic to al-Hassan's form of Palestinianism. Yasir was anxious to put the few guerrilla trainees who had come from Algeria to quick use, to stage an incident which would prove that the Shukayri-led PLO was waging only a war of words, whereas Fatah backed up its words with actions. Al-Khalidi had been the director of the Syrian Military Academy in Damascus, and enjoyed a reputation as a nerveless fighter. When Arafat heard that he was in Beirut, he asked al-Hassan to bring him to a meeting.

When al-Khalidi sat down with the others, Arafat confessed that none of the Fatah leadership, himself included, possessed the proper military experience to implement Fatah's guerrilla war plans. "We have some men, we have the desire, and we can obtain the weapons," Yasir said. "But we do not have the knowledge." He thought that because the West Bank contained the largest concentration of Palestinians and was closest to Israeli population centers, it should be the focus of Fatah-sponsored *fedayeen* activity. Then, perhaps carried away by his own long-bottled-up fantasies, he stitched together an ambitious scenario of Fatah growth over the coming years, culminating in what he claimed would be the annihilation of both Israel and Jordan through a popular revolution from within, and the establishment of an autonomous Arab Palestinian state in their place. In concluding the rendering of his vision, he invited al-Khalidi to become commander of military operations for Fatah. "When our revolution is complete," Yasir coaxed, "you will become commander in chief of the armed forces of Palestine."

Al-Khalidi declined the invitation. In his view, the very professionalism Fatah hungered for proved that the tiny organization had no workable military potential. He was also troubled by Arafat's revolutionary timetable, which, in al-Khalidi's words, "spanned only a few years. The man was talking as though liberation was just around the corner. A few guerrilla actions against Husayn and against Israel and the population would rise in a storm of battle and suddenly there would be a nation called Palestine. He was totally unrealistic. I told him that such a revolution would take years, perhaps decades, that he might not live to see it. He said, 'Ah, no, you are mistaken, I will live to see it, we will all live to see it.' He wanted to start guerrilla actions immediately, to take away the prestige of the PLO, to cause difficulties for Husayn, for Nasser, to provoke a war with Israel. I told him that if he wished to conduct guerrilla warfare from any Arab country, the population must be painstakingly prepared for such activities before action could begin. Otherwise he would earn the hatred of the population, because it would be they who suffered from enemy reprisals. It would be self-defeating, I told him. For instance, the West Bank. Without the support of the people, the people would shun his fighters, they would betray them to the authorities, and soon there would be no more Fatah to lead the revolution. He became very angry at my warnings. He shouted and cursed and insulted me. 'We have no time for those who seek to discourage us,' he said. 'We have had our fill of people telling us what we should not do! Tell us what we should do, or get out!' Well, I got out. But as I was leaving I mentioned the only thing that came to my mind. I said go to the Syrians. I thought the Syrians, with their new regime, would be the only ones interested in Fatah. They were just as impatient as Arafat and al-Hassan. And I was right."

The offhand suggestion was immediately discussed by the Fatah founders, and enthusiasm for it mounted rapidly. "It was one of those things that became 'Of course, why didn't we think of it before?' " recalls Nabil Rashmiya, a young trainee from Algeria who was present at several of the meetings. "Faruq al-Qadumi had a relative in the Syrian intelligence group that was working Beirut. The Syrians were already trying to infiltrate the camps of Lebanon to organize Palestinian guerrillas. Faruq said he had learned this from his relative. This made Yasir mad. 'Why did you not tell us this, you idiot?' he said to Faruq. 'Don't you realize the Syrians are doing the same thing we are? Don't you realize it is a perfect opportunity to make contact with the Syrians?' And Faruq replied, 'I did not say anything because I thought we decided long ago that we would make no alliances with Arab countries.' And Yasir came back, 'You thought, you thought! You, Faruq al-Qadumi, are not qualified to think. You are an idiot. You leave the thinking to me!' There followed a vicious argument between everyone about collective leadership and equal say. Finally it was resolved. Yasir kept saying, 'We must be flexible, that is the key to our mission, revolutionaries must be flexible, like a coiling snake.' "

Al-Qadumi was dispatched to tell his cousin that Fatah was interested in getting Syrian backing. Within a month Gaeth Hafez, a functionary of Syria's Deuxième Bureau—an Arabized version of the French colonial secret police that had operated in Syria before World War II—arrived in Beirut from Damascus and tracked down the Fatah leaders at Dekwaneh.

On December 30, 1964, Yasir Arafat, Khalil al-Wazir, Faruq al-Qadumi, and Syria's Gaeth Hafez met at Ein al-Helweh, a Palestinian refugee camp near the port of Saida in southern Lebanon. During the previous six weeks Hafez had recruited a dozen residents of Ein al-Helweh and other nearby camps. Mostly young men in their twenties who scratched out their livings as smugglers and petty thieves, their names and identities had been on a list secretly acquired by Hafez, through his Deuxième Bureau connections, from the Lebanese police, who made it a practice to keep track of the criminal element among Lebanon's large Palestinian population. Hafez had offered the twelve steady wages in exchange for their services as guerrillas, and had sent them to a camp on the Syrian-Lebanese border for two weeks of rudimentary training in infiltration techniques. Now they were to earn their pay.

Hafez had been appointed by the Deuxième Bureau to act as liaison between the Syrian government and Fatah. He had once been a member of the French Foreign Legion, had fought against the Viet Minh in Indochina in the early 1950s, and was considered one of Syria's top experts on guerrilla warfare. He was an officious, domineering man, and after some resistance by Yasir Arafat and the other Fatah founders he had worked out a plan of guerrilla action to be carried out against Israel in the name of Fatah.

The first action was meant to be symbolic as well as real—he was sending a team of six of his recruits across the Lebanese-Israeli border to blow up a section of the Israeli National Water Carrier, the canal through which flowed the waters of the Jordan River diversion project, in the Beit Netopha Valley. The team was to leave the camp that morning, and Hafez, Arafat, and the others were busy writing an announcement, entitled "Fatah Military Communiqué No. 1," taking responsibility for the raid and characterizing it as the opening round in the new Fatah war of liberation.

The communiqué was completed a few hours before the team's scheduled departure. Hafez had it run off on a camp mimeograph machine, then sent Arafat and his cohorts back to Beirut to distribute copies to the city's many newspapers the following day—the day the explosion was due to occur.

Unbeknown to any of them, however, in the hour before departure one of the members of the secret demolition team decided that the mission was too dangerous. He disclosed it to Lebanese security officers in charge of the camp and the entire team was arrested. In the meantime, Arafat and his cohorts had reached Beirut and dropped copies of Military Communiqué No. 1 into more than fifteen newspaper mailboxes. The following day the papers gave front-page prominence to the raid and Beirut buzzed with excitement at the first news of the group that called itself Fatah. The day after that, however—New Year's Day, 1965—Lebanese authorities privately informed the papers of the arrests at Ein al-Helweh and it became known that the Fatah claims about the raid were untrue. It was to be the first of many false claims and exaggerations, and was an inauspicious debut for the "storm," as the communiqué described it, that Fatah was about to unleash on Israel.

Yasir returned to Ein al-Helweh furious with Gaeth Hafez. The Syrian had planned for such an eventuality, however; he had infiltrated a second demolition team of five men into a camp at Irbid in Jordan, and when he learned of the first group's arrest he sent a message to Irbid ordering the backup team into action.

On the night of January 2 the backup group, now reduced to three men by the defection of the other two, crossed the Jordan River at a shallow spot and set out for the nearby Beit Netopha Valley. Dressed in makeshift uniforms and wearing black-and-white checked *kaffiyeh* (the traditional headdress of Arabs from Palestine), they avoided Israeli border patrols and reached the water canal by midnight. Placing their cargo of ten dynamite packs against the canal's dike, they inserted and fused the detonators, and then crept away. By dawn they were back across the Jordan.

Again the canal escaped damage. An Israeli watchman discovered the ineptly disguised explosives later that morning and removed the detonators. A border patrol followed the tracks of the intruders to the Jordan and observed the trodden reeds that betrayed their point of entry. At that time the Israelis did not make it a practice to pursue saboteurs across borders, so the patrol drove away and submitted a routine report. Neither the three saboteurs, making their way back to Irbid, nor the Israelis were aware that the incident, however abortive, was the signal for the beginning of a new stage in the Arab-Israeli conflict.

28

Becoming Abu Ammar

News coverage of the non-exploit at Beit Netopha provoked an immediate furor over Fatah in the Arab world. From a little-known organization, containing at the time less than a hundred members and sympathizers, it was launched on the wings of first a false and then an exaggerated newspaper account into wide celebrity. The original newspaper reports, based on Military Communiqué No. 1, described extensive damage inflicted on the Israeli Water Carrier. The follow-up accounts modified the claims, but by then the impression had been made. Fatah immediately announced that the non-exploit was "the opening shot in the Palestinian Revolution."

Opinion was divided over the operation, and over Fatah itself. As earlier, the governments of Egypt, Lebanon, and Jordan issued statements of disapproval, based on fears that such unilateral actions would bring Israeli reprisals against their territories. Only Syria praised the action; but then, of course, Syria had engineered it.

The Arab press and radio were, on the other hand, generally expansive in their praise of Fatah. Employing Arabic's most vivid and bellicose phraseology, they glorified Fatah during the following weeks and aroused widespread sympathy for its "revolutionary aims."

Arafat and his fellow founders were unable to capitalize on the favorable publicity, however. After news of the actual raid on Beit Netopha was made known, six of them were arrested and imprisoned for more than a month. Nevertheless, they were aware of what they had achieved. "It made our time in prison worth every minute," Arafat says today. "We became convinced that we were truly the wave of the future, and that there would be no turning back."

Also arrested was Gaeth Hafez, but he was immediately released after a diplomatic protest from Syria. While Hafez worked on getting the Fatah leaders out, they busied themselves behind bars expanding and refining their plans.

"That was the time when they all decided to take on new names," recalls Assam Sarraj, a Palestinian who says he was imprisoned at the same time and was recruited into Fatah by Salah Khalef, his cellmate. "Almost everyone they came into contact with they brought into Fatah. But they themselves remained a force apart, like a separate organization. They professed to be a collective leadership, but it was Arafat who seemed to have the most sway over everyone else. One day the Syrian, Hafez, came to visit, and he brought two journalists to interview the leadership. Yasir and Khalid al-Hassan were not there—they had been taken elsewhere for questioning. The journalists interviewed the others, and they wanted to know who the leader was. Salah Khalef, Khalil al-Wazir, the others, they all insisted there was no single leader, that it was a collective leadership. But the journalists kept demanding that for publicity purposes there must be a single leader. Finally Hafez stepped in and said they could write that Arafat was the leader, that most of the ideas were his.

"Later," says Sarraj, who has since left Fatah, "when Yasir heard this he was angry with Hafez. He called a meeting of the founders and berated them for allowing their names to be revealed to the public at large. 'We have many enemies,' he said, 'we must operate anonymously. We must let Fatah speak for us, not individuals among us.' Then he proposed that they all take new names, in fact new identities."

Arafat's new-identity idea was based on his youthful experiences with Majid Halaby, the man who had given him the name Yasir and who had taken for himself the name Abu Khalid, and also on his exposure to the secret-identity practices of the Ikhwan. He announced that they should all assume new names in the interests of security and anonymity.

He chose the name Abu Ammar, another name Majid Halaby had bestowed on him when he had taken the name Abu Khalid. Khalil al-Wazir chose Abu Jihad—*jihad* meaning "holy war" in Arabic. Salah Khalef chose Abu Ayad. Khalid al-Hassan, according to Assam Sarraj, did not think too much of Yasir's idea and resisted a name change. So the others in the group imposed one on him—Abu Said. Faruq al-Qadumi chose Abu Lutuf, and Muhammad Yusef became Abu Yusef. Neither Zuhayr al-Alami nor Kamal Adwan, the other two founders, had been jailed, but they were assigned new names in absentia.

The group—with al-Hassan mildly dissenting—agreed to use the new names exclusively thereafter when referring to one another. "You must remember," says Arafat today by way of explaining the reasoning behind his idea, "we were being interrogated intensely by the Lebanese police while we were in prison. None of us had been in Lebanon for very long. We were not well known, and the Lebanese weren't sure of what they had on their hands. I was determined to make it as difficult as possible for them to be able to trace our backgrounds. In this way we could protect our families. It was also useful for reducing the journalists' need to single out particular ones as the leaders of Fatah. It made them respect our desire for the collective image."

While Yasir and the others were in prison, Gaeth Hafez engineered a few more infiltrations by hastily recruited layabouts from Lebanon's refugee camps. On January 14, 1965, a two-man team finally managed to detonate an explosive charge under the Israeli National Water Carrier, thus vindicating the claims of two weeks earlier. On February 28 another team blew up a grain silo at the settlement of Kfar Hess.

The Lebanese released Yasir Arafat and his cohorts from prison in the beginning of March on the promise of Hafez that they would not remain in Lebanon. Upon his release Arafat was taken by Hafez, along with Salah Khalef and Faruq al-Qadumi, to Damascus to meet a Syrian army colonel, Sulayman Faqr. Faqr was the man in charge of Syria's program for Palestinian guerrilla agitation against Israel, the principal point of which was to embarrass both Nasser of Egypt and Husayn of Jordan, who was felt by the new Syrian regime to be, like his grandfather before him, insufficiently anti-Israel.

Faqr greeted Arafat expansively and explained that since the recent raids had been so thoroughly identified in the Arab public's mind with Fatah, even though they were basically Syrian, the Syrian regime had decided to take advantage of the circumstances to build Fatah into a large-scale guerrilla organization. Members of the Syrian junta had read some of Arafat's pronouncements in *Our Palestine* and saw in Fatah a potentially valuable instrument of its

Baathist policy. If the Fatah leaders cooperated, Arafat was told, they would soon have at their disposal a large force of trained guerrillas.

Yasir agreed to the proposal, but expressed misgivings about Hafez's practice of hiring refugee-camp ne'er-do-wells to become the actual guerrillas. "Our political message was making an impact," he says today, "but we had yet to inspire any large impulse on the part of the people to become fighters for the cause of liberation."

Go, then, and build up a cadre of committed fighters, he was told. Colonel Faqr promised him unlimited funds and other forms of aid to tour the refugee camps in Jordan for the purpose of recruiting guerrillas. "We will continue to send teams recruited and trained by Hafez against the Zionists," Faqr said, "and Fatah will receive the credit for each success. Soon you will have refugees waiting in line to join you."

Even as they were meeting, another Syrian-backed raid was brought off—this one against the desert town of Arad in Israel. Again Fatah received the credit, despite the fact that Arafat and his colleagues had nothing to do with it. Ignored were the raids that failed. Hafez and Faqr on several occasions dispatched demolition teams which, instead of crossing the border, hid their satchel charges in caves on the east bank of the Jordan and then returned to Irbid, the usual starting point, to tell of their success and to collect their pay. Since Hafez would deluge Arab newspapers with accounts of each raid as it was supposed to be taking place, these aborted missions received the same prominence as the actual raids. By April the entire refugee population, along with non-refugee Palestinians, were under the mistaken impression that Fatah possessed a mighty guerrilla army.

The Israeli government was under somewhat the same false impression. Israeli intelligence services had not taken notice of Fatah until late 1964. Inflammatory anti-Israeli articles were routine in the Arab press, so when Israeli intelligence began to peruse the pages of *Our Palestine,* little concern was expressed, although the articles by Arafat and others were clipped, photostated, and distributed to other departments of government. It was only after the Kfar Hess raid in February of 1965, with its accompanying publicity in the Arab press, that the Israelis began to consider Fatah seriously. They rightly suspected that Arafat and his co-leaders were receiving help from the radical Syrian regime, but they tended to credit Fatah with more size and influence than it actually possessed.

Throughout April and May, Colonel Faqr established guerrilla staging centers near Kalkiliya and Jenin in West Bank Jordan. When King Husayn learned of this, he protested bitterly to the Syrian government, but to no avail. The Syrians loudly accused Husayn of being heir to that element in the Arab world—the Hashemites—which had originally been responsible for selling out Palestine. Syria insisted that Israel, and indeed Jordan itself, or at least the West Bank, were still legally Syrian territory; since Husayn refused to join wholeheartedly in the liberation struggle, since he had a vested interest in remaining outside the fight to annihilate Israel, the Syrians would carry the banner alone. Any protest or interference by Husayn would be considered a subversive act, warned the Syrians, and would bring wholesale Syrian wrath down on Husayn's head. Husayn temporarily withdrew his protest, although he sent a secret communication to the Israelis disclaiming any responsibility for the fact that most of the guerrilla raids were originating in Jordan.

Arafat and his Fatah co-leaders, in the meantime, had slipped across the Syrian-Jordanian border and were touring refugee camps, distributing leaflets and attempting to indoctrinate and recruit guerrillas for training in Syria. Harking back again to his days with Majid Halaby, Arafat revived the concept of *asifah*—"the storm"—and began to call Fatah's still barely existent guerrilla force Asifah. Coupled with the publicity Fatah was garnering through the guerrilla actions organized by Hafez and Faqr, the idea began to take hold in the camps through which Arafat moved.

His first real recruiting success did not come, however, until June of 1965. On May 25 a "Fatah" raid on Ramat Hakovesh in Israel's Sharon Valley resulted in three Israeli deaths. The following night "Fatah" guerrillas blew up a house in the town of Afula. In reprisal, Israel sent an armed force into West Bank Jordan and destroyed Colonel Faqr's new staging camps near Jenin and Kalkiliya.

The Syrians were pleased. They were aware that the Israelis suspected them to be the moving force behind the raids and had grown apprehensive lest Israel strike back at their territory. That the Israelis did not dare assault their strong defense network along the Syrian

(Golan) Heights frontier but instead chose to attack weaker Jordan meant, in their view, that their strategy to embarrass King Husayn and, by extension, Nasser was working. Consequently the regime decided to enlarge the scope of guerrilla activities and gave Colonel Faqr the green light to begin a serious expansion of Fatah.

Faqr called Arafat and his cohorts back to Damascus for a progress report. He berated them for their slow recruiting progress and outlined Syrian plans to step up guerrilla activity. "It was a humiliating experience for Yasir," recalls Ahmed Khailana, a Palestinian who was a recent inductee into Fatah and who accompanied Arafat back to Damascus. "The Syrians condescended to him and the others, shouting instructions and orders at them. Faqr called Yasir an idiot for not taking advantage of the Israeli raids to generate enthusiasm for Fatah. Yasir complained that recruiting was difficult because the elders in the camps would not cooperate. Faqr said he wanted no excuses. He told Yasir that he would give him and the others one last chance to organize a force, and if he didn't do it quickly the Syrians would forget about Fatah and start their own liberation group.

"Then he brought in Muhammad Araka. Araka was a Palestinian working for the Syrian government as a spy against King Husayn. He knew his way around the camps better than anyone, and he had good contacts with Palestinians who were members of the Jordanian government. Faqr said that he was appointing Araka to take charge of Fatah until Yasir and the rest of us learned how to recruit. Yasir and Khalil al-Wazir protested, but Faqr said that if they didn't follow Araka's instructions he would have them arrested.

"Yasir and Khalil gave in. They knew they had little chance of success without Syria. When they informed the others about Araka, there was much arguing. Khalid al-Hassan said that Yasir was selling out their principles of remaining independent. Salah Khalef refused to work under Araka. Yasir finally won out. He said Fatah needed the Syrians' help, but that they would use the Syrians in the same way the Syrians used them. Once they got Asifah organized, they would declare their independence. It was the best thing that could have happened, because once Araka took over, the recruiting really began to build up."

Little is known today about Muhammad Araka except that he was a violent anti-Zionist and was murderously ruthless in his methods. It is said that he employed the full weight of his Syrian sponsorship in an attempt to carry out the assassination of King Husayn of Jordan; but even while he was planning that, he was also plotting with more extremist elements among the Baathists to overthrow the Syrian leaders who sponsored him. "He had two priorities," says Ahmed Khailana, who today mans a Palestinian information office in Europe. "The first was to kill Husayn. The second was to kill Israeli leaders. From the things that he told us, I am sure that his main interest in building up Fatah was in the hopes of fomenting a revolt against Husayn. He believed Jordan needed to be liberated before Israel could. I understand his hatred of Husayn came from the fact that Husayn's grandfather had had Araka's father killed back in 1949, when his father was working against the annexation of the West Bank."

Araka led the party of Fatah leaders back into Jordan in June of 1965 and quickly showed them the most expedient way of overcoming the resistance of the camp elders to their recruiting efforts. This was to have them killed. Their first stop was at the large camp in Irbid, where Yasir found that in his absence Syrian propagandists, using the Israeli reprisal raids on "innocent" Arabs in Kalkiliya and Jenin, had whipped up enthusiasm for Fatah. Araka quickly saw to the murder of two of the camp's leaders who had been counseling against guerrilla action on the ground that the people who would suffer most would be the inhabitants of the camp. The remaining camp elders thereafter fell silent, and Araka opened a Fatah recruiting office in what had formerly been a recreation tent at the center of the camp. Leaving Faruq al-Qadumi and Kamal Adwan behind in the company of two of his Syrian assistants to continue the recruiting drive, Araka, with the other Fatah leaders in tow, then moved on to another large camp near Amman, the Jordanian capital. There he repeated the same process, leaving behind Salah Khalef and Muhammad Yusef. From there he, Arafat, al-Hassan, and al-Wazir crossed the Jordan and settled into the West Bank camp of Nuweimeh, between Jerusalem and Jericho. Soon Arafat and al-Wazir were installed there, unopposed by the camp's leadership, with instructions from Araka to produce two hundred able-bodied recruits within the month.

Araka's blitzkrieg methods were very effective. The camp's elders were easily intimidated by Araka, and Arafat and al-Wazir rapidly found themselves with almost total authority over the youth of Nuweimeh. They took to calling compulsory meetings of all male camp residents under forty and conducting indoctrination lectures in Fatah ideology. Those who demonstrated early enthusiasm were appointed as personal aides to enforce attendance at meetings, and within a matter of weeks Nuweimeh was a solidly developing Fatah outpost.

By mid-August, Arafat and al-Wazir had enlisted more than their quota of two hundred potential guerrillas and shipped them off to Syria for training. Word of the expanding Fatah influence at Nuweimeh spread to the other camps of the West Bank and into the cities and towns as well. Simultaneously, continued raids into Israel—some actual, others only fictional, but all carefully credited by the Syrians to Fatah—further sharpened West Bank awareness of the new guerrilla organization.

In September, Arafat and al-Wazir, leaving a small cadre of trusted converts behind to oversee Nuweimeh, moved on to camps in the Hebron area. There, using the techniques learned from Muhammad Araka, they managed to have almost as signal a success as they had at Nuweimeh, setting a pattern of recruitment they would pursue over the next two years in the service of Syria's hardening desire to bring an end to the decade-long span of Arab inaction over Israel—inaction which was the fruit, as the Syrians saw it, of Egypt's leadership of the Arab world.

29

The Syrian Connection

Arafat's next stop was Gaza, where he, Salah Khalef, and Faruq al-Qadumi were sent in the company of several of Colonel Faqr's Syrian intelligence operatives, under phony passports, to recruit and organize in the camps there. Nasser had taken a strong stand against Fatah and had even had the government-controlled newspapers of Egypt try to discredit Arafat by disclosing his former Ikhwan association and labeling him a "tool of the Zionists," a phrase that Arafat himself had grown fond of using in the pages of *Our Palestine* to denounce *his* enemies. The effect of Nasser's campaign was the opposite of the one intended; it provided Arafat with instant fame throughout Egypt. And when the Syrian propaganda machine fired back, using statements it attributed to Arafat, comparing the deeds of Fatah to the mere words of Ahmed Shukayri and his Egyptian-sponsored PLO, it produced rising sympathy for Fatah as well.*

Arafat and his colleagues had considerable success during the three months they spent in Gaza. By now they had their message down pat and had gained confidence and proficiency in the intimidation techniques learned from Muhammad Araka, who was back in Damascus helping to put the final touches on an impending extremist coup. Their efforts were aided, of course, by sensational press reports of continuing Fatah raids into Israel. Although many of these raids were still either nonexistent or totally ineffectual, the momentum of credibility had been established and few Arabs doubted the accounts.

Recruiting efforts were given an additional boost late in 1965,

*While in Gaza, Arafat and the other Fatahists were required to conduct their recruiting more or less secretly because of Egyptian intelligence surveillance. It was at this time that the system of code names Arafat had instituted was put into everyday practice.

when reports were circulated by the Western press that Israel had devised a process for making nuclear weapons. The news ignited the Arab world, and even Nasser began to talk about the need to begin a "preventive war" against the Jewish state before it could actually produce atomic weapons.

Syria seized on Nasser's declarations to again play up what the Baathists viewed as his impotent temporizing and his unworthiness as spokesman for the Arab world. Syrian propagandists announced that the idea of a preventive war was another of Nasser's usual half-measures designed to deceive the Arab public; what would once and for all solve the problem of Zionism and Palestine was total war. At the forefront of a total war, went the Syrian line, would be Fatah, whose guerrilla actions would harass, demoralize, and weaken Israel until the armies of the Arab nations, operating under the Unified Command, "met in Tel Aviv."

By the beginning of 1966 Arafat and his cohorts, still recruiting in Gaza and Jordan while using Syrian funds and printing facilities, had more enlistees than they could handle. The recruits were now being promised a regular monthly stipend and, during their training in Syria, many of the amenities of life that were lacking in the refugee camps. Arafat himself began to become somewhat of a cult figure in the camps. Constantly on the move from camp to camp, he had taken to living out of the back seats of the dilapidated automobiles he and his aides commandeered. Usually dressed in soiled khakis and wearing a checked *kaffiyeh,* he increasingly became the prize of Arab journalists, who sought him out for interviews in underground locations, faithfully printed his hard-hitting anti-Israel statements, and described an austere life of physical hardship and personal sacrifice made particularly severe by his renunciation of women, wine, and other temporal pleasures. "I am married to Fatah," he was often quoted as saying. "Fatah is my woman, my family, my life."

As he perceived the effect the newspaper stories were having, he further cloaked himself in an aura of mystery and danger. He refused to talk about his past or his family, insisting that "I was not born until I became Abu Ammar," and threatened death to any writer who mentioned his blood relationship to Haj Amin. He continued to disclaim himself as "the" leader of Fatah, resorting to muddled dissertations on the glories of collective leadership. But it was his very volubility on the subject, while the other founders remained generally dour and uncommunicative, that marked him as the true leader of Fatah. His colloquies flowed with traditional Arabic eloquence, exaggeration, and bombast. But they were spoken in a dialect filled with syntactical and grammatical crudities, so that when he delivered his pronouncements he sounded to his listeners much as a British or American labor leader, speaking the language of his constituents, sounds in English. "I am the Palestinian people," he often declared, "and the Palestinian people are me. It makes no difference who I am, it is what I am that matters. Any Palestinian could be Abu Ammar. Therefore Abu Ammar is all Palestinians."

As he came into contact with more and more reporters, Arafat further learned to appreciate the virtues of personal enigmatism. Irony, contradiction, unpredictability—these, he realized, were the qualities the emissaries from the Arab press thrived on. So he began to mix his pedantic intensity and humorlessness with a kind of proletarian charm dredged up, says his cousin Abud al-Qudwa, who was present at some of his interviews, from his memory of Majid Halaby. "It was amazing to watch the change that came over Yasir once the journalists began to come around. In private he was as uncommunicative as I had always known him. He looked especially on members of his family with contempt, but he was also abrupt and superior with those who were close to him. When a journalist would appear, however, he became expansive and warm. He pretended to treat us all like old friends, making jokes, telling stories, as though we were all great comrades. As soon as the journalist left, he would turn cold and distant again until the next one showed up. He was very clever. He fooled many of the writers into thinking he had this great charm which made us all devoted to him. He was also that way with the boys he was recruiting. He would be very solicitous and friendly, and as he became more well known this would make a great impression on the boys—that the great Abu Ammar would be so concerned with them. But once they declared their loyalty to Fatah he would ignore them."

Arafat managed to deceive the Arab press on another matter as well. Pleased with the publicity he was receiving as leader of Fatah and as mastermind of Asifah, Fatah's guerrilla arm, he took care to conceal the fact that the real power behind the two groups lay in the hands of Colonel Faqr and Muhammad Araka in Damascus.

This became clearly evident within the guerrilla movement in mid-1966. In February of that year Faqr and Araka were part of the coup that ousted the existing Baathist government and installed an even more extremist military junta headed by General Salah Jedid. The coup came about for many reasons, most of them deriving from religious and clan differences with the Baath party, but it was sparked by the fact that the incumbent leaders had begun late in 1965 to show a softening in their challenge to Nasser's leadership. Once the new regime was established, it immediately sent emissaries to Russia to express solidarity with the aims of Soviet communism and to seek arms. The Russians, having experienced difficulties in their efforts to penetrate the Middle East through Egypt, responded positively to the Syrian approach and concluded an arms-supply deal that also called for a large-scale Soviet presence in Syria.

Shortly thereafter, Arafat and his Fatah co-founders were summoned back to Damascus by Colonel Faqr and told that, in the interests of stepping up the new regime's war plans, the operations of Fatah and Asifah were being placed under stricter Syrian control.

By now the "collective leadership" of Fatah had expanded to include about forty men, most of whom had joined in the previous year and had been appointed to various policy and tactical committees. Arafat and the seven other founders had formed themselves into an executive committee, each founder heading one of the subcommittees, but the second-rank leaders had begun to have a voice in decisions. Faqr's decree caused an uproar within the committee structure when Arafat called a meeting in May to announce it. Several of the founders, notably the perennially argumentative Khalid al-Hassan and Salah Khalef, having grown resentful of the publicity Arafat had been receiving, protested on the ground that acceptance of the Syrian move would mean a further erosion of Fatah's already compromised independence. Arafat, on the contrary, lobbied for acceptance of Faqr's decree, insisting that it fitted well into Fatah's rationale of provoking a war and that Asifah was not yet strong enough to conduct guerrilla warfare on its own.

The dispute became more bitter during the following weeks, and no decision was reached. Arafat remained obdurate, pleading with Colonel Faqr for more time until he could convince the dissenters.

Al-Hassan and Khalef, in the meantime, along with those they had persuaded to their point of view, began to plot the removal of Arafat from his position as final arbiter.

The plot was unnecessary, however. Colonel Faqr, impatient with what he considered to be the inconsequential deliberations of the Fatahists, decided to take matters into his own hands. He appointed one of his military aides, a captain in a Palestinian unit of the Syrian army named Yusef Urabi, to take charge of Fatah and instructed Arafat and the rest of the leadership to thenceforth take orders from him. Urabi tried to go one step further. He sent a message to all Fatah cells in Syria that he was dismissing Arafat and his co-founders and was himself assuming the leadership of the organization.

Faqr's and Urabi's actions disabused Arafat of the idea that Syria had Fatah's best interests in mind and served to re-unite him with al-Hassan and the other dissident leaders. According to several Fatah members who were present in Damascus while these events were unfolding, Arafat personally sent an assassination team to Syria's Yarmuk refugee camp, where Urabi had set up headquarters, to kill him. When the assassination took place, a squad of Palestinians loyal to Urabi descended on Arafat's hideout on the eastern outskirts of Damascus to revenge the murder. A pitched gun battle ensued in which several of Arafat's bodyguards were killed. Before the Urabi loyalists could break into the house in which Arafat was hiding, however, Syrian police intervened.

Arafat nevertheless was arrested on orders of Colonel Faqr, and a day or two later eleven other Fatah members, including al-Hassan and Khalef, were rounded up. The other Fatah leaders fled Damascus for Lebanon. Arafat, Khalef, and al-Hassan remained in prison throughout the summer while Faqr tried to persuade them to obey his wishes. In the meantime, the Syrian General Command continued to send increasing numbers of terrorists through Jordan and into Israel, crediting most as Fatah operations but some as raids by other liberation groups that had sprung up as rivals to Fatah and come under Syrian sponsorship.

Late in August, Arafat, al-Hassan, and Khalef agreed to cooperate with Faqr and were released from prison. Their agreement was merely a ruse to secure their release, however. Once free, they immediately smuggled themselves into southern Lebanon, where they found haven at Nabatiyah, another refugee camp. There they learned that there were now two Fatahs operating: their own, which had been decimated by the events in Syria and had shrunk in number to only about thirty men, including the founders; and the one in Syria, now fully controlled by the Syrian General Command and containing most of the guerrillas they had recruited.

The discovery came as a singular blow. Nevertheless, Arafat and his associates—but especially Arafat—had become through the press and radio solidly identified in the mind of the Arab public with the exploits of the Syrian-controlled Fatah during the previous year. Since Syria continued to attribute most of its widening terrorist raids to Fatah, without distinguishing between Arafat's branch and its own, Arafat and his cohorts found it a simple matter to let the credit for the "Fatah" activity in Israel, which was gaining ever-wider notice in the press, devolve upon themselves.

Toward this end they began to seek out Lebanese journalists, who broadcast their "secret" presence in Lebanon and wrote interview stories which left the impression that Arafat and the others—but again especially Arafat—had come to Lebanon to repeat the recruiting and organizing successes they had achieved in Syria, Jordan, and Gaza, and at the same time to continue to act as supervisors of what were really the Syrian-mounted "Fatah" forays into Israel.

The Syrians, although they had secret agents in Lebanon trying to track Arafat down, did not wish to reveal any discord in the guerrilla movement. So they remained quiet about Arafat's claims to the Lebanese newspapers. (Many of the terrorists operating under Syrian control actually believed they were still under Arafat's auspices.) The Syrian silence only served to inflate the credibility of Arafat's claims. Soon his star began to rise again, this time among the more than 100,000 refugees living in the squalid camps of Lebanon.

Arafat and his co-leaders, however, were without funds, having lost their Syrian financing. To remedy this, they began to tour the Palestinian community, begging, threatening, and otherwise soliciting contributions to the cause. Soon they were able to establish an office in Beirut, from which they launched a new recruiting operation. At the same time, they recognized the necessity of making a new alliance, for by themselves they were militarily too feeble to achieve anything.

Toward the end of 1966, Egypt's Nasser, in an effort to counter rising criticism from Syria, had done a turnabout, suddenly coming out in favor of guerrilla action against Israel and authorizing Ahmed Shukayri's PLO to begin terrorist activities. Throughout the early months of 1967, Israel was subjected to increasing *fedayeen* terrorism, both from Jordan by Syria and from Gaza by Egyptian-supplied PLO elements. Not surprisingly, Arafat and his Fatah co-founders made a turnabout too. They sought and gained an alliance with the PLO. It was short-lived, however, for within months the intensifying machinations between Syria and Egypt as they vied for leadership of the Arab world resulted in all-out war with Israel.

30

The Transformation of Yasir Arafat

One of Yasir Arafat's favorite boasts is that had it not been for him and his colleagues in Fatah, the June, 1967, Arab-Israeli war would not have taken place, and that the issue of the "Palestinian people" would thus not have become the central focus of the Middle East conflict.

As we have seen, this claim is in reality rather an empty one. It was the series of increasingly extremist Syrian governments seeking to dilute the influence of Nasser, and perhaps also endeavoring to purge the deeply ingrained sense of national shame and frustration stemming from Syria's original loss of Palestine, which precipitated the war. Without doubt Syria used Fatah, or at least the idea of Fatah, to help achieve its objective of war, just as it used several other guerrilla liberationist groups it sponsored after jailing Arafat. But Fatah itself—the original Fatah of Arafat and his co-founders—had little to do with the war.

Nevertheless, aside from the Israelis, if there was any other entity that benefited from the war it was the original, albeit truncated, Fatah, and to a lesser extent two or three even smaller rival groups. The history of the 1967 war and the events that have flowed from it down to the present time have been well and extensively documented elsewhere. In the following pages, therefore, I will summarize the highlights of Arafat's rise to world prominence and attempt to put the final brush strokes on the portrait of the man as he is today.

Arafat and his colleagues watched helplessly from their various refugee outposts in Lebanon as the Israelis made a quick shambles of the Arab war effort. Almost the day the war ended, however, they were on the move. So complete was the Israeli victory, so thoroughly humbled were the Arab nations, that at first it seemed that at least another decade would pass before Israel would be threatened again. The Western world for the most part exulted at the Israeli victory, posed as it was in David-and-Goliath terms, and overtly smirked at the pitiable performance of the Arabs. But anything the Western world approved of automatically provoked the disapproval of the Eastern world, namely Russia.

Major spoils of the Israeli victory were its conquests of the Gaza Strip and West Bank Jordan and its takeover of the entire city of Jerusalem, which it publicly resolved never again to give up. Tens of thousands of additional refugees had fled into East Bank Jordan as the Israelis secured their grip on the West Bank, swelling existing refugee camps there and causing more to be established.

Although thoroughly beaten, the Arabs were unbowed. The week after the fighting ended, the drumbeat of anti-Israeli rhetoric began again to dominate the Arab press and radio. The newspapers of Beirut, by far the most numerous of any Arab city, provided an open forum for anyone who wanted to indulge in the rhetoric of revenge. Perceiving in the Israeli occupation of the West Bank and the Gaza Strip an opportunity to finally give Fatah ideology front-page substance, Arafat and his colleagues hounded the newspapers for space. The papers, vying with each other to print the most inflammatory and therefore the most newsworthy statements possible, gave the Fatahists all the linage they wanted. Within weeks Arafat, the principal spokesman, was a household name in Lebanon.

His basic theme was "the Palestinian people." Giving the impression that Fatah—the much larger "Fatah" of the Syrians which had earlier been identified with him in the public mind—had come through the war stronger than ever, he vowed that the organization would become the primary instrument in the creation of a Palestinian state—notwithstanding the recent overwhelming defeat. "Out of the ashes of this disastrous war will rise the phoenix of a free Arab Palestine," he declared. He bitterly criticized the Arab states for failing to unanimously support the Palestine liberation movement and, playing on the shame of the Egyptians, Syrians, and Jordanians, demanded that they, as well as the Lebanese and the rich Arab oil countries of the Persian Gulf, "put us at the forefront of the revolution."

In the Arab states involved in the war, the leaders' first reactions to the defeat were to execute or imprison many of the military people they held responsible for it. In Syria, Colonel Faqr and Muhammad Araka, along with dozens of others, were quickly dispatched and a new hierarchy installed in the Syrian General Command.

At a summit conference in August of 1967, called by Nasser to reassert his leadership and to debate future Arab policy with regard to Israel, the Arab nations re-declared their refusal to recognize the Jewish state and their intention to renew the war at some future date. At the same time, they endorsed the interim usefulness of guerrilla action and promised to support, with money and arms, any and all *fedayeen* groups willing to come forth.

The Fatah leaders in Lebanon leaped at the proposal. In September, Arafat arranged to have himself invited back to Damascus under safe-passage guarantees. There he was summoned before Syrian Premier Salah Jedid—his first meeting with a major Arab leader—and was cleared of all charges stemming from his difficulties with Colonel Faqr. He was then asked to address a Baath party conference. His speech was by turns vitriolic, compassionate, sarcastic, and sympathetic; he came down heavily on the failure of Syria to fulfill its ancient responsibility to the Arabs of Palestine and exploited the dishonor he claimed all Arabs should feel as a result of the frustrated nationalist aspirations of the Palestinian people.

It was, in the mood of the time, a daringly arrogant speech, but it worked. Rather than being hauled off and shot, Arafat was roundly praised. Within the week he was given a commission by Syria to take over the remnants of Colonel Faqr's Fatah, weld it to his own, and commence action. There would be few strings attached. The new consolidated Fatah, now five to six hundred strong, would belong solely to Arafat and his co-founders. They would receive Syrian training, arms, money, and military advice, but would remain independent. The only condition was that they not send missions into Israel from Syrian soil.

Contrary to Arafat's expectations, Fatah expanded slowly, despite ever-widening endorsements and support by Arab countries. One problem was the rival organizations which sprang up in the wake of the war—most notably the Popular Front for the Liberation of Palestine (PFLP), which had grown out of the old-line Arab National Movement centered at the American University in Beirut and was led by Georges Habash, a Christian Palestinian doctor who, like Arafat, had received Syrian support before the 1967 war and had tailored his political ideology to that of the extremist Baathists.

Another problem was the fact that despite the Syrian commitment to Fatah, the government decided to organize its own guerrilla group, both to demonstrate its faith in the *fedayeen* idea and to provide itself with a counterweight to Fatah in case the latter became too powerful.

Yet another problem was the still predominant apathy with regard to *fedayeen*-ism and liberationism within the Palestinian populations of the various Arab states. The Palestinians—refugees and non-refugees—had lived for years with the unfulfilled promises of the Arab states. There was little in the rhetoric of the *fedayeen* leaders to make them believe that things were going to change.

Finally, there was the problem of the Israeli military occupation of the West Bank and Gaza. In Arafat's view these two areas represented the most fertile ground on which to sow the seeds of insurrection and guerrilla warfare, to "win the minds and hearts of the people living under the sword of the oppressor," as he put it. Indeed, beginning late in 1967 he spent a great deal of time secretly circulating throughout the West Bank, organizing, with very little success, Fatah cells in the towns and villages. The Arabs of the West Bank who had not fled ahead of the Israeli conquest discovered that the occupation was not much harsher on them than when they were under Jordanian administration. Resigned to centuries of foreign domination of their homeland, and eyewitness to the power of the Israeli military machine, they found little sustenance in the revolutionary rhetoric of Arafat and other spokesmen for liberation, moderate or extremist.

It took an incident early in 1968 to give Fatah the boost it needed and to secure for Arafat the prestige that had continued to elude him. The incident took place in March.

Since September of the year before, *fedayeen* terrorist raids had been on the upswing, particularly against civilian targets in Israel and the occupied territories. To promote solidarity and enthusiasm for Fatah, Arafat had managed to institute the idea of martyrdom into the *fedayeen* mystique, again copying the example of his early-day hero, Majid Halaby. In orthodox Islamic dogma, death is often thought of as a reward, particularly when it has heroic dimensions. The liberation of the homeland was indeed a heroic objective; thus any death in the service of that objective was viewed as ipso facto heroic, elevating the deceased and his family survivors to positions of fame and honor. Arafat and his co-leaders used this concept to encourage volunteers for guerrilla missions and to instill in them the necessity of avoiding capture. With some it worked, and when reports got back to the Fatah leaders of the death of a guerrilla, he would be declared a martyr and his family would be looked after. With most, however, it didn't work; many terrorists were captured by the Israelis and grilled. By the beginning of 1968 the Israelis had a rather thorough knowledge of Fatah—its makeup, its leadership, and especially the locations of its staging bases in Jordan.

After a busload of Israeli children were wounded by a guerrilla-placed mine on March 8, 1968, the Israelis decided to retaliate with a view to wiping out a major Fatah staging base in the village of Karameh, just north of the Dead Sea in East Bank Jordan. On March 21 a large force of troops and tanks crossed the border and descended on Karameh, other units sealing off escape routes. Arafat was at Karameh, the Israelis had learned from captured *fedayeen,* and a special detachment was assigned to take him alive, if possible.

Unanticipated by the Israelis was the fact that the regular Jordanian forces of King Husayn would intervene. Israel had let the Jordanians know that their advance on Karameh was directed against the *fedayeen* only and that the king should not interpret it as an invasion of Jordan. But Husayn, walking a political tightrope in the Arab world over the issue of the Palestinians, felt obliged to make a gesture on behalf of the *fedayeen,* even though he feared and resented their expanding presence in Jordan. So he ordered his nearest armored forces to counterattack.

At the beginning the Israelis easily took control of Karameh, killing close to two hundred Palestinian guerrillas. But as they sought to withdraw they were confronted by the Jordanians, and a pitched battle followed. A few surviving guerrillas joined the Jordanians; but most fled, including Arafat, who commandeered a motorbike and escaped northeastward to the town of Salt.

The Israelis suffered relatively stiff casualties and a considerable loss of armor in the battle with the Jordanians, and the incident received worldwide notice. In the aftermath of the 1967 war, once jubilation over the Israeli performance had died down, a mood of dismay over what was thought by many to be Israeli intransigence had begun to develop throughout the Western world. This was particularly true among those of the younger generations engaged in leftist anti-war and anti-imperialist movements. Suddenly Israel, viewed only a few months earlier as the David to the Arab Goliath, became itself the Goliath, while the hapless Palestinians assumed the role of David. The Israeli assault on Karameh reinforced the image. In many quarters the Israeli setback was cheered and sympathy for the Palestinians mushroomed.

Arafat and his fellow Fatahists lost no time in exploiting this sentiment, both within and without Arabdom. Arafat had finally experienced the ultimate danger—the sound, the flame, and the blood of battle. That he had made his departure early, leaving hundreds of his minions to die and bleed behind him, mattered little. He arrived in Salt, his heart aflutter with both relief and excitement, bearing exaggerated tales of *fedayeen* heroism against the enemy. When, a few days later, the Israelis disclosed their casualties, he rushed to Damascus to impress upon the Syrian regime the ability of Fatah to stand up to the might of the hated Zionists. The Syrians were not about to argue. They knew it was the Jordanians who had fought the battle, not the *fedayeen,* but the Jordanians were the last ones they wished to credit. So they congratulated Arafat and lavished praise on Fatah for the world to hear. The Arab press, then the foreign press, picked up the story, and soon the myth of the Fatah "victory" over the Israelis became fact.

The incident and its attendant publicity mobilized the Arab world around the *fedayeen* movement, bringing it a sharp increase in recruits and a massive influx of funds from almost every Arab nation. It also catapulted Fatah, and Arafat, to worldwide attention. Foreign newspaper and television teams poured into Lebanon and Jordan to send back to their readers and viewers scenes of freedom fighters, many of them mere children, in training; of *fedayeen* martyrs' funerals; of the impoverished inhabitants of the refugee camps; of Arafat and his lieutenants lecturing their interviewers on the justice of the Palestinian cause and the "legitimate rights of the Palestinian people."

In the years following Karameh it was all uphill for Yasir Arafat, although the climb was not without peril. Fatah representatives toured Europe throughout the rest of 1968, setting up cells in almost every major city and enlisting foreign students to the cause. Others canvassed the Arab oil states, prying larger and larger amounts of money out of the treasuries of sheikhs who were rich beyond imagination. Fatah power and influence multiplied, spawning envious rivals who often tried to depose Arafat and, failing that, sought to outshine Fatah by exceeding its capacity for terror and spreading it beyond the Middle East.

In February of 1969, Arafat cemented his hold on the *fedayeen* movement by gaining control of the PLO, still nominally an adjunct of the Arab League but discredited since 1967 because of the cowardly behavior and vacuous rhetoric of its leader, Ahmed Shukayri, during the June war. (It was Shukayri who had invented the slogan "We will drive the Jews into the sea," although today he denies that he meant it literally.) He organized the PLO into a Fatah-dominated organization and then set out to incorporate rival groups into it and persuade the Arab world in general to recognize it as the "only legitimate representative of the Palestinian people."

Arafat and the Fatah PLO began to receive moral and material support from the Soviet Union, China, and lesser communist powers, but their quest for pan-Arab recognition fell short because of intensifying internal rivalries and their increasingly outspoken contempt for King Husayn of Jordan. Husayn reacted in the fall of 1970 by declaring war on the *fedayeen,* who were by then swelling his country in such numbers and with such audacity that they seemed about to take it over. In a series of battles beginning in September and extending into 1971, his army seriously depleted *fedayeen* ranks and drove the survivors back into Syria and Lebanon, thus earning their eternal enmity.

The liberation movement spent much of 1971 regrouping and re-expanding, centering itself in Lebanon under even firmer Fatah-PLO control. Re-armed by Russia and to a lesser extent by China via Syria and Algeria, Arafat and his subleaders established ties with other guerrilla and revolutionary movements the world over. At the same time, they launched a new wave of commando activity against Israel, this time mostly from the Arqoub region of southern Lebanon, which rapidly became known as Fatahland. Their aim was the same as in the pre-1967 years: to provoke another war and bring the Palestinian issue further to the forefront of world awareness.

This time Arafat and his colleagues were much more in control of the movement, but although the hoped-for war indeed came, in October of 1973, they again had little to do with its provocation. In fact, they were as surprised as the rest of the world when the Egyptian army made its daring foray across the Suez Canal and the Syrians knifed through the Golan Heights.

The 1973 war and its aftermath completed the ascendancy of Arafat. The Arab world, although it won little militarily, achieved a great deal psychologically and in the diplomatic and economic spheres. Shortly after the war another Arab summit conference was convened, this time at Rabat, Morocco. Egypt and Syria were angry at King Husayn of Jordan for failing to open a third front by attacking across the West Bank; they believed their success would have been greater had the Jordanians been able to distract a large part of the Israeli army. In the months leading up to the Rabat conference, Arafat and his Fatah-PLO cohorts excoriated Husayn and insisted that by his inaction he had abandoned Jordan's claim to the West Bank—that the West Bank and its population could only be represented by the Fatah-PLO. The Arab leaders, anxious to punish Husayn for his inaction, viewed Arafat's demands sympathetically and passed a resolution acknowledging the PLO as the "only legitimate representative" of the Palestinian people.

The resolution effectively removed Jordan from the tangled Palestine question and gave official Arab recognition to Arafat and the PLO. With such recognition, Arafat proceeded then to achieve the climax of his career—an invitation to address the United Nations General Assembly in November, 1974, on the question of Palestine.

The UN of 1974 was rather a different animal from the UN of 1948, which had voted for the creation of Israel (and also of an Arab Palestinian state). Its political complexion had changed markedly with its expanded membership, which included many nations created through revolutionary wars of independence. To the old-line Western nations, which had dominated the UN in its early years, the invitation to Arafat was an embarrassment they could do little about. To Israel it was, of course, an outrage. To the majority of nations, however, many of them born of terrorism and guerrilla warfare, the Palestinian cause was a kindred one and Arafat a kind of spiritual brother. Indeed, the very man elected as president of the General Assembly during the session in which Arafat was to speak was himself a former Algerian terrorist.

As Arafat stood before the General Assembly and accepted its welcoming ovation, he was, in the eyes of many, a sympathetic figure. Dressed in his familiar soiled khaki windbreaker and checkered *kaffiyeh,* which hid his totally bald pate, and with a holster on his hip, he read his carefully prepared speech—the product of the combined efforts of his closest Fatah colleagues—in an alternating compound of stentorian and pleading Arabic. It was a speech of contrasts—truths and untruths, historical accuracies and inaccuracies, threats and mollifications—all symbolized by the image he used to conclude it: the gun and the olive branch.

Epilogue

It is a starry, crystalline night in Beirut in January, 1976. On the terrace of a villa on a hillside overlooking the city, Yasir Arafat, huddled against the chill, is conversing with a wealthy Lebanese newspaper publisher. The publisher, a Christian, is pleading with Arafat to secure the release of an elderly aunt and uncle who had been kidnaped a few days before by Palestinian guerrillas. The publisher is in the process of learning what few people know—that Arafat has lost all authority over the various guerrilla organizations that make up the Palestine Liberation Organization. Arafat is embarrassed by the publisher's almost hysterical importunities. The man had often entertained Arafat at his home and had always opened his newspaper's pages to him.

Arafat looks down on the once brightly lit city. The glow of the many fires that pock its now black expanse is reflected in his large, doleful eyes. He turns to the publisher and, in Arabic, says, "I am sorry, my friend, but I am taking my orders from—" and he mentions the names of two men in the Syrian High Command. "There is nothing I can do for the moment. I am powerless until all this" —his arm sweeps toward the distance—"is over. I tell you this in utmost confidence, as a friend. If you breathe a word of it, you will be killed. I will not be able to stop them [the Syrians]. They have their agents everywhere."

Arafat's next visitor is an American journalist. As the journalist steps onto the terrace from the villa, he is quickly surrounded by half a dozen members of Arafat's retinue. Two bodyguards, who had been lingering in the shadows, move in close, their Kalashnikov automatic rifles nestled loosely in their arms. The journalist's first question is about the United States' promise to veto the forthcoming United Nations Security Council resolution to recognize the PLO. The amber light from the city below glints in Arafat's eyes as they harden and narrow.

"We have exhausted our patience with the United States," he hisses in luxuriantly accented English. "We have tried diplomacy, as you people in the West have insisted. But, I ask you, what has it got us?"

Arafat picks reflectively at the stubble on his chin for a moment, casting a glance at one of the men standing behind the journalist. Then, in a measured, bitter tone, he continues. "Remember this well. We were responsible for the '67 war. We were responsible for the '73 war. We were responsible for the oil embargo. The Palestinian people will not be denied their just due. If the United States still refuses to recognize the legitimate rights of my people, we will then be forced to bring about a new war. You ask how we intend to react to the veto? What is happening in Lebanon today is nothing as compared to the blood that will flow in Israel in the next war. You can tell your people that I say there will be another war, very soon. And this time it will not just be Arabs fighting Zionists. Each time you deny us, you in America come closer to your own holocaust."

The journalist asks: How soon is soon?

Arafat ponders the question for a moment. One of the bystanders moves over to him and whispers in his ear. Arafat nods, and then smiles at the journalist. "We understand you have elections this year. For president, eh?"

The journalist himself nods.

"Well, you see, we understand that this veto you are predicting will be done for your own internal reasons, political reasons. It would be unpopular in your country to recognize us in an election year. We are told that any politician who recognized us would commit political suicide because of the Zionist press, eh? So—I tell you this. We will wait to see who is your president. When your election is over, we will see what happens then. If your new president does not take immediate steps to recognize us, we will have no choice but to start the new war. And you remember my words carefully. It will be the third world war. You will have only one option. That is to recognize us, and guarantee immediately our right to have a sovereign state. If you fail this, then it will be the third world war.

And as your children are consumed in the flames of nuclear obliteration, you will wish you had listened to me."*

This is a different Arafat—cocksure, expansive, threatening. With the publisher he had been apologetic, almost meek, projecting impotence.

Which, today, is the real Arafat? The man who claims he can call down a world war at will? Or the man who confides to a distressed acquaintance that he is under the thumb of the Syrian government?

Perhaps the answer lies in *The Protocols of the Elders of Zion*—that famous counterfeit tract manufactured by the secret police of nineteenth-century Tsarist Russia to justify their anti-Jewish pogroms—a dog-eared Arabic copy of which Arafat carries around with him and constantly quotes to visitors to impress them with his vision of Zionist treachery. The words are:

> It is by grafting the sense of our apparent power onto the hearts and minds of the people that we will gain real power. What would otherwise be nothing more than a potentiality in the eyes of intelligent men will become an actuality in the vision of the masses. Hence it is our task to spread ourselves throughout the world and to exploit the natural anxieties of the unlettered and superstitious, to plumb the depths and prod all the dark corners of their dungeons of fear, to habituate them to accept as real and without question that which is only phantom in its substance. There are too few of us and too many of them for us to hope to dominate by the force of our numbers. To dominate by inference, by the inference of our potency, is the road we will travel. . . . Our goal will be to force the inference of our power to become our power until the world trembles at our feet and obeys us.

*This account was given to me by the Lebanese publisher's mistress, an Arabic-speaking European woman who had accompanied the publisher to the villa. On their arrival, the woman had been ushered to a room on the second floor of the villa to wait while the publisher spoke to Arafat. The room directly overlooked the terrace. I have known this woman for many years, and have every reason to believe that her account is accurate.

Index